MW00413051

DREAM CHASERS

DREAM CHASERS

IMMIGRATION AND THE AMERICAN BACKLASH

John Tirman

The MIT Press   Cambridge, Massachusetts   London, England

MIT Press books may be purchased at special quantity discounts for business or sales promotional use. For information, email special_sales@mitpress.mit.edu.

Set in Stone serif and Univers by the MIT Press. Printed and bound in the United States of America.

Library of Congress Cataloging-in-Publication Data are available.

ISBN 978-0-262-02892-9

10 9 8 7 6 5 4 3 2 1

to the memory of my friend and teacher Howard Zinn

CONTENTS

ACKNOWLEDGMENTS

My biggest debt is to my colleagues at MIT, and particularly the Center for International Studies and its director, Dick Samuels. Thanks are due to the patient John Covell of the MIT Press, and to Robin Straus, my literary agent, for realism and well-timed cheerleading. I owe much to many people in New Bedford, Massachusetts, and Tucson, Arizona (most of whom are named in the accounts of those two cities), to old friends Tracy Bachrach Ehlers, Nick Bromell, and Anna Badkhen for advice and encouragement, and to two anonymous reviewers who provided much-needed criticism. My daughter, Coco, rode the Sonoran Desert with me and prompted me to explain what was happening on the border. Most of all, I express my admiration for the many thousands of activists who work with little compensation (and too little respect) for justice and, yes, a better world.

1 RAID: THE SECOND GREAT MIGRATION AND THE CULTURE OF RESISTANCE

Of all the hot issues that have burst upon the landscape of American politics, illegal immigration is in many respects unique. It is both a domestic issue and a global concern. At its roots, it involves economics, politics, and culture. It is intertwined with the American homily that we are a nation of immigrants, one of the sturdiest glories of our national narrative. Unlike other current controversies (for example, those over climate change, the Middle East, and health care), it has been at the center of the American experience for hundreds of years. Even when there were no laws governing immigration, influxes of certain races or ethnicities stirred heated opposition and decades-long discrimination by the privileged white culture, initially Protestant and conservative, even as that dominant class expanded rapidly and violently across the continent. Another hardy pillar of the national narrative, that we are a "nation of laws, not men," came to clash in many ways with immigration politics, whether the entry of the immigrants in question was technically legal or not. Immigration has had a tumultuous history, one in which some groups have been intermittently scapegoated and made "illegal" by sudden changes in the rules that govern entry.

As we look back at that history after more than 130 years of unevenly conceived restrictions, we see the ebb and flow of immigration law and enforcement as shaped by racial and ethnic prejudice, class distinctions, and economic exigencies. Immigrants from China and elsewhere in East Asia were excluded from entry as early as 1882 by the Chinese Exclusion Act, the first of its kind, which was prompted by the large-scale Chinese immigration that by the time of the act had brought so many Chinese to California that they constituted 25 percent of the labor force. The East Asians would be a primary target of all exclusion laws, including the draconian measures of the 1920s, which prohibited immigration from East Asian countries altogether. Most Asians were denied any chance to become naturalized citizens—this from the first naturalization law in 1790—and without that possibility, immigration was denied as well.

When immigration flows became especially strong at the end of the nineteenth century—just about the time that the western frontier was thought to be closing—alarms about undesirable immigrants prompted hysterical political and social reactions. One notable effort, in many ways revealing of how anti-immigrant sentiments have always manifested, came with the formation in 1894 of the Immigration Restriction League. The League, founded by three Harvard alumni, proposed a literacy requirement for entry. "Watching with anxiety as immigration increased sharply in the 1880s and 1890s, League members had lost faith in the nation's ability to assimilate newcomers into its political, social, and cultural fabric," a Harvard archivist notes. "They associated immigration with the socio-economic problems of their increasingly urban and industrialized society—crowded tenements, poverty, crime and delinquency, labor unrest, and violence." The migrants from Southern and Eastern Europe were, the Harvard men claimed, "inherently unable to participate in self-government or to adopt American values."[1]

By the first decade of the twentieth century, an anti-immigrant sentiment was in full bloom in US politics. The Dillingham Commission, a joint House-Senate committee created in 1907, concluded that immigrants from Southern and Eastern Europe (including Italians, Greeks, Poles, and Russians, many of them Catholic or Jewish) were a threat to American culture and should be tightly regulated. It invented the National Origins Formula, a quota system by which immigration was limited to 3 percent of the number of people of a nationality already in the United States by 1910 (when most of the immigrants were Northern and Western Europeans). The quotas were included in the exclusion laws of the 1920s and weren't reversed until the major immigration reform of 1965.

The anti-immigrant sentiments that reigned in elite circles for about a century and were codified in law were significantly based on race, on the fear of diluting some distinctive American character. The concerns about the lowly tenements and all their social ills in New York and other urban magnets were often cast in terms of the unclean and untrustworthy immigrant, while it was industrialization and rapid economic expansion that brought the low-paid workers to the city: the immigrants were merely fulfilling their longtime economic role of cheap labor. The dominant white culture that cried out against diluting the American character was the same class that needed immigrant labor to sustain their enterprises and their often sumptuous lifestyles. "Lower" class and "race" (or unwanted ethnicities, or non-Protestants) were differentiated and made the "other"—dirty, licentious, undeserving.

Much of that mix of racial and class prejudice, blaming the victim, exhortations about white superiority, and manipulating the rules of the game for economic advantage remain the characteristic qualities of the immigration debate today. The debate—really a cacophony—centers on how to deal with the influx of immigrants who enter and remain in the United States without authorization. The immigrants in question are almost all Latino, from Mexico and Central America (Guatemala, El Salvador, and Honduras in particular), and now number about 11 million present without authorization. But the social and political discourse is really a much broader take on immigration. It involves the same issues that mobilized the Immigrant Restriction League so many decades ago: these Hispanic immigrants and their progeny—now numbering more than 50 million, including those who are "legal"—are changing the American dream, the culture of the Protestant white Europeans who "settled" and built the country. In this account, they are fundamentally at odds with the key traits of being English speaking, hard working, and patriotic.

It is, in short, an epic culture clash. Illegal immigration is usually depicted as an issue of legality, economics ("stealing jobs"), strains on social services in border states, and the political ramifications of reform efforts (that whoever leads reform will gain the electoral favor of Hispanics). These matters surely count in the calculations of political leaders. But they don't account for the vociferous opposition to "illegals" and reform efforts alike. The opposition is based mainly on the cultural ramifications of immigration from south of the border. Once this is more clearly understood—and the other, rickety excuses for opposing reform are set aside—the debate can be waged on those grounds and remedies can be more easily imagined and adopted.

This book is aimed to look directly at the cultural dimensions of immigration from Latin America. I regard the issues of culture in two ways. First is the way in which the cultural resistance has occurred. As the numbers of Latinos in the United States has increased, the dominant white culture has retaliated and resisted in several complementary ways: marginalizing Latinos (whether "legal" or not), disparaging the aspirations of immigrants, degrading their contributions to the American economy and American society more broadly, and rounding up unauthorized immigrants and putting them into a shameful detention and deportation system. This is what I call "the raid mentality," an ideology about immigrants that seeks militant, even violent, solutions to a social phenomenon that causes few actual problems. I write about raids, particularly one action by federal immigration agents in the Massachusetts city of New Bedford in March 2007, which illustrates so much of what is wrong about the raid mentality.

The consequences of that raid and so many others have only brought misery to some immigrants but have not gainfully addressed the issues of unauthorized immigration. The raid mentality ignores both the causes of the immigration it seeks to police and the long-standing traditions of American businesses seeking and indeed facilitating immigration to satisfy their need for labor. To justify the inhumane practices of the raids, large and small, at the border and within the interior of the United States, a cohort of opponents—most of them affiliated with right-wing media outlets—dehumanizes the immigrants, their claims, their history, and their needs. The politicians and opinion-makers who disparage Mexican immigrants and oppose reform (because all bipartisan reform packages include some forgiveness for unauthorized immigrants already in the country) propose militant measures like vastly upgraded border security, racial profiling, and deportation of all "illegals." The resistance to immigration, I argue, is at its core an outcry against anything that sullies the opponents' view of what it means to be an American.

The second way of explaining the role of culture in the immigration controversy is to regard the Latino[2] flows into the United States as the Second Great Migration. The Great Migration describes several periods of African-American migration from the old Confederacy to the North and the West mainly during six or so decades of the twentieth century. The Great Migration, which was spurred by the continuing mistreatment of former black slaves and their progeny in the South, changed the racial compositions and the social and cultural dynamics of Chicago, Detroit, New York, and other Northern cities. The Latino migration, mainly from Mexico but also significantly from Central America, Cuba, Puerto Rico, and the Dominican Republic, has been equal or larger in scale and arguably as significant in reshaping parts of the country demographically, as well as US politics, and American culture. It bears many similarities to the Great Migration even as there are important differences, and comparing the two sheds light on the cultural resistance to Hispanic immigration.

As several scholars have shown, such cultural resistance or reaction is measurable in attitudes about use of English, habits of living, work ethic, loyalty to the United States, and other concerns. What I believe has been less articulated is how cultural resistance is the *sine qua non* of nativist sentiments, and that this is evident in all the political battles for reform, in the localized skirmishes over school pedagogy, and in the way the news media regard the issues of illegal immigration. And reform takes us only so far. As with the case of blacks now decades after the Great Migration and a century and a half since the Emancipation, cultural attitudes and social practices change only gradually.

As long as the raid mentality remains the centerpiece of the political and cultural resistance, attitudes are likely to remain rigidly unmoving, and reform efforts will fail.

The Great Migration is one of the grand, consequential stories of American history. Scholars sometimes divide it into different parts, but generally it is depicted as the migration of blacks from the South—the old Confederacy—to the North and the West between about 1910 and 1970. In those decades, 6 million African-Americans migrated away from the sharecropping trap that white landowners and other elites had set for them. That system, similar in important respects to the *encomienda* system of Spanish and Spanish-descended landowners in Latin America, was informally called "Jim Crow" (after a stage character who had highly exaggerated black characteristics). It was a system of grinding agricultural labor, debt peonage, little if any educational opportunity, an absence of government services, and formal segregation. Entirely based on race, the system actually grew harsher as the South entered the twentieth century. "Challenges to the supremacist regime—even of the trivial sort—could unleash furious rampages enacted by hooded thugs who generally took their cues from men and women who claimed impeccable respectability," wrote one historian. "Everywhere black Southerners found themselves forced to play out the galling rituals of subordination."[3]

The subordination was economic—the sharecropping scheme was a recipe for increasing black farmers' indebtedness—but it was even more a vast and deep social and cultural system of oppression. Formal segregation meant inferior schools, hospital access, ill treatment in any and all public settings; but it also meant that contact between whites and blacks could be punished severely, even when innocent and initiated by whites, and it was the darker race that would suffer the lash, the jail cell, the noose.

It was in many ways remarkable that blacks put up with such treatment for so long, but any hint of rebellion was crushed with terrifying violence. Indeed, as Isabel Wilkerson showed in her fine history of the Great Migration, *The Warmth of Other Suns*, even the act of leaving the South for the North involved perils that many blacks found intimidating, including detention and other harassments. The northward movement was aided by recruiters "who were getting paid a dollar a head to deliver colored labor to the foundries and slaughterhouses of the North,"[4] but it was more than those agents or the boll weevil that decimated the cotton economy that drove the grandchildren of slaves northward. In the 1920s, the Chicago Commission on Race Relations actually asked the migrants why they made the move, and their answers were straightforward. Typical responses were "some of my people were here," "for better wages," "better living," "more work," and "to get away from the South."[5] It was accelerated by the First World War and the need for labor in the factories up North, but once established in those industrial cities, the migrants had created social networks that made it easier for the next wave to join them. The passage was difficult, usually in dilapidated, filthy, blacks-only railroad cars, but the promise of a better life essentially emptied the South of young black men, and soon of young black women.

What awaited them in Cleveland, Baltimore, St. Louis, Chicago, New York, and other urban and industrial centers was not paradise. Northerners harbored racist sentiments, too, if less vicious and institutionalized compared with the South. Informal segregation was exacted mainly through housing discrimination, which then led to segregated neighborhood schools, services, and commerce. The black neighborhoods were underserved by city governments, black workers were paid less than white, unions would shun black participation, and social strictures remained, if less violently enforced. "Unknowingly, the migrants were walking into a headwind of resentment and suspicion," Wilkerson noted. "They had emerged from a cave of restrictions into wide-open, anonymous hives that viewed them with bemusement and contempt."[6] Still, life was far better in the North, economically and socially, and the Great Migration's persistence into the 1970s is proof of that. Statistics show clearly that in the last 75 years the incomes of blacks have increased substantially relative to those of whites, and that a black middle class has taken root—achievements not to be taken lightly. There remains much that is wrong with this picture, including chronic wage differences based on race and a troubling downward mobility for many blacks born into the middle class. Compared with the Jim Crow South, however, the progress is indelible.

The picture is more complex than income statistics, however. What transpired with this migration, particularly after the Second World War, is both the apotheosis of this vast movement of people in the civil rights and black power movements and the continuing scourge of white racism and marginalizing of African-Americans. They were escaping the desperate conditions—economic, social, and cultural—of the old South; they were welcomed, at least conditionally, as inexpensive labor in the Northern industrial cities. Culturally, they were brought into a wilderness, in which they reinvented themselves, but in all aspects of daily life their invisibility, their lack of recognition as fully American citizens, and the relentless assaults on their dignity were burdens that weighed heavily for decades. Black literature and philosophy at the time the Great Migration matured—Ralph Ellison's *Invisible Man*, Richard Wright's *Native Son*, and Lorraine Hansberry's *A Raisin in the Sun*, for example—reflected these deep frustrations and depicted what Langston Hughes called "a dream deferred." Later, Malcolm X was even more unsparing. "Some people wonder 'Well, what does Mississippi have to do with Harlem?'" he said at a Harlem rally after Mississippi blacks had been denied a place at the 1964 Democratic National Convention. "America *is* Mississippi. There's no such thing as a Mason-Dixon Line. It's America. There's no such thing as the South. It's America. If one room in your house is dirty, you've got a dirty house ... . Don't say that that room is dirty but the rest of my house is clean ... . You have authority over the whole house. The entire house is under your jurisdiction. And the mistake that you and I make is letting these Northern crackers shift the weight to these Southern crackers." He went on to say "Every senator from a state where our people are deprived of the right to vote, they're in Washington, D.C. illegally ... . The brothers and the sisters in Mississippi are being beaten and killed for no reason other than they want to be treated as first-class citizens."[7]

The Great Migration sent millions north into an unstable and often hostile human ecology. Blacks remained politically disenfranchised until the Voting Rights Act, and even then equal access to housing, education, and the vote were hindered in many jurisdictions. They were able to work and earn more than in the dead-end economy they suffered in the South, but nonetheless often found themselves in dire poverty, with poor social infrastructure granted to them by the white ruling elites. But they also faced a cultural resistance that was ferocious and often nearly as violent as in the South, a resistance borne of racial difference and the sense among many middle-class and working-class whites that they were losing out to blacks who were taking over the cities, poisoning the young, taking undeserved benefits, and corrupting the American way of life. Poor, crime-riddled, falling-down neighborhoods and an absence of educational routes to better lives (not to mention sheer hostility such as I witnessed firsthand in the hateful anti-busing riots in Boston) were harsh realities that greeted these migrants and their children and grandchildren.

The entire sweep of the Great Migration—what sent those millions northward and how they adapted to a better but still hostile environment—is remarkably similar to the second Great Migration of Latinos over more recent decades. The structure of oppression in the places of origin, the difficulties of migration, the ambivalent reception, the contingent status with respect to legality, the unequal treatment compared with whites, the difficult and frequently contentious relationship with police, the poor conditions of education and housing, the suffering of racism and discrimination, the constant harassment of blame-the-victim posturing, and the raid mentality that passes for problem solving in the political establishment—all these elements are the same. There are, of course, significant differences. But the two migrations bear a striking resemblance to each other and in the social, cultural, and political resistance that rose in the receiving states. What does that tell us?

At a minimum, it illustrates common features of reaction. That reaction is political (attempts to deny the vote, legality, citizenship, or the capacity to organize), social (opprobrium regarding mixing races or ethnicities, discriminatory bars to housing, exclusion from social institutions), economic (job discrimination, wage differences), and cultural (biases in educational curricula, disrespecting and demonizing cultural traditions of migrants, conflicts over use of language, and contentious understandings of history). The forces of reaction are often working in tandem to exercise denial: discrimination in housing makes more possible poor educational facilities, for example. Social segregation enables dehumanizing attitudes. Cultural disrespect—declaring a subculture as not being American—is a means to delegitimize a group. And so on. As we regard the growth of the Latino presence in the United States—more broadly than some border towns, more permanently than seasonal workers—we increasingly see the same dynamics of the reaction to black migration now attending the brown migration. And those two words, 'black' and 'brown', denote much in and of themselves.

The way the reaction to illegal immigration has manifested indicates most clearly that the resistance is mainly one of cultural difference and exclusion (a broader scope than racism alone) rather than economics or politics.

When Georgia passed a tough law targeting unauthorized immigrants, for example, the reasons given by the bill's sponsors revolved around the use of hospitals and schools. "They are illegals, they are going to use our services," said one, implying that immigrants don't pay taxes and therefore have no purchase on taxpayer-supported institutions.[8] In fact, most unauthorized immigrants do pay taxes (through payroll deductions) and often overpay, because they cannot claim refunds. Schools, moreover, aren't off limits because of a Supreme Court decision thirty years ago that stated flatly that children who are not in the country legally are nonetheless entitled to education. In the cases of hospitals and schools, there is no legal or economic basis for exclusion. It is the animus toward "them" using "our" services that rankles the anti-immigrant forces, much like the thought of "coloreds" using "white" rest rooms was abhorrent to Southerners. In 2011, Alabama passed a law that, among other measures, mandated a census of unauthorized immigrant children in public schools; it was widely seen as a tactic of intimidation, and indeed school attendance dropped sharply.

Many of the state and local laws passed in the last ten years to punish unauthorized immigrants[9] have been focused on schools and hospitals and other social services like food stamps and drivers' licenses. Some are redundant—food stamp eligibility for non-citizens is already limited by federal regulations. And some possess a certain irony, as with the charge that illegal immigrants cost taxpayers because they use expensive emergency-room care in hospitals; one of the key reasons the Affordable Care Act ("Obamacare") was passed was to reduce the use of emergency room treatment for the uninsured (the vast majority of whom are white citizens).

By the end of 2011, 306 laws and resolutions had passed state legislatures restricting or excluding the presence of unauthorized immigrants in 45 states; in 2012 and 2013, this juggernaut continued, often redundantly, and with only a handful of gubernatorial vetoes. As many as 1,400 bills were introduced annually. (Not all these laws are anti-immigrant, however, and most of them are in effect neutral.) Few of the laws and resolutions have much teeth, said one analysis. "The far greater impact has been social, Hispanic groups say. Laws targeting illegal immigrants have reflected and even intensified the rising anti-immigration movement, both in statehouses and on the streets. The result is a legislative record from Arizona to Florida that hasn't made much of a mark on illegal immigration, but has fueled a populist backlash against it."[10]

While the numbers of local laws seem excessive, the resistance to immigration, especially Latino immigrants, stems from the longtime animus toward newcomers that has often been quite vociferous in American political culture. It is unlikely that this animus is particular to Latinos; if large influxes of Arabs or Indians made up the "illegals" in our midst, the reaction from nativists would be equally fierce, possibly more so. The years of Chinese exclusion are proof enough of that, as was the prejudice against Jews, Slavs, Irish, and others from Europe. Mexicans and Central Americans are much more like most Americans than Chinese, Arabs, Indians, or many others, as they are Christians of the New World, and many share some common history. The fact that they nonetheless stir such passion in nativists demonstrates the depth of xenophobia.

Whatever the spark, the fire that rages in the right-wing discourse about unauthorized immigrants is fueled by a deeply embedded American habit of suspicion and fear. The historian Richard Hofstadter captured this in his brilliant 1964 essay "The Paranoid Style in American Politics." What was once an obsession with Freemasons or communists or Jews or blacks is now visited upon Latinos, replete with the conspiracy theories that keep the anti-immigrant fires burning—the notion, for example, that Latinos immigrate to lay the groundwork for a takeover of the lands once belonging to Mexico in the American Southwest.

Whereas the likes of the John Birch Society and other extremists were significantly marginalized for much of American history, they now dominate the Republican Party. How this has come to pass is probably due to an inchoate anger stirred by the hollowing out of the middle class, stagnant income growth for most Americans, the rise of groups and ideologies that challenge old notions of "family values," and the gradual decline of American hegemony in much of the world. What is also different now is the rise of well-funded right-wing media outlets that use reactionary sentiments to promote an agenda that is part cultural and part economic. The latter is fostered by wealthy conservatives who promote their own interests by politically mobilizing anti-gay, anti-immigrant, anti-science, and broadly anti-government turmoil. These are the Koch brothers, the Rupert Murdoch empire, the Scaife family, and hundreds, perhaps thousands, of others. They have built an alternative structure alongside the Republican Party that pushes it toward militancy and obstruction, preying on a constituency confused by the cultural changes and unwittingly willing to vote against their own interests of better health care, a clean environment, good schools, well-paying jobs, and so on. This has always been true, the millionaires manipulating the masses (and quite evident in many countries abroad where elites enflame ethnic tensions for their own benefit), but in the United States it has been perfected tactically through political action committees, redistricting congressional seats, creating disconsolate groups (often under the rubric "Tea Party"), and linking issues in the conspiratorial manner—for example, rousing anti-science sentiments about evolution that then feed skepticism about climate change.

Right-wing media outlets enable this resentment and paranoia to work so well politically. Murdoch's Fox News and *Wall Street Journal*, talk radio, and blogs convey these messages frequently every day. And the anti-immigrant tirade fits neatly into the old Confederacy's inveterate racism. It always rises to a fever pitch when reform is afoot. The complaints are uniformly shared—the illegal aliens are about to be granted amnesty, possibly even citizenship, jumping the line ahead of other would-be immigrants, costing taxpayers trillions, stealing jobs at a time of high unemployment, unwilling to learn and speak English, smuggling drugs, dropping "anchor babies," becoming welfare queens or gang members or even revolutionaries or terrorists. These charges, most of which are untrue or irrelevant to the immigrants, are elaborated endlessly. They are easy to make, because the immigrants have little if any voice in the news media and because pro-reform politicians are cautious in their defense of new legislation.

The animus isn't limited to immigrants, but is often even more heated when taking on those pro-reform politicians, or even someone outside the reform debate. Laura Ingraham, one of the more popular talk radio entertainers, lashed out at Supreme Court Justice Sonia Sotomayor for not calling unauthorized immigrants "illegal aliens." "Why do we have a Supreme Court Justice whose allegiance obviously goes to her immigrant family background and not to the US Constitution?" Ingraham fumed. "So we have no rule of law. We are going to pick and choose who has to follow the law in the United States."[11] What to call unauthorized immigrants has nothing to do with law or the Constitution. Sotomayor was born in New York to Puerto Rican parents; all Puerto Ricans are US citizens. But even this detail of how to refer to these migrants is a "hot button" for the right wing, so much so that it warrants a baseless on-air attack on a Supreme Court justice.

Ingraham focuses frequently on one of the right wing's most tendentious claims: that the English language is under assault because of the immigrants' use of Spanish. She insisted to a caller that English was in decline because of Mexican "jingoism," for example, as a leading edge of their scheme to retake the American Southwest.[12] It's a common theme among conservative commentators. Michelle Malkin, a ubiquitous commentator on immigration issues, celebrated a restaurateur who was an "assimilation warrior" when it came to English-only commerce: "No dumbed-down pictographs for the idiocracy. The choice at Geno's is simple: Sink or swim. Learn English or eat somewhere else."[13]

Malkin and like-minded bloggers have focused ample attention on the so-called Dreamers—young Latinos brought into the United States without authorization by their parents and who now seek legal status. The Dreamers, in this view, aren't victims of circumstance, but perpetrators of a scam. "The open-borders progressives' 'DREAM Act' is an electoral nightmare," Malkin wrote in her blog in 2010. "It's not just an illegal alien student bailout. It's a 2.1 million future Democrat voter recruitment drive. The 'path to citizenship' dangled by Obama is a superhighway to generations of big government-birthed, identity politics-nursed dependents."[14] So, no special treatment for these non-victims. No bilingualism. No tolerance for the "thugs" who fly Mexican flags at rallies. No reform. No compromise on an endless insistence that the border is insecure and that the feds are not enforcing immigration laws. The solution these conservatives offer is 100 percent rooted in the raid mentality—round them up, deport them, militarize the border even more.

Then there is the omnipresent threat of terrorism from the southern border: "systematically lax enforcement of our immigration laws combined with suicidal political correctness paved the way for the September 11 terrorist attacks," Malkin wrote in 2012.[15] This has been one of the key alarms sounded by the nativists—that lax border security and criminal Latino gangs constitute an existential threat of terrorism. The terrorism narrative was powered by a confluence of anxieties and misperceptions. Illegal immigration had implied job insecurity for native-born Americans. Physical security, the security of the homeland from political violence, was newly attached to the Mexican border only after September 11, 2001. (Criminal violence from drug smugglers or gangs was more familiar if sporadic.) This concern about terrorism only seemed to peak after the war in Iraq had become a ruin of violence and terrorism. It was a long way from Baghdad to Nogales, but the displaced anxiety of war violence and the inability of war supporters to acknowledge the colossal toll in Iraq bubbled up to the surface on our southern border just as President Bush's 2006–07 reform effort got underway.

The allegations about Islamic terrorists crossing the border include allegations that al-Qaeda, Hezbollah, or other such groups were sending members to the nether zone of the golden triangle of Argentina, Brazil, and Paraguay for training in "how to act Hispanic" and to speak Spanish so they could blend in with Mexicans illegally entering the United States. Others saw Iran's new alliance with President Hugo Chávez of Venezuela as an indicator of ill intent, and warned of Hezbollah sleeper cells that on command from Tehran could "light up the place," as one congressman alleged. Another rumor held that al-Qaeda had training camps just across the border in Mexico. Similar hysteria appeared when the al-Qaeda offshoot known as the Islamic State (IS) became a target of US military action in 2014; conservatives relentlessly alleged, with no proof, that IS terrorists intended to furtively cross the border from Mexico.

That such charges were basically nonsense didn't degrade their utility to the anti-immigration crowd. No one who crossed the Mexican border illegally has been arrested for engaging in an act "Islamist" violence. A senior official for border security told me that the notion of al-Qaeda operatives slipping across the Rio Grande is without foundation. Forging the link between terrorists and illegal immigration served to heighten fears and to equate immigration with the most traumatic moment in recent American history, the al-Qaeda attacks of 9/11. (The attackers were significantly in violation of their visas, and the broad federal effort to "securitize" immigration ensued right after the attack, mainly through closer scrutiny of those seeking entry for any reason and monitoring visa compliance.) So the dread of a takeover by Latinos was braced by the newfound dread of terrorism and a Muslim infiltration more broadly. The latter was at the root of dozens of legislative efforts at the state and municipal level to ban the use of Sharia, Muslim religious law, in courts. Mosque burnings and other hate crimes against Muslims increased in frequency. Terrorism became an article of everyday politics, with its own homeland security state and subsidy-consuming industry. While different phenomena, Latino immigration and Muslim "infiltration" and political violence abroad were conflated into the same threat—the threat of overwhelming the "real America." The remedies for these threats were almost identical: raids in the United States, massive raids (i.e., war making) in Muslim countries.

The mixture of general xenophobia and specific distrust of Muslims plays out vividly when immigration is a hot political topic. During the attempts at reform in 2006–07, the right wing mobilized opposition to the Bush plan in part by linking (in their depiction) lax border security and the Muslim threat to American security. Malkin derided the nation's largest Muslim human-rights organization, the Council on American-Islamic Relations (CAIR) and its active support of Bush's efforts and protests of the growing number of questionable local laws. In a 2006 blog post titled "Muslims for Open Borders," she wrote: "Many interesting characters are showing up at the illegal alien demonstrations against immigration enforcement. Black Panthers ... [and] America-bashing Muslim activists."[16] What is especially telling about this post and many others like it is the explicit conflation of those accused of terrorist links—and CAIR often is so accused, unjustly—and "open borders." And, indeed, in a 2006 Gallup poll, two-thirds of respondents said terrorism was one of their major concerns about illegal immigration, equal to its effects on jobs available to Americans.

The strategy of intertwining fear of Muslims and fear of immigrants continued to resonate long after the 9/11 attacks. When two men of Chechen origin detonated two home-made bombs near the finish line of the Boston Marathon in April 2013, their immigrant status and their religion—Islam— quickly came into play. Not only did conservative commentators pound the two for their Muslim beliefs (which appeared to be rather superficial); they also made much of the fact that they were immigrants. That they had been refugees from the Caucasus violence, legally in the country, and brought here as children did not deter the instantaneous baying for new restrictions on immigration. "It is interesting that at this moment, we are considering legalizing or giving regularized status to millions of people," Laura Ingraham said a day after the bombing. "Pretty much none of them have gone through any rigorous background checks."[17] Several members of Congress said that the bipartisan immigration-reform package should be slowed down in the aftermath of the Boston incident. And the reliably caustic Anne Coulter remarked to Fox's Sean Hannity that the immigration system is bringing in more "losers, murderers [and] welfare recipients."[18]

The Boston bombing and the subsequent hyperbolic talk about immigrants did affect the public's perception of the urgency or prudence of immigration reform. According to the results of a Quinnipiac University poll released two weeks after the bombing, 23 percent said their opinion had changed about providing a path to citizenship for undocumented immigrants, although a majority still supported citizenship.[19] The upshot of this is that anti-immigrant activists consciously use the threat of terrorism—a minuscule threat to begin with—as a bludgeon against immigration reform. It parallels closely the right-wing discourse on crime. By any measure, violent or property crimes committed by unauthorized immigrants (and legal immigrants) are far fewer than those committed by native-born Americans. Yet crime as an immigrant-borne threat is one of the incessant mantras of the anti-immigrant crowd. "There is a massive cover up underway across mainstream media outlets regarding the viciousness and frequency of crimes committed by illegal immigrants,"[20] Laura Ingraham said in defending Representative Steve King's infamous comment about most Dreamers being drug smugglers.

I regard this nativist reaction to unauthorized immigration at some length for two reasons. First, the right-wing media outlets have shaped a large segment of the public's attitudes on many issues through bold and clear ideological messaging. The death of immigration reform in 2007 and the difficulty of achieving reform in Obama's second term are due in no small measure to the persistent opposition voiced by conservatives in the media. The second and more important reason is the tenor and substance of this voice. The predominant concern of the right pivots on cultural and social issues: crime (and the ultimate crime, terrorism), English-only versus bilingualism, despoiling American education, and separatism. The last, the *reconquista* and Aztlán fantasies—the notion that the Southwestern US is to be taken back by Mexicans, and the mythical land of Aztlán reborn—are a particular affront to those who think they are struggling to preserve the American Way of Life because it encompasses a complete rejection or over-turning of history and culture. However absurd it is (and nearly all Latinos understand perfectly well that it is absurd), *reconquista* and Aztlán appear frequently in right-wing discourse as demonstrations of Latino treachery.

Remarkably, public opinion about illegal immigration has shifted some-what in a more progressive direction, although it sends mixed signals. Most striking is fairly consistent support for a path to citizenship, even among many Republicans, in questions about legislative reform. About one-third of respondents favor deportation, but consistent majorities support allow-ing unauthorized immigrants to remain if meeting certain conditions (pay-ing a fine, learning English, and so on), in a variety of polls taken in 2013 and 2014. Support for the Dreamers is high, except among Republicans. Support for stronger border enforcement is high. Very clear majorities reject the provision of federal benefits like health care to immigrants who are not citizens. And the public is ambivalent about allowing more legal immigra-tion generally.

That latter sentiment is one in transition, however, as a consensus has begun to form on the employment effect of illegal immigration. For years, the economic issue was front and center.[21] Illegals, the argument went, are stealing jobs from native citizens. This was clearly the sentiment in the 2006 Gallup poll cited earlier. But as more and more research has shown, the employment impacts are slight if there are any at all. Economists have come to the view that the illegal workforce—about 8 million—performs jobs that enhance overall productivity and growth by permitting US-born workers to concentrate on tasks at their skill level and businesses to expand to meet higher demand. Unauthorized immigrants broadly don't compete for the same jobs as US-born workers, although there may be some effect on African-American workers without a high school diploma. Overall, immigrants' effect on the workforce is to raise employment and wages. This would be even more so if legalization were legislated.

There are ample numbers of anecdotes about this—factories raided and emptied of undocumented workers, and little hope of replacing them with Americans (one story had a majority of the replacement workers at a meat-packing plant failing drug tests). Gradually this set of stories has changed opinion, as has testimony like that given by Mayor Michael Bloomberg of New York that his city would come to a standstill if all unauthorized immigrants were prevented from working there. Such a shift was evident in a striking exchange between Laura Ingraham and George Will during a television program in 2014, when Will, a conservative stalwart, argued that immigration was desperately needed for economic growth.

The holdouts on this issue are groups such as Federation for American Immigration Reform (which is anti-reform) and the Heritage Foundation, the bloggers, and the right-wing activists who have a grip on the Republicans in Congress. The claim to be pro-worker is difficult to maintain when one votes against raising the minimum wage, against extending unemployment benefits or food stamps, and against most employment-generating measures. When arguing with George Will, Laura Ingraham cited the lack of assimilation as the first concern. And the ground of empirical economic evidence has slipped away from the nativists altogether.

This is not all good news for immigrants or reform. If ameliorating measures such as better educational opportunities don't provide some ladder for upward mobility, the use of Latino immigrants to perform the lowest-end jobs for the minimum wage is a recipe for a semi-permanent servant class. But the apparent fact that the public doesn't regard "job stealing" as a mortal threat to the United States is good news for reform and for social acceptance of immigration.

If the cultural dimensions of resistance to immigration trump economic reasons, what of the politics of immigration? Is the nativist resistance more political than cultural? Without a doubt, politics is always prominent. The barrier to reform in Congress became as much about denying President Obama an important victory as it had to do with immigration. The rejectionists who are particularly vociferous about the cultural wounds they think illegal immigration visits upon the United States are the same rejectionists on health-care reform, measures to deal with climate change, financial sector reform, economic stimulus, and so on. The hindering of immigration reform is part of the conservative package using obstruction to thwart the Obama administration and Senate Democrats.

I will take up the politics of reform in a later chapter, but it's worth considering where cultural, social, and political categories set and overlap. Cultural and social interactions are not regulated by the state (or shouldn't be), but there is considerable influence of one upon the other in any case. The state determines, for example, pre-college curricula in history, social studies, and other topics that can influence thinking about immigration. Social interactions tend to increase tolerance and respect for diversity, but the reality of how immigrants settle into the United States tends to minimize such social intercourse. Unauthorized immigrants in particular wish to lower exposure to people they don't know or are outside their own group. Upholding cultural traditions that have been brought in with immigration can cause social frictions and retaliation from nativists, but gradually they tend to be seen as part of the "gumbo" of American social life by those in the community, even if a minority sees them as a threat. The right-wing discourse about assimilation—that it is a necessary condition of acceptance, even entry—is framed as a social and cultural value, namely belonging based on cultural submission.

Politics enters this in two straightforward ways. Political leaders can play off of anti-immigrant or pro-immigrant sentiments to gain votes and build political power. This is what has happened in the hundreds of anti-immigrant laws and resolutions across the country, in which politicians respond to or stir cultural sentiments (about English, education, history, and so on) and translate those sentiments into law, regulations, or political exhortations. An interesting debate is surfacing as to whether law itself is a cultural or political expression; technically, it is political in the sense that it is a function of legislatures, governors, and courts, but it is often an expression of cultural anxiety or disapproval. The same can roughly be claimed for the idea of citizenship, a political manifestation of belonging and acceptance and sovereignty, but who is given legal entry and a path to citizenship is also a matter of cultural acceptance, as the history of immigration law and citizenship clearly shows.

So what is "political" in the sense of governance, making law, and setting the terms of citizenship is very much intertwined with cultural values and perceptions. There is also the matter of the sudden emergence of

Hispanic political power, as evidenced particularly in the 2012 presidential election. A great amount of talk has been heard since then about the need for Republicans, who lost the Hispanic vote by 50 percentage points, to participate in immigration reform to win over Hispanic voters. Twenty-three million eligible voters are Hispanics (including Puerto Ricans on the mainland), up from 13 million in 2000. They made up 17 percent of the population in 2012, but only 10 percent of those actually voting, yet the trend is upward for both, and it is expected that by the middle of this century the country will be 27 percent Hispanic. It's a sizable and growing block of voters that by some reckonings should be conservative, given the importance of religion and entrepreneurship to many. But for now, they vote Democratic, mainly because they see the Democratic Party as the natural supporter of immigrants (particularly in contrast to the sharply hostile rhetoric of many Republicans) and despite the record number of deportations during the Obama administration. In this sense, then, the "political" has to do with the growing power of Hispanics. This partly explains why Republicans resist a path to citizenship, even one that is 12 to 15 years long, because they believe those immigrants will be Democrats.

What I argue in this book, however, is that the primary source of resistance to immigration is cultural, and that this plays out in many ways—in curriculum battles, in identity politics (of the nativists *and* the immigrants), and in the controversies over the Dreamers and reform generally. A structure of oppression that sent millions northward from Central America and Mexico was and is an economic system—originally the *encomienda*, now neoliberal globalization—but it has been enabled and sustained by social and cultural norms and coercion. This structural argument is mirrored in the Great Migration of African-Americans, which was also a response to and reflective of a system of oppression rooted in cultural and social norms and practices, and nourished by law symbiotically connected to that oppression. Many scholars would no doubt object to this comparison of the Great Migration and the Hispanic immigration. The black migration was borne of unspeakable cruelty in the antebellum South and its aftermath, and was, of course, an *internal* migration. But I believe a comparison is useful to underscore the structural similarities and responses, which are striking in their resemblances: the white/Anglo resistance is primarily cultural and manifests in remarkably identical ways. This is what we call a natural experiment. The resistance to blacks in Northern cities could be considered an outlier in the migration experience generally in the United States; after all, the Irish, the Slavs, and other immigrants faced prejudice before integrating successfully into the fabric of American society, politics, and economic life. But the enormous numbers of Hispanics migrating to the United States, legally or not, has stirred a reaction much more akin to the pervasive and abiding social/cultural rejection and low-wage-labor acceptance greeting African-Americans than to the nineteenth-century immigration from Southern and Eastern Europe. And in this similarity there are vivid lessons about how society manifests its ambivalence about immigration today.

In chapter 2 I delve into what I regard as the most illustrative example of a cultural clash of significant scale that one can find in the United States today: the curriculum controversy in Tucson's high schools. A Mexican-American studies program, by most accounts a valuable and motivating course of study for Chicanos, was banned outright by the Anglo political establishment for being anti-American. The curriculum, mainly Mexican history and literature, gave students a stronger sense of identity and self-worth. The Anglo politicians, feeling threatened by that emergent identity, reacted by, in effect, raiding the Tucson school board and holding it hostage through a threat to withhold state funding if the curriculum wasn't thrown out. The controversy reveals much about the cultural contours of the immigration cacophony.

In chapter 3 I take up what I call the "raid mentality" by discussing a raid by agents of the federal government on a factory in the Massachusetts city of New Bedford. The 2007 raid by Immigration and Customs Enforcement police netted 360 arrests and ultimately resulted in the deportation of 161 Central Americans. The same story could have been written about a dozen other places in the United States. Why raid that particular factory? Was the harshness of the agents' tactics related to a political agenda? What happened to the people arrested, placed in detention centers, and deported? What happened to their families? Did it "solve" the problem of illegal immigration in any significant way?

In chapter 4 I contrast the reactions of an older generation of unauthorized immigrants, those who stay in the shadows, and the new generation of educated but unauthorized youth who have taken up their own civil rights cause. These so-called Dreamers have altered the immigration debate on their own as few others have managed to do. They confront the raid mentality and the passivity that it forced upon their parents and grand-parents. They bear similarities to the black activists and the Chicano rights advocates of the 1960s and the 1970s—classic social movement organizing to "speak truth to power." But their generation is also beset by a small minority that is trapped in violent street gangs.

In chapter 5 I return to a theme mentioned here and teased out some in the accounts about New Bedford and Tucson: how economic globalization has created the conditions of desperation that drives migrants north across the US border. I focus on Guatemala and Mexico. The case of Guatemala (the majority of the arrested in New Bedford were Guatemalans) is revealing because its difficulties were in part the consequence of US intervention, first to oust an elected leader that Washington didn't like, and later to support a series of strongmen who committed what the United Nations has called a genocide of the indigenous people. War combined with "neoliberal" economic policies have devastated the rural communities and prompted about a million peasants to take the long and dangerous journey north to the United States. This migration has been recently punctuated by tens of thousands of children making the trek without their parents in order to escape drug-gang violence. A similar story describes Mexican emigration, and although war plays a role in Mexican history, of course (not least the United States' seizure of half of Mexico in 1849), the main stimulus to the movement of people north nowadays is the drab economy. It's an economy that has been a laboratory for neoliberal policies as embodied in the North American Free Trade Agreement (NAFTA), but, as is so often the case with these policies wherever they are applied, a few people do very well and a great many people are left behind, their communities disrupted, their ways of life unsustainable. So they emigrate.

In chapter 6 I consider the current debate on immigration reform in the United States. The improbability of actual reform's being passed by Congress is plain, but the dynamics of reform are worth reviewing. The inadequacy of the response by politicians in both political parties is particularly apparent. The politicians talk border security and little else—the raid mentality—and conduct a hollow debate about citizenship, while the actual drivers of illegal immigration get no notice in Washington. That translates into no reform (as long as the extreme conservatives control the House of Representatives) or reform that deals only partially with those unauthorized immigrants already here, but not prevent others from coming.

In chapter 7 I discuss two arguments that are central to the immigration discourse. One focuses on "legality," and I review that concept to challenge the rigid way it is used in current popular discourse. That includes the surprisingly supple notion of citizenship and belonging. Perhaps a growing recognition of the fact that the "crime" of illegal immigration is actually a misdemeanor, a minor civil infraction (technically "entry without inspection"), will soften the rigidity around legality. I then take up the hot-button issue of the use of the Spanish language—an issue that has become a linchpin of the nativists' distress with Latino immigration generally.

I conclude the book with discussion of some hopeful signs that the immigration imbroglio is gradually being resolved in many corners of American society. Surveys indicate a surprising amount of support for reform, and even citizenship, for those here without authorization. Some cities and towns now have "welcome committees" for new immigrants, and other cultural efforts to embrace the controversy creatively are evident in film, television, and music. Many of the old bugaboos based on racial stereotypes—that Mexicans are lazy or thieving, for example—may be giving way to an appreciation of how much of the US economy is dependent on their low-wage labor. What I see is the beginning of a "norm cascade"—a change in what we believe is the correct values regarding immigrants, what they contribute to society, and how they should be treated. Optimism about solving the problem of illegal immigration ebbs and flows, but what seems to remain year after year is a deep fissure in the American identity as a nation of immigrants. There is, on the one hand, ample evidence that the United States is indeed such a nation, one that is replenished constantly and with increasingly diverse immigrants. But at the same time, the resistance to Latinos particularly indicates deep animus toward newcomers who are in some ways different from the dominant white culture, and this has always been true even as the contours of "dominant white culture" have shifted over the decades. Black migration was resisted for similar reasons—as a threat to the self-concept of a white nation. And, as with that "threat," the resistance has been built on manipulating law and mounting raids.

The title of this book, *Dream Chasers*, is meant to convey two intertwined aspirations. The yearning for the American Dream is, of course, a commonplace in popular discourse. But it does have a deeper resonance when it comes to immigration, and, indeed, the resistance to immigration. Our expectations about the dreams immigrants harbor about America may be quite mistaken, conditioned by our own sense of exceptionalism. Many of those who enter without authorization or overstay visas do so simply to work, and don't plan to stay. So their dreams really have to do with a better life in Mexico or Guatemala or wherever they came from and hope to return to. Many others do pursue the dream of a better life in the United States, of course, and no doubt many come merely for work and end up staying because their lives here fulfill some of their dreams—a good education for their children, job opportunities, freedom from crime, or other reasons. The millions of native-born European-origin Americans who are sharply critical of "open borders" or "amnesty" and oppose reform also have a dream. Their belief in the American Dream is one in which all Americans speak English, adopt American values, and are here legally. It is easy to disparage this as a reactionary stance, but it persists as a powerful cultural vision and actually shapes much of the politics of the immigration debate. This book does not seek to judge these dreams; rather, it seeks to see them as the apotheosis of cultural and historical understandings of race and ethnicity, place and belonging, privilege and oppression. And these understandings are resilient: to borrow a popular phrase, dreams die hard.

One of the more disturbing implications of the arguments I consider in this book is that what has happened to black America—to some tragic extent a group struggling to reinvent itself culturally but mired in economic and political disadvantages—may also be the fate of Latino America: a permanent "underclass" hindered by low educational achievement and high unemployment, dead-end jobs, and increasing problems with drugs and crime, all of which acts in a reinforcing cycle. What Daniel Patrick Moynihan once reported about the black urban ghettos, that they were a "tangle of pathologies," is the nightmare scenario for Latinos, too. Tough neighborhoods in East Los Angeles and Newark, among many other cities, attest to this possibility. Legalizing those who aren't now authorized to be here might not prevent that scenario if the cultural and social biases harden, or if reform and border security and conditions in the prime sending countries don't perform, because the unauthorized will continue to find a way to join us. Without reform, however, the chance that the Latino experience here will be more similar to the black experience, rather than less similar, increases.

2 RAIDING THE SCHOOLS: THE RIVEN SOUL OF ARIZONA

Dolores Huerta didn't realize the storm of dust she was stirring when she spoke at Tucson High School that day in April 2006, the day she said that Republicans hate Latinos. She was speaking in a state that was not just dominated by Republicans, but by the large and growing extremist wing of the party. Huerta, then 76 years old, was legendary among Mexican-Americans. She co-founded the United Farmworkers Union with César Chávez and became one of the most vociferous and effective advocates for the rights of workers, women, and Latinos anywhere in the world, with a list of legislative achievements that dwarfs most activists and, for that matter, most legislators.

Huerta was in Tucson as part of a two-day recognition of the rights of undocumented immigrants, with the students and others marching the day before she spoke. She reminded her high school audience that the undocumented are the people doing the hard work of taking care of the elderly and children, cleaning homes and hospitals, and they deserve to be citizens. "We didn't cross the border," she told the Tucson youth, who answered in unison with her, "the border crossed us." And along the way, she uttered the provocative remark "Republicans hate Latinos."[1]

It didn't take more than a few hours for the right wing to respond in full throat, demanding an investigation and questioning, typically, on the basis of money—who was paying for Huerta's visit? Who paid for the school buses to take students to hear her? Arizona Superintendent of Public Instruction Tom Horne got wind of this and sent a deputy, Margaret Dugan, to Tucson High to counter Huerta's comments. When students realized that no questions would be permitted at that talk, 200 of them stood up during the assembly, duct tape covering their mouths, and walked out. Horne blamed the budding ethnic studies program for the disrespect, and spent the next three years trying to bring it down. Legislative attempts to ban ethnic studies failed until Obama was elected and lured Governor Janet Napolitano to Washington to become Secretary of Homeland Security. With the conservative Jan Brewer as governor, Horne successfully pushed through bills banning ethnic studies.

But not all ethnic studies. Just one, in just one place: Chicano studies in Tucson.

Horne had political ambitions, and was elected attorney general in 2010, but one man's career trajectory doesn't explain the depth and breadth of controversy stirred by banning this ethnic studies program. True, as superintendent from 2003 to 2010 he pushed hard for English-only instruction and the traditional canon of Western civilization, but these are standard tropes of the right wing. His final act as superintendent at the end of 2010 was to ban the Mexican-American program. The uproar this caused may be unique in the annals of American education.

Arizona was in the throes of an anti-immigrant frenzy at the time. The 2006–07 reform effort by President Bush had spiraled up passions on all side of the illegal immigration debate, and this never subsided in Arizona, which had been passing bills and referenda to stop the "invaders of American sovereignty" for several years. When Napolitano went off to Washington and the full impact of the economic downturn that began in 2007 was ripping through Arizona and the rest of the country, a bill like SB 1070, Support Our Law Enforcement and Safe Neighborhoods Act, was almost inevitable. Introduced in January 2010 and passed only a few weeks later, the law made it a crime to aid illegal immigrants and enabled police to stop and ascertain the legal status of any individual. Its provisions were so stark that the Justice Department challenged its constitutionality, and by 5–3 vote the US Supreme Court overturned several of the worst provisions. Such measures included police power to detain and demand papers for anyone who they suspected were in the country illegally, making it a crime for such immigrants to solicit and perform work. One provision was upheld—the right of police to check immigration status of someone arrested for other crimes—but the Supreme Court generally insisted that immigration was a federal matter and states couldn't concoct their own rules. Justices Antonin

Scalia, Clarence Thomas, and Samuel Alito issued a sharp dissent that said "If securing its territory in this fashion is not within the power of Arizona, we should cease referring to it as a sovereign State"[2]—a view that harkened back to the Civil War and the South's insistence on absolute states' rights.

The ruling didn't much discourage the Republican politicians who were riding high on anti-immigrant sentiment. Governor Brewer signed SB 1070 and never failed to defend it fervently, and famously made headlines by wagging her finger at President Obama in a tarmac tirade. Obama had recently declared that out-of-status immigrants who were brought to the United States as children would not be deported, and Brewer retaliated by denying them driver's licenses, saying that they had no right to public benefits. (As it happens, the State of Arizona had already issued some 40,000 licenses and ID cards to such immigrants in the previous six years.) Another well-known politician, Maricopa County Sheriff Joe Arpaio, had been touting himself as "America's toughest sheriff" since his election in 1992, and he demonstrated his toughness by his abuse of Mexican immigrants in particular, keeping them in oven-hot jails and living by his own interpretation of the Constitution. Harsh raids and harsh treatment are his hallmarks, earning rebukes from Amnesty International and lawsuits from the Justice Department and others. Among his many violations was suppressing evidence in more than 400 sexual abuse cases, many of them in Latino communities and most of the victims children. The list of lawsuits and charges against him, for everything between corruption and staging a fake assassination attempt on himself, would fill its own book. He was reelected for the fifth time in 2012 by a seven-percentage-point margin.

It is this septic political atmosphere in which the anti-immigrant sentiments were nurtured, and that gave rise to the bill targeting Chicano studies for elimination. By 2010, when John Huppenthal won election as Arizona's new superintendent of schools, controversies about several of the state's legal measures the state had taken to stop illegal immigration were in full swing. Huppenthal ran on the issue of taking down Tucson's Chicano studies program. Horne ordered the program to be ended, and within days Huppenthal was in office to enforce that order. "Huppenthal immediately challenged Tucson Unified School District in a long-running dispute over its ethnic-studies curriculum, saying he agrees with his predecessor, Tom Horne, that the district needs to change or eliminate it," the *Arizona*

Republic reported a few days into 2011. "'That class is symbolic of a broad cultural conflict,' said Huppenthal."[3]

On that, at least, the superintendent was absolutely correct.

The ethnic studies program came about in part because of a desegregation order. In a federal court ruling aimed at racial desegregation in 1978, Tucson began a long and contentious journey to balance the city's schools and spent nearly a billion dollars to comply. After three decades, the performance of African-American children—6 percent of the district's population, many of them progeny of the Great Migration—had not improved and dropout rates continued at high levels. What had changed was the ethnic composition of the Tucson schools, namely soaring Latino enrollment, now almost two-thirds of the student body, and diminishing white enrollment, down to about one-fourth of the school population.

That demographic earthquake shook the curriculum, too, by unsettling the old ways of looking at history. Even in the 1980s, middle schools and high schools were still teaching the "great men" stories of how the West was won and the nation governed, and the sense of entitlement of white settlers so prevalent in politics was reflected in the official pedagogy for children. Arizona was especially ripe territory for the national myth of the frontier, the abiding story of white, Christian settlers who tamed the wilderness and subdued the savages who inhabited it. The Frontier Myth began with the Puritans, who believed their encounter with the wilderness was divinely ordained, and the ideology of the frontier had scarcely changed in the 300 years to Arizona's inclusion as the last of the lower 48 states in 1912. The Frontier Myth included among "savages" not only the indigenous peoples that European-origin settlers encountered and nearly exterminated on the march west, but also the Spanish-origin Mexicans and mestizos who had populated Arizona for hundreds of years. The education of school children in Arizona, as elsewhere in the United States, repeated this myth, but there the "savages" were a majority of the student body.

The desegregation order occasioned a new look at the curriculum, and that brought with it ethnic studies—black, Native American, and Mexican-American—and the inevitable challenges to the dominant white paradigm. The order was ended in 2009, opening the door to Horne and Huppenthal's ban on ethnic studies, but a federal judge re-imposed the sanction in 2012, stating that the school district should "develop and implement culturally relevant courses of instruction designed to reflect the history, experiences, and culture of African-American and Mexican American communities."[4] That was the crux of it, the assertion that the relevance of education to the students was morally compelling and practically crucial, as educators sought to keep students in school and boost their achievement by appealing to how they saw themselves in American society.

As it developed over the last several years, the Mexican-American Studies (MAS) program certainly took up an alternative view. Where Mexican-Americans and other Latinos fit into American society was depicted as an oppressed minority, relegated to second-class jobs, education, housing. The story of immigration and identity in this case was not one of capture from a faraway place, enslavement, and another hundred years of Jim Crow, as it was with African-Americans, but a claim to sovereignty over the territories of the Southwest along with the equally downtrodden Native Americans. The Mexican heritage of the area is long and deep. Spanish conquistador Coronado and priests established outposts as early as the sixteenth century, and presidios, including Tucson in 1775, were created in southern Arizona. When Mexico won its independence from Spain in 1821, Arizona was indeed Mexican territory, as was New Mexico, until the Mexican-American War. Parts of the state, including Tucson, remained Mexican territory until the Gadsden Purchase in 1853 set the current borders. So it can be said, and is often invoked, that Arizona was Mexican before it was American. And the way the United States got it was an act of classic imperialism.

For generations of American schoolchildren, the Mexican-American War is a brief interlude between the founding and the Civil War—a small triumph of Manifest Destiny (the term was coined for this war) by a president whose four-year administration is taught in schools as the "era of good feeling." James K. Polk, an Andrew Jackson protégé elected on a promise to annex Texas and California among other lands in the west, sparked a war in 1846 by sending General Zachary Taylor to a disputed area along the Rio Grande. Provoked by Taylor's men, a small contingent of Mexican troops attacked, and the war was on.

America's first foreign war ended quickly, thanks to the superior firepower its industrialized base afforded. Within two years it was over, and Polk demanded and received California, Utah, part of Colorado, New Mexico, and Arizona, with the Gadsden Purchase completing the task. (The war also produced one of the great treatises of dissent, Henry David Thoreau's

"On the Duty of Civil Disobedience," written to protest the war and slavery.) In effect, the war with Mexico began with the American expansion into Texas, which was annexed in 1845; thus, within about a decade, the United States had won, by violence, about half of Mexico.

The war was in keeping with the Frontier Myth, and during the war the popular press and politicians depicted the Mexicans as savages standing in the way of young America and its restless dynamism. This set of attitudes didn't differ greatly from descriptions of the Wampanoag or the Apache, although Mexico was a significantly urban culture with obvious European influences. The idea of annexing all of Mexico was unpopular in the United States because the prospect of incorporating so many dark-skinned people was distasteful. This racism was quite in the open, a given of the debate. In the end, of course, just the territories mentioned earlier were taken by Polk; in all of these, "only" 75,000 Mexicans lived. The specter of racial contagion was contained. (When the United States warred on the Philippines half a century later, the same resistance to annexation appeared, also based on race; in fact, even the "anti-imperialists" were significantly motivated by racism.) The Frontier Myth, as explained by its leading expositor, the cultural historian Richard Slotkin, "permitted racial warfare as a means of achieving progress" but "envisioned such wars as involving extermination or displacement of small bands of savages by civilized men, not conquest and integration of another populous culture into the American system."[5] But the debate over annexation, for our purposes, was a sideshow. What is important about the war for Texas and the Mexican-American War is the indelible fact that the borders *did* move, and the abiding attitudes of the privileged white culture depicted Mexicans as savages, much like African-Americans or Native Americans.

The rough history of US conquest led in the 1960s and the 1970s to the rise of Chicano activism, which created its own myths of identity and longing. The relatively harmless myth of Aztlán, an Aztec-based narrative of a paradisiacal land of forebears, was invoked as a foundation story that actually has nothing to do with the indigenous tribes of Arizona and even less to do with Spanish-descended. More serious is the brash notion of *reconquista*, which has come to convey the compelling reminder, as Dolores Huerta said at the Tucson High School assembly, that "we didn't cross the border, the border crossed us." *Reconquista* is a marginal, if potent, claim that the territories seized by the United States in the nineteenth century are lands inhabited in large numbers by Latinos and that they have a right to their own sovereignty. Few Mexican-Americans subscribe to *reconquista* as a political goal, but it's a powerful cultural avatar. It says, in one word, "This was our land, not yours, you took it through violence, and some day it will once again be our homeland." Of course, the land was actually inhabited exclusively by indigenous tribes, not by Mexicans per se. "The problem with Mexican-American studies," according to the Indian activist Mike Wilson, "is that it imagines this land as Aztlán, and I say that this is our land."[6]

The right wing in the United States cites occasional references to *reconquista* as proof of disloyalty and even treason among Latinos. *Reconquista* has become the right's key to understanding Mexican-American activism, everything from political action like voter registration to anti-Arpaio organizing to the Tucson MAS curriculum. (Of course, no such alarm was sounded when petitions to secede from the United States became briefly epidemic after Obama's reelection or when Texas governor Rick Perry indicated his support for secession.) Patrick Buchanan wrote in 2006 that the Mexican government was behind the plot to recapture the US Southwest. The *reconquista*, he explained, is not to be accomplished by armed force, but "by a nonviolent invasion and cultural transformation of that huge slice of America into a Mexamerican borderland."[7]

Recapturing a lost homeland is scarcely a new fantasy, although it can be a slippery slope politically. The legitimacy of Israel's taking of its pre-1967 land was based on an ancient claim, and few of those who decry the Mexican-Americans' claims would dispute Israeli sovereignty. The *reconquista* and Aztlán imaginary reflects something much more profound than a political program, about which it scarcely has credibility, however. There is something about those concepts that resonates across the political spectrum. And it derives from the encounters of the nineteenth century.

The idea of Mexicans and Mexican-Americans as savages persists in collective memory and in contemporary stereotypes: it is the stuff of what many Latinos see as the oppressive atmosphere in the United States today. The Mexican-American War and the Texas war for independence salted and preserved these depictions, or, one could say, the mythologizing of those conflicts from the Northerners' perspective. Among the sturdier cultural paragons of this era is the rogue adventurer Davy Crockett, who was turned into a classic American hero at the defense of the Alamo; most Americans of a certain age can recall the Disney version, which portrayed Crockett the last man standing against the Mexican hordes.

As Slotkin and other scholars explain, the mythologizing of the Texas war of independence and of Davy Crockett and Sam Houston as quintessential "frontiersmen" was a conscious political project, sometimes (as in the case of Crockett) conducted by those being mythologized. Sam Houston, a vastly more consequential figure in history than Crockett, nurtured more ordinary self-embellishments, but disdained Mexicans and Tejanos. "The vigor of the descendants of the sturdy North," he told his troops before the decisive battle of San Jacinto, can never "mix with the phlegm of the indolent Mexicans." Texas' declaration of independence similarly disparaged Mexicans as "unfit to be free" and "incapable of self-government."[8] Such sentiments have led some historians to see secession as a "race war" rather than the glorious triumph of upstart Americans itching to free themselves of the yoke of the backward Mexicans. (Some historians even see the conflict as representing a "European civil war" between Northern Protestants and Southern Catholics, a plausible idea insofar as anti-Catholic prejudice was strong throughout the nineteenth century.) The glorification of the Texas experience—which was, of course, the triumph of immigrants and the triumphalism of the Mexican-American War that was its possibly inevitable consequence have been long-running tropes of the Frontier Myth and Manifest Destiny. These stories, infused into American popular culture ("Remember the Alamo!"), required not only adoration of American bravery and love of freedom but also attribution of the opposite qualities to Mexicans. And the wars of 1836 to 1848 encompass and represent the standard story of America's westward expansion with regard to Mexico. This mythologizing far surpasses the story of Aztlán in importance, but it is scarcely acknowledged as mythmaking in American culture.

Late in the nineteenth century and early in the twentieth, Arizona aspired to statehood but was held back by old-fashioned imperialists such as Senator Albert Beveridge of Indiana, who regarded the racial/ethnic mix of Arizona and New Mexico as unsuitable for full membership in the American nation. It was, of course, a mix of Mexicans, Apache, Tohono O'odham, Hopi, Navajo, and many other indigenous tribes and the Anglo settlers who had come particularly since the Gadsden Purchase and who increasingly dominated the state politically and economically. Beveridge and his kind thought this mix was, in the familiar phrase, incapable of self-government. "Throughout the two-decade struggle to become a state," the historian Eric Meeks writes, "Anglos in Arizona honed an argument ... that the indigenous and ethnic Mexican populations would have little role in government. As Arizonans sat down to write a constitution, this argument manifested itself in explicit, exclusionary policies designed to relegate non-whites and those who did not speak English to second-class citizenship ... . Racial inequality was not simply an unfortunate corollary to full statehood; it was built into the very identity of Arizona from its inception."[9] The entire discussion of Arizona's admission to the Union was predicated on the widely accepted assertion that only true Americans—white, European-origin settlers from other parts of the country, by then a majority—would be capable of ruling; the Mexicans and the Indians would provide labor but were incapable of more.

And these images and the ideas behind them persisted. For decades, as the anthropologist Bárbara Cruz writes, the image of the indolent and corruptible Mexican was embedded in American teaching: "[S]chool history textbooks tend to portray Latin Americans as alternately violent, passive, lazy and unwilling to assimilate into mainstream US society—when they are included at all."[10] And the schools themselves have reinforced such messages among the Latino children by assuming that schooling was a temporary stop before assuming the life of a young mother or store clerk or lawn boy, or worse. Studies show that, unlike many immigrant groups, each successive generation of Mexican-Americans performed worse in school than their predecessors. "For a majority of [this] high school's regular (non-college-bound) track, schooling is a *subtractive process*," the researcher Angela Valenzuela explained in a 1999 study. "It divests these students of important social and cultural resources, leaving them progressively vulnerable to academic failure."[11] The force-fed assimilationist curricula leave these students cold, and their lack of achievement shows it.

So, quite predictably, the Tucson school controversy spun around sideshow issues such as discussions of Aztlán or the *reconquista* instead of the Anglo mythmaking that is the standard text. John Huppenthal, as a state senator, had introduced a bill (HB 2281) calling for a ban on ethnic studies, a major tenet of which was that ethnic studies promoted the overthrow of the US government. The other provisions of the bill were closely aligned with that notion—for example, a ban would be imposed if such an educational program promoted group identity over individual identity, was designed to teach a specific ethnic group, or promoted resentment against a class of people. Huppenthal, and Tom Horne before him, had repeatedly alleged that all these violations were occurring in Tucson. Anti-Americanism and its tributaries—ethnic solidarity in particular—were equated with the *reconquista* movement and similar cultural outbursts.

Was the program of instruction in Tucson anti-American? Much of the controversy boils down to that question.

The MAS program was introduced into the high school curriculum in 1998. It gradually became a popular alternative to standard American history courses because (in the words of Sean Arce, one of the program's founders) in the old course of study "students didn't see themselves in the curriculum—what does it have to do with me or my family?"[12] Another teacher who went through the Tucson schools as a youngster notes that "it validated the struggle of folks who were just like me, the immigrant story, the story of not quite fitting in to this American fabric."[13] This is the core concept of such studies programs, the purpose of which is to provide a "place" for those typically marginalized in American society. It instills a sense of affirming identity, of feeling there is value in being Latino or African-American or female in a country that has been largely dominated—and whose historiography has been dominated—by white men of European origin. It's no wonder, then, that the MAS program grew to include large numbers of students—2,500 at one point, nearly 20 percent of high school enrollment. And it's no wonder that two of the popular texts of the program were Paulo Freire's *Pedagogy of the Oppressed* and Howard Zinn's *People's History of the United States.*

In different ways, Freire's book and Zinn's both encapsulate the promise of the MAS program as well as its provocations. Freire's celebrated 1970 tract is provocative precisely because it pivots on a new vision of the practice of education. The book (written by a Brazilian educator and social activist) became popular as a kind of complement of liberation theology and similar leftist movements that regarded post-colonial dominance by capitalism and the United States particularly as a cultural as well as an economic and political phenomenon. The "the pedagogy of the oppressed," Freire wrote, is

a pedagogy which must be forged with, not for, the oppressed (whether individuals or peoples) in the incessant struggle to regain their humanity. This pedagogy makes oppression and its causes objects of reflection by the oppressed, and from that reflection will come their necessary engagement in the struggle for their liberation. And in the struggle this pedagogy will be made and remade.

He continued:

The central problem is this: How can the oppressed, as divided, unauthentic beings, participate in developing the pedagogy of their liberation? Only as they discover themselves to be "hosts" of the oppressor can they contribute to the midwifery of their liberating pedagogy. As long as they live in the duality in which *to be* is *to be like,* and *to be like* is *to be like the oppressor,* this contribution is impossible. The pedagogy of the oppressed is an instrument for their critical discovery that both they and their oppressors are manifestations of dehumanization.[14]

This struggle in Latin America, despite its many decades of political independence from Spanish imperialism, reflects a common paradox of postcolonialism. That is, the old ways die hard, not only the tendency of the *ancien regime* to exercise privilege and even dominion, but so too with the habits of the oppressed—of deference, of passivity, of not wanting to rock the boat. This was the central tragedy of Jim Crow: after the Civil War, the system of white domination was in some ways even worse than slavery. The attempt to emerge from this gripping condition of "divided, unauthentic beings" took more than 150 years in Latin America, as one strongman replaced another throughout the hemisphere until the debt crisis spurred a new, democratic populism in the 1990s and the 2000s. Something roughly similar happened to African-Americans, who migrated from the South but also asserted themselves politically in cities where they were a majority, often to be disappointed by activist leaders turned corrupt mayors. The same might be said of Africa. Eventually, the divided self, the urge to "be like the oppressor," is resolved and leads to normal politics. (One twist of history for African-Americans is that the triumph of Barack Obama is outside the historical experience of most black Americans, as he isn't a descendant of slaves.) For Latinos in the United States, their political power was unrealized in part because their own identity was unformed, which is also true of African-Americans, but for different reasons. By seizing upon the opportunity to explore their identity—where they came from and why—the Mexican-origin children in Tucson were also laying claim to political authenticity. This struggle is at the root of all Latino activism, whether for curricular or immigration reform or political rights: to shuffle off the inherent oppressiveness—as a state of mind as well as an objective condition—of post-colonialism.

The language of oppression was enough to send Horne and Huppen-thal through the roof, of course; that any Americans were caught in a sys-tem of oppression was a heresy and could never be acknowledged, even as the oppressive circumstances of slavery and male chauvinism were readily apparent. The notion that Latinos were oppressed by the dominant Anglo culture was simply unacceptable to the dominant Anglo elites. Freire's peda-gogy, moreover, demands that a student examine this oppression critically. Students who do so will be more engaged than if they were merely studying from afar the oppression of others, and that engagement is a splendid form of learning likely to lead to activism—specifically, protest of the oppression and the oppressors. Such pedagogy will, of course, cause anxiety in the edu-cational hierarchy. Couple it with books like Zinn's *People's History*, which gives voice to oppressed peoples from throughout American history, and you have an exhilarating mixture of liberation and self-realization.

John Huppenthal (who held degrees in engineering and in business admin-istration) was a state senator before his election as superintendent of Arizo-na's public schools. During his nearly 20 years in the legislature he authored more than 200 bills on education and sat on several relevant committees, so he came to be superintendent with a long interest in learning. In most respects, he is a conventional Arizona Republican politician. He considers his achievements as the state's top education official to be the A-to-F grad-ing system for schools and districts and enacting "school choice," a favor-ite conservative cause to create a publicly funded alternative to the public school system, which they believe has been corrupted by teachers' unions. But what Huppenthal probably will best be remembered for is his decision to close the Mexican-American Studies programs in Tucson.

Upon becoming superintendent, Huppenthal immediately took up Tom Horne's charge that the Tucson Unified School District (TUSD) was in viola-tion of the law he had guided through the legislature. (Horne, as attorney general, made this official as soon as he entered that office.) After sending two investigators to Tucson, Huppenthal issued his finding:

A school district or charter school in this state shall not include in its Program of instruction

any courses or classes that include any of the following:

1. Promote overthrowing the US government;

2. Promote resentment towards a race or class of people;

3. Are designed primarily for pupils of a particular ethnic race; and

4. Advocate ethnic solidarity instead of the treatment of pupils as individuals.[15]

Under the second provision, the team from the Arizona Department of Education (ADE) investigating the curriculum's use in Tucson found that "reviewed materials repeatedly reference white people as being 'oppressors' and 'oppressing' the Latino people," and "reviewed materials present only one perspective of historical events, that of the Latino people being persecuted oppressed and subjugated by the 'hegemony'—or white America."[16] Similar charges were made with respect to subsections 3 and 4. Huppenthal ordered that TUSD bring the program into compliance with state law within 60 days or lose 10 percent of state education funding, or about $15 million, a sum that Tucson couldn't afford to lose.

The school district and the MAS teachers and students took strong exception to the findings and appealed the superintendent's decisions. Two students, writing in a local newspaper, put it bluntly: "Huppenthal defied the findings of the audit he himself ordered that cost taxpayers $170,000," wrote Asiya Mir and Ryan Velasquez. "Huppenthal distorted the facts."[17] That audit, by a large consulting firm based in Florida called Cambium Learning, did in fact find the Mexican-American Studies program in compliance. Indeed, the auditors' conclusions were quite positive overall: The programs, it stated, "were designed to improve student achievement" and had "valuable course descriptions aligned with state standards, commendable curricular unit and lesson plan design, engaging instructional practices, and collective inquiry strategies through approved Arizona State Standards."[18] There was virtually no evidence, said Cambium, of the kind of resentment-stirring racialist ideas that Huppenthal later asserted. Apparently dissatisfied with the audit, Huppenthal sent two of his staff to Tucson to review the MAS program, and it was their visit that triggered his finding of non-compliance.

At an appeals hearing later in the summer of 2011, it became clear there was a certain element of "he said / she said" when judging the validity of the investigations. The two staff members, John Stollar and Kathy Hrabluk, asserted that Cambium had inadequately looked at the program and was misled by MAS teachers. But under questioning by Richard Martinez, a lawyer representing MAS, Stollar and Hrabluk acknowledged that they "never observed any classes or read any of the books they cited and they drew their conclusions only from class materials," according to a news report.[19] While others testified against the program, the confluence of Huppenthal's rejection of the Cambium report and his use of his own aides' less-than-credible methods led logically to the perception of a political agenda. As two students put it in a "special to the *Arizona Daily Star*," "Huppenthal should explain the inconsistencies and lack of transparency in how, we believe, he misrepresented the audit's findings. ... Huppenthal and the state may attempt to destroy our classes through discriminatory political distortions, but they can never lock us out of our education, history and culture."[20]

The assessments, the finding, and the appeal in the spring and summer of 2011 were magnified by an extraordinary outburst of student activism that led to MAS students occupying a school board meeting, a national attention-getter and an action that both galvanized the community and polarized Arizona more than ever on the issue of ethnic studies.

The occasion was a school board meeting in the squat, two-story Tucson school administration building in a nondescript residential neighborhood in the center of the city. The school board, which had long supported the Mexican-American Studies program, if warily, was divided on Huppenthal's actions. The previous December, it had passed a resolution backing the program by a vote of 4 to 1. But by spring it was clear that the board had a tiger by the tail, and controlling it wasn't going to be easy.

"In April, I foresaw a train wreck coming," school board member Mark Stegeman later recalled, "so I proposed to expand and revise MAS, to make it an elective. This caused a huge commotion. The issue was so polarized by this point that the proponents weren't willing to make any concessions." Stegeman thought the Cambium assessment was inadequate because MAS teachers would not cooperate with what they saw as a Huppenthal gambit, but said the "audit give a fairly clean bill of health, that MAS was not breaking the law, and this put Huppenthal in a bind."[21] But then the students' action at the April 26 school board meeting ratcheted up the visibility and emotions of the issue.

It was Stegeman's proposal to change the credit for the MAS courses (mostly in Mexican and Chicano history and literature) from fulfilling requirements for graduation to being electives—in many respects more a symbolic alteration. But the students saw this as an affront and as likely to be a first step toward eliminating MAS. "Since February, we've been just put on the back burner," Eliza Mesa, one of the protesters, told an interviewer. "We have asked for meetings with them. And we've done civil discourse. We've done that. We've done it peacefully. And it seems, each time, that it just goes in one ear and out the other." She and other students organized a group called UNIDOS (United as Non-discriminatory Individuals Demanding Our Studies). "This [electives] resolution was very, very last-minute on their part, and it was completely against the stances that they've come out against HB 2281," Meza continued. "The resolution was going to be voted on, and as we knew prior that three of the five board members were going to vote for the resolution to be passed, and only two of them were in support of us. So we were aware completely that if we didn't stop the vote from happening, that the classes would be turned into elective courses that wouldn't have been able to count as a core credit upon graduation for the students at the high schools."[22]

Dozens of MAS students arrived at the April 26 school board meeting, packing the small meeting room, which normally held about fifty people. Just before the board members were to take their seats at their courtroom-style desks, nine students, in a coordinated action, ran up to the desks, chained themselves to the chairs, and began to chant in unison with most of the others in the room to "fight back" against the attempt to suppress their program. The loud, raucous scene earned national news coverage, much of it favorable to the students. "I can't remember any students in my high school who wanted to learn something so bad that they hijacked a school board meeting," a blogger on the Daily Kos wrote.[23] The *New York Times* and other national news organizations picked up the story. Critics were active as well. "Just as the Tucson school board was about to hold a meeting to vote on making the now-outlawed racist and anti-American curriculum an 'elective,'" a right-wing blogger known as Gateway Pundit wrote, "La Raza activists and teachers sent in students to shut down the meeting and chain themselves to the chairs. Yet another example of why La Raza must be stopped."[24] It had not been the first sign of student activism on these and related issues, as Tucsonians from middle school to veterans of the Chicano movement took to the streets to march against SB 1070 and HB 2281. So the school board sit-in was, if novel, not unprecedented.

A week later, the school board convened with a sizable police presence. Many of the police were in riot gear. Access to the building and to the meeting room was limited. The students and other supporters of MAS were there in large numbers, too. The specter of riot police guarding a school board meeting in the United States was harrowing for people on all sides of the issue. "We screwed up," Stegeman said later. "It was overkill. The police overprepared. They arrested an old Latina who stood up and spoke out-of-turn. We came out looking terrible."[25]

After Huppenthal's shut-down order, the school board voted to appeal, and the controversy continued to boil. At the appellate hearing, Stegeman dug a deep hole for himself by describing the Mexican-American program as "cult-like," a characterization based on his reading of the popular philosopher Eric Hoffer. But attention at the appeals hearing was riveted on the assessments by Cambium and Huppenthal's lieutenants. On the one hand, an independent auditor (Cambium) found the program in compliance with state law and producing good educational results; on the other hand, an evaluation by the Arizona Department of Education found that MAS had not complied. The nub of the state's case against TUSD was that the program didn't provide the right materials to Cambium, that very few hours of instruction were observed, that teachers had a heads-up when Cambium was to visit, and, on the whole, Cambium could therefore not make a rigorous assessment. The testimony and some of the materials used in the program were alleged to show a strong bias that geared the program to Mexican-American students (possibly excluding non-Latinos) and dwelt on oppression as an ingrained habit of white America.

A few months later, the administrative law judge hearing the appeal, Lewis Kowal, found for the Huppenthal order. The law, Judge Kowal wrote in December, "permits the historical (objective) instruction of oppression that may, as a natural but unintended consequence, result in racial resentment or ethnic solidarity. However, teaching oppression objectively is quite different than actively presenting material in a biased, political, and emotionally charged manner, which is what occurred in MAS classes. Teaching in such a manner promotes social or political activism against the white people, promotes racial resentment, and advocates ethnic solidarity, instead of treating pupils as individuals."[26]

That "oppression" may be the subject of instruction if racial resentment or ethnic solidarity is depicted as a "natural but unintended consequence" of the oppression was an interesting use of reasoning. The Mexican-American Studies program, Judge Kowal alleged, was promoting such resentment and solidarity. A paradox of the entire controversy, of which Kowal's decision was just one piece, is that those trying to suppress the MAS program probably were promoting more racial resentment and ethnic solidarity than anything taught in the classrooms.

What Superintendent Huppenthal, Governor Brewer, and the many other Arizona Republicans horrified by the MAS program may not realize is how deeply and widely debated "multiculturalism" has been. It is a concept and a practice that has earned brickbats from the right, to be sure, but plenty of criticism from the left as well. The ethnic studies movement was very much a part of multiculturalism, even though as a fairly sturdy undertaking—long established in many venues—it could stand on its own without the philosophical trappings that multiculturalists bring to the table.

What so offends Huppenthal and others (something that is hotly debated throughout Europe, by the way, mainly with respect to Muslim immigration) is that treating students as individuals—formerly a given of American political thought, as Judge Kowal put it—is challenged by the ethnic identity-making and solidarity that multiculturalism do indeed promote. The political values of the Enlightenment hinged on the rights of the individual, not least because they were formulated in reaction to monarchical or ecclesiastical dominance. And there was very little ethnic awareness as these ideas were promulgated by Locke, Hume, Montesquieu, and others, because it was a discourse between Englishmen, Scotsmen, and Frenchmen, men of a certain class. (Sectarianism was rife, however, and was generally viewed as a bad thing; one of Locke's great essays, "A Letter Concerning Toleration," argued for religious liberty—that is, for not suppressing Catholicism in late-seventeenth-century England.) So we were bequeathed these political ideas, which were new and powerful when the nation was born, and we are lucky that we were: the values of individual liberty, rights against arbitrary action by the state, rule of law, and popular sovereignty have proved remarkably durable and fair.

A political architecture that is designed to constrain the state leaves much untrammeled beneath, usually a good thing, but a space that nonetheless is open for social and economic discrimination and, yes, oppression. In fact, political oppression was allowed as well, because the Constitution failed to outlaw slavery until 1867 and, after the Civil War, the Supreme Court and the political system didn't end the practice of Jim Crow and also failed to guarantee equal rights for women. So the long undoing of the structures of slavery, Jim Crow, sexism, and other forms of oppression, which is still in progress more than two centuries after the Constitution was ratified, is a project that exposes the notion of a nation-state governed by universal values of freedom and democracy as, shall we say, contestable.

Multiculturalism arose to challenge the denial of rights of citizenship, of belonging and integration, which Huppenthal and others insist cannot be examined through the ethnic lens.[27] It arose in significant part because of the steady influx of East Europeans, Africans, Arabs, and South Asians into Europe after the Second World War. There the "crisis" of multicultural societies gave rise to attempts to provide a sense of belonging to immigrant communities while permitting them to maintain cultural cohesion. In the United States, which absorbs immigrants as a matter of course, it became an issue mainly as a consequence of African-American activism, feminism, and the early Chicano-rights movement. Here it was less a problem of diminishing the potential for religious conflicts. Instead, controversy rose because a "resident" minority was brought here by force and kept in servitude for centuries, and a very large minority that was also resident to some degree was long welcomed as cheap labor. Unlike most of the migrants to Europe, the minorities in the United States were "recruited." And the two groups, those whose heritage was African and those whose heritage was Latin American, were by far the largest (with the exception of women) to feel at odds with the dominant white political, economic, and cultural structure.

For the most part, the multiculturalism project is the work of liberals who welcome this diversity and see it as a strengthening of society. Some useful research of the effects of ethnic diversity on economic performance and the provision of public services suggests a mixed picture. Many economists regard ethnic diversity as a net plus for the economy, but as exacerbating a persistent problem of equitable distribution of public services.[28] More broadly, diversity is regarded, as in biological systems, as a positive good, enriching societies and making them less insular and more connected to the world in a globalizing age. But even here the principle of diversity radiates a certain ambivalence.

The values of the Western political tradition of Liberalism—open societies, rule of law, popular sovereignty, and the like—have long been posited as *universal* values that should apply everywhere at all times. This Liberal universalism (with 'Liberal' capitalized to distinguish it from current everyday liberalism; even American conservatives are Liberals) was derived from two earlier philosophical traditions: those of Christianity and Ancient Greek philosophy. Christianity's power as a proselytizing religion stems from its claim to universal validity. (The same is true of Islam, one of the reasons they clash.) The Greek philosophers also saw their rationalism as a universal truth. So Liberalism's claims about, for example, the frequently invoked list of human rights are claims to all-encompassing and privileged status as a set of principles that should not be constrained by local practice or tradition. It isn't surprising that the most widely applied standard is the UN's 1948 *Universal* Declaration of Human Rights.

This universalism is what we grew up with, so the notion that there can be other, equally important values that govern ordinary life and politics isn't readily recognized as a valid possibility. A growing appreciation for pluralism attenuates this a little, but pluralism as a political value has typically acknowledged that different, autonomous groups exist (whether ethnically based or not) and will vie for a seat at the table of political power. There is an attempt to expand that definition to be inclusive and see pluralism as an active engagement of different groups in dialogue without sacrificing their ethnic or religious distinctions (notably through the Harvard Pluralism Project), and this could rightly be considered as the leading edge of multiculturalism—not merely "separate but equal" existence, but distinct and engaged with each other in society.

Multiculturalism as an exercise in acknowledgment and respect has been largely successful. This merely recognizes that immigration has brought many cultures and subcultures to the United States and that these cultures and subcultures are increasingly honored as legitimate parts of the "salad bowl" (rather than the "melting pot") that is now American society—ethnic diversity alongside the diversity of family structures, sexual preferences, and the like. It is worth noting that many studies of the "contact hypothesis" have shown that the more one group is exposed to another in everyday living, and especially in the workplace, the less each is likely to sustain harmful stereotypes about the other.[29] Multiculturalism runs into greater resistance when it lays claims to special rights. This, again, has been less of a problem in the United States than in Europe and some other countries. The adjustment of laws to recognize different religious holidays or requirements (for example, to butcher animals only in certain ways, or to wear a veil) are special rights, but they rarely impinge on what we consider to be the basic human rights that are protected for all citizens. We can imagine, however, special rights' being claimed for sexually repressive or discriminatory practices, such as denial of certain jobs for women, on the basis of ethnic traditions or religious strictures. Because such claims violate basic human rights, they wouldn't be tolerated in the United States.

The ethnic studies movement in the United States never insisted on special rights apart from the claims of Chicanos and other ethnic minorities to know their own history and to make that history, literature, and language available to anyone else who wanted to learn. (Indigenous cultures, of course, can and do make claims about sovereignty that to some extent are honored in American governance; this can get sticky with respect to Latinos, insofar as so many of them descend from indigenous peoples.) In the rather complex discussions about the role of diversity, pluralism, and multiculturalism in Western societies, Chicano studies is a rather mild form of multiculturalism, an educational enhancement that builds self-esteem and a sense of belonging but in no way trumps the liberal values that have long braced US politics and society. It challenges the monochromatic view of history, but that is a stance, a pedagogy, that isn't exclusively derived from multiculturalism.

Multiculturalism has come in for criticism from the left mainly because it has emphasized cultural self-examination and identity building at the expense of other ways and means of challenging ruling elites and ideology. As the sociologist Todd Gitlin put it years ago, the left was "marching on the English Department while the Right took the White House." Anyone who attended an anti-war rally or another progressive event in the 1990s or the 2000s must have noticed that the focus of the event was dispersed among many causes and perspectives—anti-capitalist, LBGT rights, Save the Whales, and so on. But this fractiousness can't be laid at the feet of multiculturalists alone. A more serious critique does have some resonance, however, and that is that multiculturalism to some important extent replaced or elbowed aside the older concerns of left-wing organizing on the basis of economic class.

If class and economic inequality are the fulcrum of injustice in the United States (a Marxian proposition, of course, that to some degree was taken up by New Deal liberals and the like), it implies a different set of remedies than social marginalization or forced assimilation alone. American society, which is remarkably elastic with respect to social mores, could honor the traditions and languages of many cultures while still tolerating high levels of inequality. (The obverse could also be imaginable, in which economic equality was pursued alongside coerced assimilation.) And this is in fact what seems to be occurring in the United States: Inequality and multiculturalism both are increasing, though not through a conscious policy preference but rather as a result of a combination of economic and social dynamics.

Economic inequality is increasinging as a result of policies and practices that favor the wealthy and remove opportunities to secure a place in the middle classes, while the assimilationist model weakens and multiculturalism becomes more robust. What some leftist critics see as tragic in this is that dissident energy is dissipated, channeled into multicultural demands (as well as feminism and LGBT activism, to some degree). The possibility for solidarity among the disenfranchised is sharply reduced, and elites get their way nearly unopposed on economics.

Like most broad formulations, this leftist critique is oversimplified—the diminishing political power of labor unions, which were the main countervailing power, has more to with right-to-work policies and shifting sources of employment than with multiculturalism. For a left that has always suffered from fragmentation, however, the emphasis on social prerogatives (e.g., speaking Spanish) rather than organizing around economic issues is simply another crippling blow.

It needn't be that way, and often is not, since the socially marginalized groups, such as recent Latino immigrants, are also economically disadvantaged. The modest goals of multiculturalism and Latinos' perception of their economic status and needs are part of the same mix. The impetus for multicultural initiatives is the perception of being forgotten, of having to accept the dominant cultural norms and essentially give up the culture their family migrated from. Economically, many of these same groups are forgotten, too, marginalized in the sense of being regarded as the workforce only for menial jobs—maids, farmworkers, meat packers, and similar—and not seen as capable or even desirous of a higher station in life. So the two—marginalization of culture and marginalization of livelihoods—are so coincident as to be nearly inseparable. And the way to break through that marginalization is through awareness, activism, and politics.

Those who opposed Mexican-American Studies in Tucson evinced anxiety that the educational program was promoting demands for inclusion—more educational opportunities, better job potential, and related issues such as housing or ending ethnic/racial profiling—through self-awareness, activism, and, eventually, politics. Given the growing share of the Latino population in Arizona, such political activism could change governance very soon. So the practical urge to stop this activism at its source—the act of awareness—became, whether consciously or not, a fervent priority of white Arizona conservatives. And the principal point of attack was to turn the tables on those who taught about oppression by claiming that the curriculum was preaching hatred of whites and of the United States.

"The MAS program was always controversial," Mark Stegeman of the Tucson school board told me. "It was approved only on the third try. A former MAS teacher published an article in a local newspaper making strong allegations against the program," so the tension began long before Dolores Huerta's speech. "There's no question that Mexican-Americans in Tucson have been oppressed, and for some Mexican-American children, the MAS will spark engagement. But I wasn't comfortable with a program that was too politically charged. I felt what was happening was going over the line, and MAS became hard to defend."

"Curtis Acosta had a huge effect on the kids, he's charismatic, a great teacher," Stegeman said, referring to one of the high-profile MAS teachers. "But there was reverse racism in the classroom."[30] He cited some chanting, embracing Aztec myth, being rushed off to a demonstration—things that crossed a line. The traditional ways of teaching history and literature were not considered legitimate.

Sean Arce disagreed: "I refute that there was an anti-white bias in MAS. Some people are uncomfortable with non-European perspectives. Mexican-American history had been left out before. High school was a pipeline to prison; more Latinos went to prison than to college. MAS changed that."[31]

What seemed clear after the controversy roiled Tucson schools for more than two years is that the perspectives about what constitutes education were sharply discordant. When seven books were banned from TUSD— including Freire's *Pedagogy of the Oppressed*, an anthology titled *Rethinking Columbus: The Next 500 Years*, Rodolfo Acuña's *Occupied America: A History of Chicanos*, and Shakespeare's play *The Tempest*—they were marked as incendiary on the subjects of race and ethnicity. ("The state was breathing fire at this point," says Stegeman.) For the MAS teachers, they were challenging and thought-provoking, and they were taught alongside books and articles by well-regarded thinkers (Martin Luther King Jr., for one, and even some conservatives). But the great divide on this was less about race than about how to teach critical thinking in a way that engages a particular minority that had been purposefully sidelined by the majority for generations. And that would entail including their literature and history in a way that spoke truthfully to that group of alienated youth.

"It was essential to provide evidence that this was an entirely different kind of education at every conceivable instant," Acosta explained. "As students became fully engaged in the curricular experiences, the dialogue in the classes centered around how the students were perceiving the literature and how they applied it to their own lives and the world around them. Thus, critical inquiry and pedagogy became the way for students to push each other toward developing social consciousness rooted firmly in themes of social justice. Literature study in our classes became a lens to analyze our barrio, school, or world and the platform for students to generate ideas for taking action to transform the inequalities in their lives."[32]

This is straight out of Freire, and it is "anti-white" in the sense that the discrimination the students explored derived from the dominant white culture of the Southwest and the United States more broadly. It set up an inevitable clash of culture—not only ethnic culture, but of class distinctions, of difference, of situation in the social order and one's place in history. Nearly forgotten, it seemed, was the effect the program was having on student achievement; a second study by three top academics at the University of Arizona conducted a quantitative analysis of achievement on test schools, graduation rates, and college matriculation, finding in June 2012 that there was "a consistent, significant, positive relationship between MAS participation and student academic performance."[33]

The theatrics of the protagonists didn't help to cool the controversy. John Huppenthal and Tom Horne, along with the bloggers and talk show hosts who supported them, have sustained a barrage of invective against the MAS teachers that accused them of everything from poisoning youth to treason. "To defend and then expand an educational program that reveres Che Guevara, that paints American history as a series of lamentable and dishonorable events, that divides students by their ethnicities and then attempts to instill in them a defiant stance toward authority and country is a form of noxious educational malpractice," wrote a researcher at the conservative Hoover Institution.[34] Huppenthal told public radio that the MAS teachers "said they were going to racemize [*sic*] the classes using a Paulo Freirean philosopher—and he's a writer of the book *Pedagogy of the Oppressed*, and he, right in his book, talks about that word 'oppressed' comes right out of *The Communist Manifesto*."[35] Huppenthal also mentioned Che Guevara. It is striking how often the disparaging remarks reference Cold War tropes.

The MAS partisans also have been confrontational at times. Some of what is mentioned in the classroom—depicting Benjamin Franklin as racist, for example—hardly seems necessary to deconstructing racism. Fostering a sense of us versus them was bound to have repercussions. Former teachers sometimes spoke out against these seemingly militant attitudes. The political nature of the curriculum as taught offended some parents, too. According to one self-described liberal, "it seeped into every single one of the class offerings, unfortunately. So even when you had really conscientious teachers, it couldn't help but become political in nature."[36]

Whether some undefined line was crossed in some classrooms is difficult to judge; teaching the history of the subaltern to those very same marginalized groups is bound to take on a political tone, particularly in the hothouse political atmosphere of Arizona. What is more remarkable still is the attempt to deny and even denigrate the improved educational achievement of the MAS students. While contestable, the weight of evidence suggests strongly that Latinos enrolled in MAS classes were higher achievers than those not enrolled in them. By denying them the opportunity to take literature and history courses in the MAS program as fulfilling core requirements, the state was not only coercing the schools to back away from ethnic studies; in effect it was saying that their educational achievement and their career prospects were of little concern. It reinforced, in the starkest way, the lessons taught by Acosta and Arce and the other MAS teachers: that the white-dominated power structure wanted to keep Mexican-American children on the margins of society. In his filing to appeal the 2011 finding by the state superintendent, the attorney Richard Martinez alleged that in HB 2281 there was "the unmistakable message to our youth that the promise of the Constitution to protect them is equally all a myth; that the history, literature and culture of at least one group is not worthy of being taught in school."[37]

This enormous clash of constitutional rights, education theory and practice, multiculturalism, and a host of subsidiary issues continued to roil Tucson throughout 2013 and 2014 as new court orders and a new local superintendent sought to reinstate "culturally relevant" studies without violating HB 2281. In many respects the clash is reminiscent of the early tensions in Northern cities when Southern blacks were arriving in large numbers to escape Jim Crow and find well-paying industrial jobs. Many whites saw that influx as a threat that was mainly cultural, and used some of the disparaging attitudes about black initiative or capacities that are visible in the Arizona controversy. Music and dancing, sexuality and other social mores, willingness to be subservient and work menial jobs no one else wants or to live in substandard conditions—these were popular ideas about Negroes in the 1920s and for decades to come, and served to justify the informal systems of segregation that prevailed in the North. (They also mirror many more recent attitudes, which also have deep historical roots, about Arabs and Muslims generally, the depictions broadly called "orientalism.") Raising onerous comparisons of cultural "difference" while prohibiting discussion of oppression is a threadbare tactic of elites, one meant to rally their own kind and disenfranchise the upstarts.

The culture clash, in whatever dimensions in Tucson and Arizona, was a symptom or an outcome of something much larger than the teaching of history and literature. It was, at root, about the enormous flow of immigrants across the US-Mexico border.

Arizona is increasingly Latino. As in New Mexico, Texas, and California, the demographics are trending sharply toward a larger and larger share of the population tracing their lineage to Mexico or Central America. From 1980 to 2010, the percentage of Arizona's population that is Latino went from 16.2 to 29.6, and the raw numbers from 440,000 to 1.9 million. Much of the growth was cumulative, since for many years the fertility of Latinas was higher than that of non-Latinas. (The decline in the Latino birth rate began in 2008 and probably is correlated with the effect of the recession, as Hispanics generally were hit hardest economically by the downturn.) About half or more of the growth in population of Latinos was due to expanding families.

Immigration was responsible for nearly two-thirds of the growth of Arizona's Latino population in the 1990s and slightly less than half in the next decade; in 2008–09 there was a net decline in illegal immigration—as large as 100,000—because of the recession. Legal immigration to Arizona from Mexico and other Latin American countries averages about 20,000, somewhat less than the estimated numbers of unauthorized migrants, which averaged between 25,000 and 30,000 annually before the recession. About two-thirds of the Latino population in Arizona is US-born, and a little less than 30 percent were born elsewhere and are not US citizens. Interestingly, the number of Latinos native to Arizona exceeds that of native non-Latinos. (About one-seventh of the Latinos who speak a non-English language at home don't speak English well or at all.) Tucson in particular is, like Miami, a two-language city.

The final relevant statistic to be drawn from the census and from other measurements concerns economic well-being. About a quarter of all Latinos are officially poor, more than twice the Anglo rate. Those who aren't citizens are more likely to be living in poverty than either US-born or naturalized citizens among the Latino population, but it is a rate that has dropped sharply since 1990. At the same time, the highest percentage of workers classified as "blue collar" is the undocumented Latino immigrants. (These trends indicate growing acceptance—even reliance—of these workers in the labor market.) Educational achievement is skewed in similar ways. About one-third of the non-Latinos have a bachelor's or a higher degree. Only 10 percent of Latinos are college-educated, and of those who aren't citizens only 5 percent have college degrees.

The picture that these statistics draw is one of an expanding Latino population, by roughly equal measure through birth rates and immigration, and within the latter about equally through legal and illegal means. Those who are unauthorized find work mostly in manual labor and are least well compensated. Poverty is significant. English-language skills and educational performance are dodgy among the unauthorized, and even among many citizens.

Two things really stand out. One is the sheer growth of the Latino population. From 1980 to 2010, it quadrupled in size. Yet their marginal status in terms of income, education, and capacity to assimilate through language seems inert. This lends the impression, so prevalent in the right-wing media, that hordes of Mexicans are invading Arizona, legions of unskilled peasants who are poor and criminal. And one of the keys to understanding both the reality and the stereotype is educational achievement. Of those 25 years and older, just 7 percent of non-Latinos have not finished high school; whereas about 35–40 percent of Latinos don't have a high school diploma, and the percentage for non-citizens is well above 50. As has already been noted, higher education shows the same imbalance.

A lack of a high school diploma often leads to chronic unemployment and poverty, and is self-reinforcing, as children of the poor and uneducated are at a disadvantage in educational achievement as well. This relentless cycle doesn't yield assimilation, and the change in educational achievement is very gradual—nationwide, from 2000 to 2011, the percentage of foreign-born Latinos graduating from high school improved from 18 to 25, but those with some college or college degrees nudged forward only slightly: The percentage of Latinos getting college diplomas rose from 8.4 to 10.2. This slow growth was reflected in overall income. For the entire United States, Latinos as a whole had a decline in real income from 2000 to 2010; for those of Mexican origin, median household income declined from $43,200 to $38,700, more than 10 percent.[38]

For Mexican-Americans in Tucson, these statistics have immediacy in the lives of the parents and students. When the results of studies of the effects of the MAS program (high graduation rates, high levels of entering college) were published, they confirmed for them the fundamental value of a curriculum and a community that not only gave hope to Latinos but also yielded concrete results. Shorn of the ideological controversy over Freire, Che, and so on, the program had accomplished what no others had: It had raised the educational achievement of Mexican-American pupils.

When Huppenthal and others opposed to the program denigrated the independent assessments and demanded the MAS program be shut down, it was yet another signal to Latino children that their futures were of little or no interest to those in power. Because Mexican-American studies were uniquely targeted for closure, this had to be seen as a hostile act of ethnic discrimination. The commotion about "anti-Americanism" in a school system run by Americans appears as an excuse to keep these students and communities "in their place." And this crusade to insist on America First pedagogy in the schools, to eradicate any Latino identity or critical thinking as a tool of education, came at the same moment when the frenzy about illegal immigration was overflowing in Arizona.

Dolores Huerta's speech in 2006 came at the peak of anti-"illegal alien" organizing and the harsh rhetoric that went with it. The Tucson controversy over ethnic studies occurred in that poisonous atmosphere. "We are in a very anti-immigrant state," observed Adelita Grijalva, the president of the Tucson school board. "The state wants to prevent school-age children who are not documented from attending. Parents must sign papers attesting to their child being a citizen, and many are fearful of this. ICE has shown up at schools."[39] In an interview, Richard Martinez, the attorney defending MAS, puts it more bluntly: "The curriculum fight became symbolic of another fight, the 'how dare they think they're not going to assimilate.' If we don't educate the Mexican-Americans, we're going nowhere. Sixty-five percent of the Tucson school district is Mexican-American. The MAS program had the throwaways. The parents are powerless."[40] Despite the lack of resources, and despite TUSD teachers who were largely white and not very sympathetic to the MAS goals, the program succeeded though the efforts of a dedicated cohort of teachers that had coalesced by the time of Huerta's speech.

But the mounting anxiety about illegal immigration was cascading into every aspect of Arizona politics. It was the time of President George W. Bush's immigration-reform effort, a reasonable plan that instantly ran into fierce opposition from the right wing—opposition generated by blogs and by long-standing nativist groups. In fevered rhetoric, those forces called the plan "amnesty" and claimed that unauthorized immigrants were coming to the United States to "drop anchor babies" and gobble up welfare, that they were criminals by definition and had among them a high proportion of violent offenders, and that the unsecured border was an open door for terrorists. None of these allegations were true, but the hostility was so palpable that the Republican president couldn't get a foothold with a Congress that should have been pro-reform.

Perhaps in reaction to the reform fracas, Arizona became the leading anti-immigration-reform state, passing legislation that would criminalize employers hiring unauthorized immigrants and mandating police to seek proof of legal status during a lawful stop, detention, or arrest. Governor Janet Napolitano vetoed the first two bills that were passed. But in 2010, after Napolitano went off to Washington to serve as Secretary of the Department of Homeland Security, the new Republican governor, Jan Brewer, signed the controversial SB 1070. The American Civil Liberties Union described the law as an invitation to racial profiling. Protests ridiculing Arizona and calling for boycotts occurred across the country, yet five other states passed laws very similar to Arizona's.

SB 1070 sparked conflicting responses in Arizona. The city of Tucson sided with one of the several individual lawsuits filed against the law; the mayor expressed concern about the economic impact of the law if threats of a boycott of Arizona tourism were to occur. Other cities came on board the anti-1070 effort. Four-fifths of the Latinos in the state disapproved of the measure, and many of them were politically activated by its passage. More respondents, nationally and state-wide, expressed support for comprehensive immigration reform than for SB 1070, although consistent majorities in Arizona backed the law. When the Supreme Court's decision was handed down, it was claimed as a victory by all sides. President Obama said "I remain concerned about the practical impact of the remaining provision of the Arizona law that requires local law enforcement officials to check the immigration status of anyone they even suspect to be here illegally. I agree with the Court that individuals cannot be detained solely to verify their immigration status. No American should ever live under a cloud of suspicion just because of what they look like."[41] Governor Brewer simply called it "a victory." She has implemented the controversial provision of asking for papers, with many innocent people—such as Dreamers—caught up in long detentions.

The entire episode illustrated not only the legislative juggernaut that the issue of illegal immigration unleashed (one consequence of which was the ban on ethnic studies) but also the fissures in Arizona's political culture when it came to the sensitive issues immigration brought to the fore—race and ethnicity, language, jobs, education, and, at root, what it means to be an American. The sheer divisiveness of what it means to be an American can be glimpsed in two sharply contrasting groups of Arizonans who work in the Sonoran Desert: the Minutemen and the Samaritans.

The Minuteman Project and its offshoots and splinters have gained considerable notoriety as a vigilante group that "patrols" the border supposedly in lieu of federal enforcement. It's a magnet for extremists, including white supremacists, and its members have been linked to several murders. One of the Minuteman Project's founders, Jim Gilchrist, was thrown out of the organization because of charges of embezzlement. The other, Christopher Simcox, was arrested in Phoenix in 2013 for sexual misconduct with three girls under the age of 10, including his daughter. Other controversies, arrests, and financial improprieties also have dogged the group. Simcox was involved in a violent domestic conflict. T. J. Ready, a neo-Nazi and an

example of the increasingly extreme drift of the nativist movement, murdered several members of his family and then committed suicide in 2012.
One of Gilchrist's successors, Carmen Mercer, was convicted of fraud in a
land scam.[42]

The idea of citizen border patrols went back nearly 30 years to when the
Ku Klux Klan began their own Klan Border Watch in California, where it
had a long history of anti-immigrant violence. And earlier "Minutemen"
had stockpiled weapons for use against a UN or Communist invasion in
the 1960s. The border vigilantes overlap substantially with right-to-bear-
arms activists, as they do with other right-wing causes, but these issues are
especially congruent. And congruent they are, too, with most of the big
conservative names in the media—Sean Hannity, Rush Limbaugh, Michelle
Malkin—lavishing praise on and giving air time to Gilchrist, Simcox, and
others. Lou Dobbs's program and other CNN programs had Simcox on 25
times. He was in many respects the perfect guest—photogenic and mission-
driven, combining the loose strands of borderland vigilantism. His own
"come-to-Jesus moments" had been 9/11 and a sojourn into the Sonoran
desert that had convinced him that terrorists were crossing into the United
States from Mexico. This, of course, added to his appeal to the right-wing
media. He was outrageous, and they couldn't get enough. As the reporter
David Neiwert recounts in a book about the border vigilantes, Simcox said
that Latino immigrants were "trashing their neighborhoods, refusing to
assimilate, standing on street corners, jeering at little girls on their way to
school."[43]

In their heyday, the Minutemen would set up stations near the border
and send out patrols to report what they regarded as illegal immigrant
activity to authorities. As a Southern Poverty Law Center report explained
when the Minutemen first started operations in 2005, "their stated goal was
to 'do the job our government refuses to do' and 'protect America' from the
'tens of millions of invading illegal aliens who are devouring and plunder-
ing our nation.'" Several of the patrollers lamented the fact that they were
barred by law from killing the immigrants crossing illicitly. "The thing to
do would be to drop the bodies just a few hundred feet into the US and
just leave them there, with lights on them at night," one of them told the
David Holthouse of the SPLC. "That sends the message 'No Trespassing,' in
any language."[44]

At about the same time, a large number of violent hate crimes against Latinos across the country were mounting, as the Anti-Defamation League has documented in detail. Much of this was tied to white supremacist groups, skinheads, and the like, a long-standing social disorder that fed into the nativist groups in Arizona and elsewhere along the border. But the Minutemen organizations were grounded in similar attitudes right from the start. It was the cultural challenge, not necessarily job competition or just the act of crossing the border illegally, that drove up the numbers of nativist groups. According to a report issued by the Anti-Defamation League, video games prevalent on nativist websites portray the Mexican immigration threat as essentially cultural. Here is a description of one such game:

Players control a gun and are charged with killing stereotypical Mexicans. Targets include a "Mexican nationalist," who carries a Mexican flag and a pistol; a "Drug smuggler," wearing a sombrero and carrying a bag of marijuana on his back; and finally a "Breeder"—a pregnant woman who has two small children in tow. Aside from the virulently anti-Hispanic themes within the game, it also hints at anti-Semitic myths such as "Jewish control" of the US through an image where the border is represented by a bullet-ridden sign showing an American flag whose 50 stars have been replaced by a single Jewish Star of David.[45]

The "breeder" aspect of this—the insistence that Latinas were coming here to have "anchor babies"—even led the national Republican Party to propose revising the Fourteenth Amendment, which gave citizenship to anyone born on US soil. "We should change our Constitution and say that if you come here illegally and have a child, that child is automatically not a citizen," Senator Lindsay Graham (a Republican from South Carolina) told a Fox News interviewer in 2010. "People come here to have babies. It's called drop and leave. To have a child in America, they cross the border, they go to the emergency room, they have a child and that child is automatically an American citizen. That shouldn't be the case."[46]

According to one news report, the increasing extremism of the border vigilantes may have been their undoing. In 2010, Carmen Mercer "sent out an e-mail urging members to come to the border 'locked, loaded and ready' and urged people to bring 'long arms.' She proposed changing the group's rules to allow members to track illegal immigrants and drug smugglers instead of just reporting the activity to the Border Patrol." "We will forcefully engage, detain, and defend our lives and country from the criminals who trample over our culture and laws,'" she exhorted the members."[47]

But the call to intensify threats and violence never materialized. Just as the punitive Arizona laws were enacted, the Minuteman phenomenon began to die off. At least, the corruption-addled organizations began to fold their army-green tents. A few weeks after Mercer's attempt to rouse the original Gilchrist-Simcox vigilantes, she closed the organization down suddenly. Gilchrist, who formed another Minuteman group in California after his ouster, was also on the ropes financially, as the Southern Poverty Law Center has documented.

Following Gilchrist's example, the vigilante "movement" merged into the Tea Party movement, just rising then to react to the economic crisis and the election of the first African-American president. While devoid of vigilantism, the Tea Party movement's thinking on immigration is virtually identical to that of the Minutemen and other nativist groups. It was a remarkable convergence, rescuing the nativist cause. The economic downturn kept Mexicans away from the United States anyway, but the Tea Party movement nonetheless insisted the unauthorized Latinos already living in the United States be deported. "A posse of Tea Party Republicans in the US Senate this week opened a new front in the crusade against birthright citizenship," ABC News reported in mid 2011, "with draft legislation that would bar children of illegal immigrants from becoming citizens."[48] The Tea Party movement in Arizona, as one would expect, focuses most of its energies on illegal immigration. As most of its members would acknowledge, the heady days of large anti-illegals rallies and high-profile border vigilantes are past. Even the highly publicized border crisis of 2014, when thousands of unaccompanied children from Central America sought entry at the Texas border with Mexico, couldn't rouse a new Minuteman movement of any significance. The SPLC reported that the number of Minuteman groups declined from 310 in 2010 to 38 in 2012. The issue remained hot through the 2012 presidential race, largely as a result of Tea Party obstruction, and the resistance to reform was unwavering afterward, with escalating wrath directed at Senator Marco Rubio (a Republican from Florida) and at the 2013 reform effort.

The Minutemen and the Tea Party movement represent a sizable portion of Arizona's political culture, but they are not dominant, although their cacophony and the Republican-dominated state government may make it seem so. A majority of Arizonans supported SB 1070, but, as has been noted, a larger majority supported a path to citizenship for unauthorized immigrants, as did the state's two Republican US senators. Indeed, there is a sizable culture of forgiveness in Arizona, significantly church-based and ethnically mixed. It is epitomized by the Samaritans, an informal group of people in the Tucson area who have organized against "death in the desert"—in effect, serving as a rescue squad for those crossing the border illegally and finding themselves in distress. They leave jugs of water and ready-to-eat food in the Sonoran hills and the scrub-pine landscape for the immigrants, report on immigrants who need medical attention, and, doubtlessly, though quietly, give other kinds of assistance, such as temporary shelter.

"Providing humanitarian aid to people in distress is not illegal," one of the Samaritans explained. "Our guiding operating principle is that of Civil Initiative, which states that our responsibility for protecting the persecuted must be balanced by our accountability to the legal order. Civil Initiative is nonviolent, truthful, wide-ranging, cooperative, pertinent, volunteer-based and community centered."[49] The water and food drops are organized in weekly meetings held at a church in South Tucson, and volunteers sign up for the treks through the desert to leave the food and water and look for trouble signs. Many of the members are middle-aged or older, and most are white. On a night I visited a meeting, there were 22 members present. Some members had been at a candlelight vigil for a boy shot by the Border Patrol. Another member reported that a local magistrate she had observed while monitoring the court system had described immigrants as "criminals and felons." There were 65 Mexicans in custody at a Tucson courthouse, she said, as a result of Operation Streamline—a practice of the federal law enforcement in which dozens of immigrants are processed through a criminal court every day, given jail time, and deported with criminal records that will make it impossible for them to return legally. (More than half of the 30,000 immigrants so prosecuted in 2012 were in Tucson.) A lot of discussion focused on the 400 gallons of water distributed, on organizing into teams, and on selling Mexican-grown coffee and T-shirts to raise money. One team found empty water bottles with "illegals" and "Go Home" written on them. The focus on water was a major concern of the group; about 170 people die in the desert each year, mainly of dehydration.

Similar organizations work in the desert and organize for immigration reform, such as Humane Borders, another faith-based community, and Direchos Humanos, which is more of an advocacy group. Direchos

Humanos is more edgy, documenting abuses by the Border Patrol (of which they say there have been 30,000 in the last several years). They deride the reform bill passed by the US Senate in 2013 for its "enhanced" border-security tradeoff: "Residents within 100 miles of the border now live within a 'constitution-free zone,'" said a June 2013 statement, "where their civil rights and liberties are consistently ignored. In their zeal for 'border security,' the Department of Homeland Security has recklessly implemented the largest waiver of law in American history, disregarding laws that protect the environment, cultural and historic sites, Indigenous sacred sites and America's public lands."[50]

The Samaritans and like-minded groups carry on an older tradition based in churches, both Catholic and Protestant, in which refugees from Central American wars and repression sought help in the United States. Much of the activism in the Tucson area is rooted in the period—mainly the 1980s—in which a "sanctuary" movement that became national in scope. It sought asylum status for many of the immigrants, who were the peasants victimized by the oppressive regimes in Guatemala and El Salvador. But it also sheltered and transported some to other locations, a kind of modern-day underground railway modeled on the abolitionists' venture to save slaves before and during the Civil War. Ananda Rose, in her splendid book *Showdown in the Sonoran Desert*, quotes a letter written by one of the movement's founders, John Fife, to Ronald Reagan's attorney general, William French Smith, to explain why the groups were openly violating US laws in sheltering these refugees: "We take this action because we believe the current policy and practice of the United States Government with regard to Central American refugees is illegal and immoral … . We believe that justice and mercy require that people of conscience actively assert our God-given right to aid anyone fleeing from persecution and murder." It was, Rose explains, civil disobedience in its grand tradition, but Fife and his co-organizer Jim Corbett called it "civil initiative"—in their words, "the legal right and moral responsibility of society to protect the victims of human rights violations when government is the violator."[51]

The citizen activism to protect undocumented immigrants draws upon the sanctuary movement, and indeed many churches and activists have organized under the banner of the New Sanctuary Movement. Whatever its name and activities, it is rooted in a long Christian tradition of Samaritanism, which is a fairly straightforward injunction of the New Testament.

As Ananda Rose points out, it is also rooted in Jewish scripture, where the reality and contemplation of migration was ever present. (Being uprooted, oppressed as "aliens," and so on is a continuous story of the Jews). But the story of the Good Samaritan, in which the stranger acts selflessly to help a man in distress, is particularly powerful, as Jesus redefines what it means to be a neighbor.

Naturally, a movement that protects immigrants and bases its work on the words of Jesus had to be attacked by the right wing. "Open borders benefit Catholic churches looking to fill their pews and collection baskets. The Vatican and American bishops, led by radical L.A. Cardinal Roger Mahony, have long promoted immigration anarchy and lawlessness,"[52] the blogger Michelle Malkin wrote in 2008. The members of these movements are quick to point out that they don't advocate "open borders," one of the many false charges used routinely in the immigration fracas. They seek "humane borders," where laws and enforcement are more mindful of the real needs for immigration and people are treated with some care and dignity.

The two cultures that clash over the Mexican-American curriculum in Tucson are at odds precisely because the lessons in the curriculum—the mistreatment of Mexican immigrants by the white settlers, in particular— are deeply rooted in the political culture as well. The denial of even the notion of "oppression" as practiced in the United States throughout its history is anathema to the European-origin Christians who pushed against the wilderness of the New World, subdued the savages, and reaped the bounty of their expansion. Mexican-Americans, like the Africans brought in chains as slaves and then later subjected to the long century of Jim Crow, were for the most part subservient to those European-*cum*-American settlers, instruments of the continental imperialism that first meant the near-extermination of the indigenous tribes.

That this drama continues to play out in the American West is itself remarkable. The lines have been rehearsed and spoken thousands of times; the curriculum is only the latest stage. The twists and turns of the drama include the contrasting versions of history, the role of racism and the privileges of "whiteness," the economic necessity of permitting immigrants to enter the United States and the loud denunciation of how Latinos steal jobs, and the growing presence of the "other"—the demographics of rapid population growth of Latinos, the proliferating use of Spanish, the political organizing of Latinos, and the coming majority of minority peoples in the United States.

The clashes that these twists and turns produce and the inevitability of a "brown America" are what Huppenthal and Horne are railing against. The specifics of the MAS reading list (Freire, Zinn, Acuña, et al.) and the alleged cultishness and political activism are the atmospherics of something much deeper in the riven soul of Arizona. A settler culture (including many retirees) with a fixed idea of American values and patriotism is challenged by an upstart culture of housemaids and gardeners—the "Revolt of the Cockroach People," to borrow a phrase—who not only claim rights they have been denied but also demand inclusion of their culture as equally, and authentically, American.

3 THE USUAL SUSPECTS: THE RAID IN NEW BEDFORD

Nothing illustrates the "raid mentality" of immigration enforcement like an actual raid.

Just at the head of Clark's Cove, along the waterfront where old textile mills and fish factories dot the small peninsula of New Bedford that juts into Buzzards Bay, is an unremarkable four-story red brick factory building that has housed enterprises long forgotten. It is unremarkable because so many buildings of that kind still stand in this legendary whaling town, many of them abandoned once textiles—for years the economic engine of the city—followed whaling's earlier decline and nearly vanished. In this building, though, textiles were still being sown into vests and backpacks for the US Army, a nice bit of business in struggling New Bedford, coming as it did with a $132 million contract. Owner Francesco Insolia won the contract with help from city and state officials, took an enormous grant from Massachusetts' Department of Workforce Development when Mitt Romney was governor, and grew to more than 500 employees to produce his army goods in what was widely known to be a sweat shop. A sweat shop with all the trappings—filthy bathrooms, draconian rules for lateness or talking or breaks, earned overtime pay never paid—an altogether substandard workplace. Insolia could do so for several years because his employees were for the most part undocumented workers, immigrants, mainly from Guatemala and El Salvador. They would work hard for Insolia and the US Army and keep their heads down. It was an open secret, of course, because New Bedford is small and jobs were scarce. But for five years Insolia and his company, Michael Bianco Inc., thrived under the nose of the military officials there and the state and city officials who poured job training funds and tax breaks into his coffers.

Then one day it all came crashing down. On a cold morning late in the winter of 2007, more than 300 agents of the Immigration and Customs Enforcement agency, known as ICE, raided the factory and rousted 362 Guatemalans, Salvadorans and a sprinkling of other south-of-the-border workers.[1] They were handcuffed and manacled, and over the course of the day were taken from where they sat on the factory floor into buses and driven 94 miles to Fort Devens, an Army Reserve base. Many spent several immobilized hours on that floor, feeling brutalized by the federal police, while others attempted to escape, some even jumping into Clark Cove to get away. Among those taken were parents of small children, about a hundred children in all, who were suddenly without parental care. The new governor, Deval Patrick, spurred by the state's child welfare agency being denied a role in the "processing" after weeks of pleading, called the whole shabby affair "a humanitarian crisis."

And indeed it was. Within hours, before lawyers could be dispatched to Fort Devens, about half of the arrested workers were flown to Texas (either to Harlingen or to El Paso) to be incarcerated in detention centers run by private contractors for the Department of Homeland Security, ICE's home department. There the possibility of being released, even with an ankle bracelet to monitor movements, was undercut by the lack of "community ties" of the detainees. Months of detention for many of the Michael Bianco workers lay ahead. About 160 would be deported outright.

In New Bedford, the reaction of the workers' families and friends was panicked. Over the course of the chaotic day, the abandoned children were identified and placed with neighbors and extended family. Many immigrant families, legal or not, hunkered down in the north-side barrio, calling in sick to the other employers—mostly the fish-packing plants—and keeping their children out of school. No one knew what was coming next. But they gathered together almost instinctively at the Parish of Our Lady of Guadalupe, the one Catholic church that offered a Spanish mass, which is part of the old St. James Church that was less than a mile from the factory. There, Father Richard Wilson and a number of social workers (including Father Marc Fallon and Corinn Williams) ministered to the shocked community and set up a kind of operations center for lawyers and other public advocates to go to work. Senator Ted Kennedy was there within a few days, as was Governor Patrick. The complex and often confused task was to make sure the children were cared for, the fractured families stable (the loss of one breadwinner being a disaster), then unravel the tortuous detention process and sort out the legalities and the prospects for a release before deportation.

The raid was one of several dozen conducted by ICE around that time, likely a "show of force" for the benefit of those criticizing President Bush for not keeping illegal immigrants out of the country. The attempt to reform immigration laws—to give the out-of-status families a route to citizenship—was colliding with a powerful right-wing backlash against any attempt to reshape the laws. The alternative to reform, or possibly a complement to it, is the raid, whether of the workplace (the most dramatic and visible) or of homes. Raid, arrests, detention, imprisonment, deportation—these constitute the raid mentality. In nearly every major raid, human-rights abuses were reported and many lives ruined for what is in effect no greater an offense than a traffic ticket. The raid sets in motion a process of criminalization that sticks with the immigrant forever, stigmatizes children, and disrupts local economies.

The immigrants themselves see the raid mentality as punitive, intimidating, and even reminiscent of the oppression they had escaped. Assimilation under such circumstances is hindered, at least for one generation, and often more. And while the many raids of the Bush administration were regarded as the high-water mark of the strategy, the numbers of apprehensions and deportations has risen in the Obama years. In 2011, for example, the Department of Homeland Security apprehended 642,000 foreign nationals, three of every four being Mexicans; 400,000 were deported—all-time highs.[2]

For the Latinos of New Bedford, the national debate and Washington politics and ICE statistics were far from their concerns in late winter of 2007. They, and the city, had to cope with the sharp economic, political, and emotional disruption of the raid and its aftermath.

New Bedford's rich history isn't apparent to the casual observer, apart from a few grand looking homes along County Street and markers of various kinds—the Whaling Museum or the fish factories or Herman Melville Boulevard. It has the look and feel of a hardscrabble New England town that belies its storied past, one built by the sea and by immigrants. It was among the first places where Europeans encountered the indigenous tribes, in 1602, when the English captain Bartholomew Gosnold bought furs and sassafras root to ship back to England. The legendary figures of the *Mayflower*—Miles Standish, John Alden, William Bradford, and others—purchased 34 shares of Dartmouth County, on the western shore of Buzzards Bay, where New Bedford itself was founded in the middle of the eighteenth century. It was from the first a whaling village as well as farming. By 1765, the town was bustling with ship building and whaling. (Less than a decade later, the first ship built there, the *Dartmouth*, was one of those boarded during the Boston Tea Party.)

New Bedford's superior position—railroads linking to the rest of the country, ample timber nearby, deep harbor—enabled it to eclipse Nantucket as the center of whaling by the middle of the nineteenth century. Just before the Civil War, it peaked at 329 whaling ships, half the entire American fleet. It benefitted from a rising demand in a new industrial age for whale oil, sperm oil, and baleen. Ralph Waldo Emerson described New Bedford's competitive advantage: "New Bedford is not nearer to the whales than New London or Portland, yet they have all the equipment for a whaler ready, and they hug an oil cask like a brother."[3]

New Bedford was the world capital of whaling, and enjoyed all its many benefits, as it also built and outfitted the ships, refined the oil, made its products like candles, and prospered mightily. "Had it not been for us whalemen," Melville wrote in *Moby-Dick*, "that tract of land would this day perhaps have been in as howling condition as the coast of Labrador." But then Melville paid New Bedford a high compliment:

The town itself is perhaps the dearest place to live in, in all New England. It is a land of oil, true enough; but not like Canaan; a land, also, of corn and wine. The streets do not run with milk; nor in the spring-time do they pave them with fresh eggs. Yet, in spite of this, nowhere in all America will you find more patrician-like houses; parks and gardens more opulent, than in New Bedford. Whence came they? How planted upon this once scraggy scoria of a country?

Go and gaze upon the iron emblematical harpoons round yonder lofty mansion, and your question will be answered. Yes; all these brave houses and flowery gardens came from the Atlantic, Pacific, and Indian oceans. One and all, they were harpooned and dragged up hither from the bottom of the sea.[4]

But the demand for oil depleted the local stock of whales and the ships needed to go far to catch their prey, oftentimes on journeys as long as two years or more—a considerable capital investment with attendant perils. This tragedy of the commons raised the prices for sperm oil and whale oil precipitously in the 1850s, nearly doubling. But what brought whaling to its knees, and quickly, was the discovery of petroleum in Pennsylvania in 1859. Kerosene was already outpacing whale oil for lighting, but it was made from coal and was costly. Kerosene from petroleum was cheap, and by the end of the Civil War, it threatened to replace the oils from whales as a source of illumination. A brief postwar boom for the whale men quickly gave way. It was plain that petroleum could be produced far more quickly and voluminously than the whale oils. In the first full year of the Pennsylvania oil wells, their output exceeded the peak amount of oil obtained from whales in any year in all of America.

The rise and fall of whaling overlapped with the rise of textile mills, which saved New Bedford from whaling's quick decline and became the city's lifeblood until the Great Depression of the 1930s. There were small mills from as early as 1799 on the Acushnet River, but it was the founding in 1846 of Wamsutta Mills that led and quickly expanded the local industry. (Wamsutta was named for the Wampanoag prince who deeded the landed that became New Bedford; he died mysteriously when Plymouth colonists detained him under suspicion of conspiracy, but it was his brother Metacom, known as King Philip, who became a warrior and nearly wiped out the English settlements in the first great war on the continent in 1675–1678.) The industry flourished and made New Bedford a leader in the production of woven cotton and other textiles; between 1881 and 1914, more than 30 companies were based there, producing prodigious amounts of product. An early-twentieth-century history of the city boasts that New Bedford was a "strong, right-living and prosperous community … . She has suffered as few cities have suffered, and triumphed as few cities have triumphed … . There is a strength and a solidity about her institutions, civic, religious, educational and cultural that satisfies, and in all that goes to make a modern city there is nothing lacking."[5]

This period piece of Babbitry was understandable. It *was* a growing city, even as whaling was all but gone (the last whaling vessel went down in a storm within sight of the city in 1924), in its stead rose the fishing industry, with nearly 5 million pounds of mackerel and cod and scallops and other sea creatures brought into the harbor in 1916. All the businesses in support of these enterprises thrived as well. But the mill owners failed to modernize and the textile industry was already struggling when the Depression ground it down over the coming quarter century. The final blow was the sale of Wamsutta in 1954. The new owner vowed to keep the plant in operation, but by 1958 closed it down and moved production to South Carolina to save costs.

During its heyday, whaling attracted seamen from many parts of the world, as Melville so colorfully depicts, but the most persistent immigration derived from the Azores, the Portuguese colony a thousand miles west of Lisbon and the most important source of foreign labor for New Bedford's seagoing industries. The flow of Azoreans, and later Portuguese from the mainland and another Portuguese outpost, Cape Verde, continued well into the late twentieth century, propelled in part by Portugal's fascist-leaning state. It was, like many migrations, a river that widened and deepened over time, for as a few and a few more came to New Bedford and Providence and Boston, they encouraged others from the homeland to join them. One can see in the nationwide statistics how this unfolded, with a doubling each decade from 1840 to 1870, then a fivefold increase in the next decade, a near-doubling again in 1891–1900, almost a tripling again in the first decade of the twentieth century, and so on, varying by the economy and conditions at home. At least half of them, and perhaps two-thirds, were from the Azores. Restrictive immigration laws in 1917 and 1924 set quotas of 2 percent for all nationalities—visas totaling one-fiftieth of the current ethnic population in the United States would be granted. Though Portuguese were surging in numbers, they still were far below British, Irish, and Germans, and other long-established nationalities. (Asians, except Filipinos, and Africans were excluded altogether.) So Portuguese immigration tailed off, from nearly 90,000 in 1911–1920 to about 30,000 in 1921–1930. The flow began again after a series of earthquakes rocked the Azores in 1957, and special legislation co-sponsored by Senator John F. Kennedy allowed more Azoreans in. In 1965, with an act of Congress that eliminated the national quota system (co-sponsored by Senator Ted Kennedy), the numbers increased again.[6]

The Azoreans and other Portuguese came because of poverty, as one would expect, and the long period of fascism in Portugal, the reign of terror by Antonio Salazar from 1932 to 1968, followed by his protégé Marcello Caetano until the regime collapsed in 1974. The two—poverty and dictatorship—went hand in hand. Salazar maintained an essentially feudal system of privilege for a small elite; he also maintained large land holdings and foreign possessions (Angola and Mozambique, most prominently). Next door to Portugal was fascist Spain. Like Portugal, it enjoyed the nearly unblemished support of the United States as a Cold War ally and a NATO aspirant. To the south was Africa. For the poor or oppressed, the lure of America was overwhelming, and one of the first ports of call was New Bedford.

By 1900 Portuguese already made up 16 percent of New Bedford's population, and the percentage continued to increase until the restrictive laws took effect. It would surge and slow again after the 1965 liberalization of immigration, but slowed after the Salazar-Caetano regime fell; the economy in New England was stagnant in the 1970s, and Portugal faced a brighter future. But by then the Portuguese, Azorean, and Cape Verdean communities were well established in New Bedford and in nearby Fall River and Providence. They constituted nearly half of the population in 1990.

Though the Portuguese were prominent in immigration, they were not alone. By 1900, the textile industry's need for skilled labor drew more broadly from Europe. English and Irish particularly swelled the workforce in the late eighteenth century, and French Canadians added to this. By the first decade of the twentieth century, 70–80 percent of the residents of the city were first-generation or second-generation immigrants. Women could operate some of the spindles, and this was favorable to the Canadians, who could migrate relatively short distances in families. Girls as young as seven worked fourteen-hour days in the mills. As the textile industry progressed, a division of sorts became apparent between the immigrants: English, Irish, Canadians, and native Yankees held the higher-paying jobs, and the Portuguese were relegated to low-skilled labor. Many of them didn't speak English. The unions, powerful by the 1920s, discriminated against them, too. This changed, slowly, as Portuguese became more integrated into society, and the unions were in decline with the mills; the fish factories remained magnets for Portuguese speakers, but in general manufacturing gradually gave way to services.

The Portuguese migration to New England subsided just as Latinos began to arrive in large numbers. Like the rest of New England, immigration from Latin America was a trickle compared with much of the rest of the United States, but from 1990 to 2010 it rose steadily. In those decades, the New England economy was more robust than most of the United States, and this alone was a magnet. For Bristol County, where New Bedford and Fall

River are located, the migrants were significantly Central American. From 2000 to 2010, New Bedford's Latino population increased by 66 percent, to one-sixth of the city's residents. (The fraction probably is even higher, as Brazilians don't always identify themselves as Latinos to census takers and unauthorized immigrants are not fully accounted for in official figures.) In 1990, it was one in fourteen. Notably, a large share of Latinos are Puerto Rican—more than half of those counted—and the remainder are almost all from Guatemala, El Salvador, and Honduras. In nearby Fall River, another recovering mill town, Latinos more than doubled in the 2010 count.[7]

Looking at figures of the 2010 census, one thing is clear: New Bedford looks like a struggling city, and a city of immigrants. More than one-third don't speak English at home. One-fifth are foreign-born. These fractions are higher than for Massachusetts as a whole. High school and college diploma holders are drastically fewer than the state as a whole; and many Latino children struggle in school. Median income is barely half of others in the Commonwealth, and the poverty rate is twice as high. New Bedford is a city on the edge.

The raid, as raids do, came suddenly and without warning. One Michael Bianco worker recalled it as follows:

I was inside when they told us to turn the machines off. When I turned to look I saw people running. I thought it was a fire or something, so I ran toward the back exit, but when I looked back I saw Immigration running toward us. There was a helicopter. There were many police. They told us, 'Don't run! Don't run!' We turned back. They told us to sit on the floor.

I got very nervous and started shaking because a man from Honduras started running in the basement," she continued, "and seven police surrounded him, they grabbed him at the neck, picked him up and threw him to the floor. They handcuffed him. Then they took us upstairs. They handcuffed us, and pushed us to the floor.

Many people could not sit because our hands were tied … . That was 8 a.m. At around 3 p.m., we asked for water. I saw them bring in many boxes of water. I thought they were for us. I asked an official to give me a little water. Another woman said, 'Yes, we want water.' He looked at me and gave me a little bottle of water. He said, 'You know, don't put your mouth on it, because many people are going to drink from there.' That little bottle was shared by about twelve people.

They treated us as if we were murderers.[8]

Many witnesses told stories about the harshness of ICE officers. A woman working in the factory informed ICE that she had a daughter who would not have anyone to care for her if she were in detention, "but they didn't care," she later recalled; "they still took me with the group." "Because some of the women who had young children, who breastfed," she continued, "[the officers] even made them take the milk from their breasts to see if it was true that they had young children. They even made fun of them. One of them told another to pass an Oreo cookie to eat with milk, that they were milking the cows."[9]

Others reported similarly harsh treatment. "When I saw that the agents carried guns, I thought they were going to shoot us," one worker told a public radio reporter. "I thought we were all going to die that day."[10] Several described the induced panic and the agents' callous reaction. "We saw these people coming and then when they started saying, 'Don't move. Nobody run,' then we realized immigration was there," a Salvadoran worker told an interviewer. "They were trying to grab everybody and people just started running like crazy. They panicked, they fell down. You found that they were pursuing people just like you were an animal. Like you would be running after a dog. They'd go after you that way." He later told an ICE agent that a seven-months-pregnant woman needed some help; the agent refused and replied that he didn't care. No food or bathroom visits were allowed, and little if any water, for seven hours or more.[11]

"I live near the plant and went there at once before the ICE raid," recalled Corinn Williams, who directs the Community Economic Development Center of Southeastern Massachusetts. "There were helicopters flying overhead and agents everywhere, and a mobile command center across the street. They put up barricades around the plant to keep families away." The Community Economic Development Center became a nerve center for the lawyers who gradually became involved and others trying to locate the arrested and their loved ones. "All day," Williams noted, "we heard from families about detainees, like the husband who had medications for his wife, who has seizures."[12]

Because the whole process of arrest and detention was taking so long and was so opaque, the community activists and family members realized in early afternoon that schools and day-care centers would be releasing children shortly, yet there was no word from federal agents as to who among the parents were detained. So the scene at Our Lady of Guadalupe was fraught with anxiety about the children, about infants without their mothers who were nursing, about older children getting out of school and going to an empty home, and about men suddenly assuming the role of two parents. As Williams pointed out, this was the first major ICE raid in which a majority of detainees were women—and young, child-bearing women at that. Father Fallon was told by ICE that Massachusetts' Department of Social Services (DSS) had been part of the planning and would make amends, but people at that agency claimed they were "not in the loop" and therefore weren't prepared.

Bethany Touré, an activist who had been on the scene, recalled that "there wasn't a lot of outpouring of emotion or crying." "It was really like vacant looks; vacant stares, kind of almost being in a state of shock," she said. "This is a people who have been so traumatized before and here is trauma again."[13] Several of the workers recalled the helicopters as reminding them of military assaults in the highlands of Guatemala or the civil war in El Salvador.

Gradually, the arrested were loaded onto gray, unmarked buses with dark-tinted windows and driven the nearly 100 miles to Fort Devens; none were allowed to speak with family members. "It was like the hunter carting away his prey," recalls Father Fallon, "returning time and again."[14] "That day was like the end of the world for me," said one worker who was eventually deported to Guatemala.[15]

Through the long day of the raid and the confusion and trauma of the days and weeks ahead, the city of New Bedford and its mayor came in for some sharp criticism for their placid cooperation with ICE (Mayor Scott Lang had known of the plans for the raid in advance) and their lack of preparations for the children. Lang blamed others. "Where was the mayor? That's what we were asking," Corinn Williams recalled. Ken Hartnett, then recently retired from editing the *Standard-Times*, the area's largest newspaper, echoed that years later: "Mayor Lang was terrible. Talk Radio—the Ken Pittman show—was stoking ideas that the Guatemalans were taking jobs and ripping off the system. Lang was on his show weekly, and should have denounced that."[16] The chief of police was, as one would expect, cooperative with ICE, but had not pursued illegal immigration as an issue for his department before.

Criticism also was directed toward Massachusetts' new governor, Deval Patrick, a Democrat who had just succeeded Mitt Romney. "Had the plan worked out," Patrick said at the time, "our expectation was to have access at the site to individuals being detained. Then we expected to have access at

Fort Devens. We didn't get that access." "Instead," one reporter explained, "DSS workers had to interview detainees after they had been flown to Texas, two days after their arrests. Patrick said it took many phone calls and help from the congressional delegation to get full access to the immigrants, causing 'a considerable amount of calamity.'"[17]

Thus, on March 6 the city of New Bedford was broken into fragments. In the south end, on the waterfront, the 300 federal agents were disposing of the 361 arrested Michael Bianco workers, keeping guard over them, denying families access, cordoning off the plant from anyone seeking information or offering to help, and finally loading the workers into the buses. The family members who were not arrested, or had legal status, tried to discover where their loved one was going to be incarcerated; some hung out near the factory in the little coffee shops to get out of the cold, or sought other refuge; some, fearful of wider dragnet, made themselves scarce. Parents or other relatives, neighbors, friends, and community activists tried to take an inventory of the dependent children and brainstorm how to deal with the ones left alone. Lawyers from Greater Boston Legal Services and other public-interest groups were scurrying down from Boston. Corinn Williams' office well north of the Michael Bianco plant became one hub of activity, as the community organizers met to build a strategy and assign tasks.

But the heart of the city moved to a church basement. The workers' families naturally gravitated to Our Lady of Guadalupe because of its Spanish language mass and the twenty-minute walk from the Michael Bianco factory. Into the austere basement of the church poured the migrant families and a small phalanx of sympathizers, mainly others originally from Central America and several community activists from the churches or welfare agencies. The basement was a veritable operations center within hours of the raid. Later, the lawyers came from Boston, more than 80 of them quickly got involved—"ICE made a mistake conducting a raid close to so many law schools," Fallon noted wryly. Hundreds of people packed into the basement, most of them distraught, babies and children crying, the meager resources of the nonprofit and faith communities stretched thin but brought to bear into the midnight hours, gathering force as word got around.

Father Richard Wilson, the parish priest, was no stranger to controversy. He had been a former aide to Archbishop Seán O'Malley during the child abuse scandal that rocked the Church. But this was a challenge all the same.

His establishing a Spanish mass had alienated old-line Irish and French Canadian parishioners. Now he had a full-blown humanitarian crisis on his hands, one that was politically fraught. The St. James Church had combined three parishes, among them Our Lady of Guadalupe, so already the house of worship that had long been thought of as "the Irish church" was drifting, in the eyes of many, toward becoming Latino. For Father Wilson, then, the raid became a test that drew upon a history of social tensions. He had already lost many of the old Irish parishioners when Our Lady of Guadalupe was founded by Puerto Ricans at St. James, and he couldn't afford to lose more. "I was at a Sturbridge retreat when our interfaith community organizer used the basement as a staging area," recalls Wilson. "I was reluctant. I was worried that a backlash would close the parish. I got back from Sturbridge on a school bus at four o'clock the afternoon of the raid. That first night, there were three hundred people here."[18]

The crisis for the families of arrested workers was twofold—children needing care if both parents were taken off to Fort Devens, and the loss of a wage earner or two. The city's officials, Father Wilson thought, had been caught unawares by the raid and hadn't been prepared, and the locals knew little about the state's rejected plea to include child welfare advocates in the ICE operation. So the panic and potentially chaotic reaction to the raid took several hours to subside to a low roar. By nightfall, community organizers were joined by the lawyers, both of which brought the reassurances, logistical help, and legal acumen to the hard tasks of finding caretakers for children and identifying who had been taken into detention. That night, a lawyer from the Massachusetts Immigrant Rights Association brought a laptop computer and recorded 288 of the names of the detained.

The children who were stranded—between 75 and 150, according to initial accounts—were located and cared for, though doing so was fitful, traumatic, and often improvised by New Bedford citizens. According to the Boston Globe, "Luis Matias came to seek help for the 9-month-old and 3-year-old daughters of his tenant, Rosa Gutierez, 26, of Guatemala, who was taken into custody. 'She's a hard worker, a good person, who came to the US to find a better life,' he said in a phone interview. 'She's a very good mother. It's inhumane to take a mother away from her children,' he said. 'She's not a criminal.'"[19]

Massachusetts' Department of Social Services, the responsible agency, had been informed of the raid in advance, but its social workers had been

denied access to the arrested MBI workers—access they needed to identify and locate the children. "They were on the scene," Corinn Williams
recalled, "but they hadn't had much prior contact with the Mayan community either."[20]

At Fort Devens, the detainees were cramped into a compound that had
been designed for 120 inmates. ICE seemed determined to ship them to
Texas as quickly as it could process them, making the work of the volunteer lawyers all the more difficult. According to a report published in the
Lawyers Journal of the Massachusetts Bar Association, "the night of the raid,
lawyers from Greater Boston Legal Services and the American Civil Liberties Union spent most of night at the Fort Devens detention facility. Even
though there were six lawyers the first night of the raid and 16 GBLS staff
and others at Fort Devens the second night, they were only permitted to
interview 31 detainees over the course of about 18-and-a-half hours before
ICE began shipping them to Texas."[21]

The ostensible reason for the hasty transportation of the Michael Bianco
workers to faraway detention camps (90 of them to Harlingen and 116 to
El Paso in the first day or two) was the lack of "bed space" in Massachusetts, though others suspected that the distance and place of the relocation
would make it less likely that the detainees could be released, as they would
have no local ties, and the lawyering would be more cumbersome. "The
government moved them to try to interfere with their rights," a lawyer representing dozens of the workers told a judge later that month. "They had
eleven months to plan this raid, and after two days they run out of space at
Fort Devens because they needed it for someone else?"[22] It was later learned
that ICE pressured detainees to sign a waiver of their rights. Since many
didn't speak English and most if not all were without counsel at the time,
this was an egregious violation of basic rights—rights to which anyone in
the United States, citizen or not, is entitled. The opportunity to post bail
was denied to many, also a violation of rights. The teams of lawyers who
descended upon Fort Devens were turned away by ICE at first and were not
allowed to see detainees until the second day, and even then only those
who requested counsel. Many of them, being from countries of rough justice, didn't know they had such a right.[23]

Reportedly, six minor children who had worked at the plant were shipped
to a detention center in Miami, Florida. Senator John Kerry of Massachusetts had called Secretary Michael Chertoff of the Department of Homeland

Security on the night of the raid and had been told that no mothers had been separated from their children, a rather obvious falsehood that signaled either a lack of organization or a lack of concern for separated families. After Senator Kennedy and Governor Patrick ripped into the Department of Homeland Security and Assistant Secretary of Homeland Security for Immigration and Customs Enforcement Julie Myers, 50–60 single parents were released on bond in Massachusetts but remained charged with illegal entry into the United States.

The families back in New Bedford were in many cases not informed of the whereabouts of their loved ones, so when Senator Kennedy appeared in the basement of St. James on Saturday New Bedford was still in a state of crisis. The Massachusetts Immigrant and Refugee Advocacy Coalition (MIRA), Corinn Williams, and other local activists, including the priests, had coped well with the unattended children. A range of services had been created on the spot, literally overnight, to fill the immediate needs of families without wage earners. In fact, the response of the community—from the whole of eastern Massachusetts—was astonishing. Not only had the lawyers come, organized by the Greater Boston Legal Services, but nursing students from the community college set up a child-care center. A food bank was set up; it operated for three months. The Community Foundation of Southeastern Massachusetts shepherded $144,000 of donations to help the workers' families to pay rent and utility bills and buy groceries. Father Wilson recalls that even the parishioners who had been so upset by the church's embrace of the Latinos donated generously to the food bank.

But the trauma of the raid was powerful all the same. A young Latino father whose wife was arrested told an interviewer that his "family was destroyed" because she was so important to all of them, especially their two young boys—a sentiment echoed by other men left with children to care for. Others spoke of the "terror within" and the despair at having left oppressive conditions in Guatemala in the belief that they would find justice in the United States. In the days and weeks that followed the raid, those families whose caregivers and wage-earners were arrested withdrew from public life, often kept their schoolchildren at home, and tried to make ends meet.

The immigrants demonstrated remarkable resilience in the face of these obstacles. One story about the New Bedford raid is particularly poignant. Ricardo Gomez Garcia, who had worked two shifts at the factory, was sent to a detention center in El Paso. He languished there while fighting deportation for six months. His wife and autistic 4-year-old son were left to a hardscrabble life in New Bedford. Ricardo was deported to Guatemala, but within days he planned his return, paid $5,000 to a "coyote" (a smuggler of migrants), and made the 25-day journey back to New Bedford for a joyful reunion with his wife and son. Then, during that first night, he developed acute respiratory symptoms and was rushed to St. Luke's Hospital. He died the next morning. He was 39 years old.

Julie Myers would deny that the raid in New Bedford had anything to do with the politics of immigration reform then reaching a crescendo on Capitol Hill. A complaint against Michael Bianco Inc. for the factory's conditions—found to be deplorable in almost every conceivable way—was lodged in the spring of 2006, and planning for a "workplace action" was launched then. Coincidentally, President Bush was under fire from his right wing for not enforcing existing prohibitions on illegal entry and overstayed visas. The Michael Bianco raid was one of several, however, carried out by ICE in 2006 and 2007, and in many respects was the most notorious. The abandonment of the children and the high-profile objections of Senators Kennedy and Kerry made sure of that. The raids continued after the reform effort collapsed. The largest of all the raids, in Postville, Iowa, in 2008, showed many lapses in judgment and operations similar to those that were evident in the New Bedford raid.

The Department of Homeland Security, which include Immigration and Customs Enforcement, was a concoction of post-9/11 angst. Representing the "securitization" of immigration in a vast new bureaucracy, it was the congressional Democrats' way of upstaging Bush on security shortly after the 9/11 attacks. Immigration enforcement had long been an ambivalent affair. The feds wanted to demonstrate some resolve in policing the southern border, but the economics of agribusiness drew in Latinos by the hundreds of thousands every year. When ICE became the enforcement mechanism, it was given a broadened mandate from its predecessor agency, the Immigration and Naturalization Service, and along with several federal agencies (the Federal Bureau of Investigation, the Transportation Security Administration, Customs and Border Protection, and the Coast Guard, among others) became the strong right arm of Washington when it came to "illegals."

Julie Myers was herself a bit controversial, and Washington gossip held that she was out to prove herself. Her credentials didn't measure up.

Heads of security agencies typically have ample experience, but she was a neophyte, seemingly picked because her uncle was chairman of the Joint Chiefs of Staff and her husband was chief of staff for DHS Secretary Chertoff. She was an attorney involved in Ken Starr's quixotic crusade against the Clintons, and she had headed a division of the Commerce Department for a year, but she had no law-enforcement experience. She was just 36 years old when she assumed office. The right wing was perhaps more upset by her appointment than any Democrat. In a blog post, one of her most pervid critics, Debbie Schlussel, wrote: "As a brilliant ICE agent friend said, ICE honchos and people like Julie Myers 'are transforming the good men and women of ICE and of DHS into a pathetic bunch of milquetoasts who are incapable of providing the most basic protections to the people of this nation.'"[24] Still, those who worked with Myers found her to be diligent and competent.

Whatever issues attending her employment, Myers certainly pushed on an open door in ordering the raid in New Bedford and others in Iowa, Colorado, Texas, Nebraska, Utah, Minnesota, and elsewhere. The raid in Postville, Iowa involved 1,000 ICE agents and netted just slightly more undocumented workers than the New Bedford raid. "In the days and months following," said one report, "more than 1,000 individuals who were not caught in the initial raid, most of Guatemalan origin, left the small town, nearly 2,300. Their departure left Postville bare, devastated the local economy, and shuttered the meat packing plant."[25] In Stillmore, Georgia, a raid at a poultry factory in September 2006 netted 300 undocumented workers. Within a month of the New Bedford raid, ICE rounded up more than 1,000 immigrants in Maryland and several locales in California. The agency busted janitors in Missouri, potato processors in Colorado, and parking-lot attendants in Virginia, among several other actions. ICE meant business, and its tactics were coming in for a lot of harsh criticism.

"Since 2006, ICE has been dispatching teams of agents into neighborhoods throughout the country as part of a ramped-up enforcement effort called 'Operation Return to Sender,'" Jennifer Bennett reported in *Slate*. "Each team must apprehend an annual quota, currently set at 1,000, of fugitive aliens. These are immigrants who remain in the United States despite outstanding orders to leave."[26] The pressure for results led to some dodgy practices in the field—warrantless searches, rough treatment, pretending to be police officers, detaining US citizens and legal immigrants. Reports of

Table 3.1

ICE "worksite enforcement" arrests.

Fiscal year	Administrative	Criminal
2003	445	72
2004	685	165
2005	1116	176
2006	3667	716
2007	4077	863
2008	5184	1103
2009	1644	410
2010	1224	393
2011	1471	713
2012	1118	520

source: Andorro Bruno, "Immigration-Related Worksite Enforcement: Performance Measures," Congressional Research Service, 2013 (http://www.fas. org/sgp/crs/homesec/R40002.pdf): 6 (data based on submissions by Department of Homeland Security).

detainees' being beaten by ICE officers are frequent, as are wrongful arrests. Lawsuits against ICE are commonplace.[27] One such action was mounted in 2011 by attorneys in Tennessee that claimed members were targeted by ICE for arrest after publicly speaking out about racial profiling, another often-made charge against the agency. In another case, the ACLU reports, "without a search warrant and without consent, the ICE agents [conducting a home raid in Nashville] knocked in the front door and shattered a window, shouting racial slurs and storming into the bedrooms, holding guns to some people's heads. When asked if they had a warrant, one agent reportedly said, 'We don't need a warrant, we're ICE,' and, gesturing to his genitals, 'the warrant is coming out of my balls.'"[28] In 2013, the agency lost one such lawsuit and was ordered to pay $1 million in damages and to rewrite its rules on home searches, which have often been conducted without proper authorization.

The more than 400,000 annual deportations during the Obama administration required some muscle, and ICE provided it. So the agency that descended on New Bedford with several hundred agents after nine months of planning was law enforcement with a mission and little patience for niceties. When one agent told a worker at Michael Bianco "We're not a social agency," that was an understatement. What happened in New Bedford was quite similar to what was occurring elsewhere in the immigration raids: families separated, detainees signing confessions without counsel after presented with harrowing options, legal residents caught up in the tussle. It was, as they say, a pattern.

Myers recalled in a 2012 interview that there "was a growing sense of frustration at the lack of workplace enforcement, no real activity at all." She continued: "I wasn't an immigration ideologue; many of these people want to work and are barred." The questions facing her as she took the reins of the agency in January of 2006 were "How can we fully support laws?" and "How can we bring criminal cases against employers?" "There were especially horrible cases—sweatshops—like New Bedford. We had to do something about the illegal workers. Nobody would be off the hook."[29]

The process for choosing the Michael Bianco plant for a "workplace action" was the same used by ICE policy makers for all such raids. A "worksite team" would identify potential raid sites and would make recommendations, which would then move up the decision chain. Once a raid site had been selected, the worksite team would work with the local ICE office. The reason for stepping up the number of raids, according to a senior DHS official, was that Congress was "on our case all the time, wanting aggressive activity." The Michael Bianco plant was not, as some conspiracy theorists have it, chosen to retaliate against Senator Kennedy, one of the most pro-immigration-reform senators. Kennedy, after all, was working with the Bush administration on the reform package. And Myers says that she worked very well with Kennedy. The raid in New Bedford was an occasion for Kennedy to trumpet reform.

The task of planning for raid fell to Bruce Foucart, the ICE Agent in Charge of the New England office, based in Boston. Foucart has been an experienced law-enforcement officer with a long list of responsibilities that stretches far beyond immigration. He has brought several human traffickers to justice, sent to jail foreign nationals for trading child pornography, and he's been involved in drug busts and other crime fighting. When the criticisms about the conduct of his forces in New Bedford reached an unprecedented decibel level—with the governor, both US senators, and a universe of lawyers, politicians, and activists chiming in—he countered in the New Bedford media a year later. "Those arrested in the MBI operation chose to break our nation's laws," he wrote. "Consequently, they placed their children in tough situations. The responsibility for this must lie squarely on their shoulders, not the agency enforcing the law." He was particularly focused on the matter of child abandonment. "Underreported or misreported is the fact that ICE worked in advance of the operation with the Massachusetts Department of Social Services to ensure that no children were left unattended. And none were. In addition, no children were placed into foster care as a result of this operation."[30]

"They stopped us every step of the way," said Harry Spence, the head of DSS, right after the raid. "ICE's rhetoric has been completely different from the truth."[31] According the DSS officials, ICE prevented their staff from engaging with the detainees at the work site and at Fort Devens. Spence flew several of his staff to Texas to interview 200 detainees, and encountered further resistance from ICE there, though that was finally resolved.

What Foucart and others emphasize is a well-established norm of law enforcement—that is, that ICE is a policing agency and some precautions are taken, but these are law-breakers first and foremost. The controversy went beyond the treatment of unattended children, however, and involved the harder issues of race, ethnicity, and class. Here, law enforcement is not the impartial instrument of law envisioned in the Weberian scheme of bureaucracy, but rather a self-generating tool of punitive justice shaped strongly by cultural currents and political expediency.

This latter depiction, while exaggerated, is most vividly apparent in the processing and detention of the arrested immigrants. In the New Bedford action and others like it around that time, the raid merely begins a long trail of "enforcement" that typically ends with incarceration and finally deportation. The arrest itself, and the processing of the arrestee, is where the game is first rigged. Many if not most of the detainees don't speak English, or speak it poorly. They are presented options that they may scarcely understand and told to choose among those options. They sign away their right to a further appeal, and are sent on their way to a detention camp. After the Postville raid, Erik Camayd-Freixas, one of the interpreters ICE had hired to facilitate the proceedings, wrote a remarkable essay that detailed how detainees were given a "choice":

The explanation, which we repeated over and over to each client, went like this. There are three possibilities. If you plead guilty to the charge of "knowingly using a false Social Security number," the government will withdraw the heavier charge of "aggravated identity theft," and you will serve 5 months in jail, be deported without a hearing, and placed on supervised release for 3 years. If you plead not guilty, you could wait in jail 6 to 8 months for a trial (without right of bail since you are on an immigration detainer). Even if you win at trial, you will still be deported, and could end up waiting longer in jail than if you just pled guilty. You would also risk losing at trial and receiving a 2-year minimum sentence, before being deported. Some clients understood their 'options' better than others.[32]

Camayd-Freixas went on to explain that the charges were more often than not unproven ("trumped up" would be the impolite term), and that the object was to move the immigrants through the system quickly. All the players knew how hollow the justice was. Lawyers weren't available until plea agreements had been signed, and once the machinery was running it was very difficult to disrupt.

What the New Bedford and Postville experiences demonstrated was that the meting out of justice is often rooted in injustice—in this case, the hasty proceedings and frightening tactics visited upon a foreign-born population that cannot understand what is presented to them in the fullest way. The charges, moreover, frequently stemmed from practices of the employer, such as making it easy to obtain or use false identification. It is unimaginable this would happen to illegal immigrants of a different sort—say, highly skilled technicians from Europe or Japan. This was documented in a 2011 study by researchers at the Berkeley Law School of the University of California, who analyzed the arrests resulting from the Secure Communities program. Secure Communities is an ICE program (piloted under President Bush, expanded quickly by Obama) that enlists local police to enforce federal immigration law; it is active in 44 states. The Berkeley researchers found that 93 percent of those arrested for unauthorized presence in the country were Latino; the percentage of the undocumented in the United States that is Latino is 77 percent, meaning that a disproportionate number of Latinos were being arrested. Eighty-three percent of those arrested as a result of the Secure Communities program are placed in detention; the overall immigration detention rate is 62 percent.[33] It isn't difficult to conclude from these and other factors that a certain amount of racial profiling is afoot in the Secure Communities effort, all the more remarkable because Muslims of Arab, South Asian, and Central Asian descent also report racial profiling is prevalent in their experience.

The ICE detention system is a human-rights debacle, and the New Bedford detainees were among its victims. The enforcement of illegal entry statutes is handled as an administrative matter, in special courts with administrative law judges who serve at the pleasure of the Attorney General of the United States. ICE has a network of 400 prisons—some of them local jails, some of them ICE "detention centers"—around the country.[34] Many of them are near the Mexican border, like the one on Montana Avenue on the northeast side of El Paso, where 116 of the New Bedford residents ended up that first week in March. The "El Paso Processing Center," across from the Lone Star Golf Club and less than four miles from the notorious Ciudad Juarez (on the other side of the Rio Grande), is a squat, nondescript blond brick building that doesn't look as if it could hold 800 inmates. The Michael Bianco workers were warehoused there, some for weeks and some for months.

Detainees don't have the access to attorneys that ordinary criminals do in federal prisons; sometimes they don't get a single phone call to seek help. They have inadequate health-care provision, as investigations have demonstrated time and again. Men and women with no criminal record are thrown into lock-ups—some of them county jails—with murderers and other hardened criminals. At any given time, 34,000 immigrants are in detention across the United States, with more than 400,000 "processed" annually. "Among those unnecessarily locked up," according to an ACLU report, "are survivors of torture, asylum seekers, victims of trafficking, families with small children, the elderly, individuals with serious medical and mental health conditions, and lawful permanent residents with long-standing family and community ties who are facing deportation because of old or minor crimes."[35] A *Washington Post* investigation found that "the medical neglect [detainees] endure is part of the hidden human cost of increasingly strict policies in the post-Sept. 11 United States and a lack of preparation for the impact of those policies" and that "the detainees have less access to lawyers than convicted murderers in maximum-security prisons and some have fewer comforts than al-Qaeda terrorism suspects held at Guantanamo Bay, Cuba."[36] The *Post* article concluded that "the most vulnerable detainees, the physically sick and the mentally ill, are sometimes denied the proper treatment to which they are entitled by law and regulation. They are locked in a world of slow care, poor care and no care, with panic and cover-ups among employees watching it happen." Among the abuses detailed in a PBS *Frontline* documentary are sexual assaults on females by guards in the privately contracted detention centers, an epidemic of rape that largely goes unreported out of fear of retribution.

The Secure Communities program has meant that anyone without papers who comes into contact with police is subject to detention. "In the absence of reform, we are left with law enforcement on steroids," said Stanford University professor Gary Segura. "That is our immigration policy." It is "on steroids" because Congress mandates 400,000 detentions per year. That's the quota, and by all accounts ICE has been geared to fill it. There were 85,000 detentions in 1995, 200,000 in 2002, and more than 420,000 in 2011.[37]

One inmate in El Paso, a Mexican journalist who sought asylum when the Mexican military threatened him for writing articles about their corrupt ways, described the experience of incarceration. "The Mexicans are treated the worst," he told a *Mother Jones* reporter. "The staff curses us and calls us rats, narcos, and criminals. The work of the prison is done by the Mexicans and Central Americans. It is ironic—the illegals are arrested for working at real jobs in the US and then they get put in prison and are made to work for nothing."[38]

ICE officials insist that their record on detention is improving and aver that the worst abuses are in the prisons run by private contractors. Julie Myers says that the raid in New Bedford forced ICE to rethink its protocols. But the improvements, such as they are, remain scant relative to the scale of the detention and deportation juggernaut. "Immigrants who do not pose any flight risk or public safety concern are routinely detained," a representative of the ACLU testified before Congress in 2013. "Congress fosters the costly over-use of detention by its inefficient and unnecessary micromanagement of ICE detention beds. FY 2012 DHS appropriations legislation increased the number of beds to their current level of 34,000. This bed mandate—effectively, a detention quota—has no basis in sound detention management and raises serious due process concerns. No other detention system in the United States, criminal or civil, specifies that a minimum number of individuals be incarcerated."[39] And none deny legal rights and humanitarian concerns so forcefully.

The boom-and-bust cycles of New Bedford brought immigrants and new industries to the town from well before Melville's time, and New Bedford's fate has long been linked to the sea—whaling, shipping, textile exports, and fishing. After whale oil gave way to petroleum, the mills revived the city. When the Kilburn Mill's two side-by-side buildings were constructed (one in 1904, one in 1910), the cotton cloth coming from New Bedford was considered a premium product. In the Great War, the city's mills benefitted handsomely, making cloth for gas masks, bandages, uniforms, and other military needs, and Killburn was one of those contracted to the government to supply the war effort. Nearly 100 years later, it was in those same buildings that Michael Bianco made leather products for the not-so-great war in Iraq—products made by Guatemalans and Salvadorans and others.

Many of the Central Americans had migrated to nearby Providence and had then gone to New Bedford to work in the fish factories. The fishing industry in New Bedford, one of the largest on the East Coast, employs about 2,000 workers. It is difficult, seasonal work, the kind of labor that is now often done by recent immigrants. In New Bedford, the fish houses had been unionized and had employed mainly Portuguese, Cape Verdeans, and Azoreans and their descendants, but the corporations broke the unions in the early 1980s, opening up employment to non-union workers. Those jobs attracted Guatemalans and other Central Americans who had found their way to Providence. As the sociologist Lisa Knauer tells it, one Guatemalan immigrant, unable to find work in Providence, went to New Bedford, slept under a bridge his first night there, and got a job in a fish-processing factory the next day; he sent word to his family and friends, and gradually the numbers of Maya K'iche from Guatemala in New Bedford increased.

Men came first, as is usually the case with immigration; women followed. The men often made several trips back and forth, a long and perilous journey for an unauthorized immigrant. As the migration theorist Douglas Massey has explained, the raised barriers to entry as the illegal immigration debate intensified had a paradoxical impact—immigrants, no longer easily able to cross the border for seasonal work, stayed in the United States, brought their families in, or made new families as permanent residents. That is particularly true of Mexicans, but Central Americans have followed the same pattern. Now women make up half of the foreign-born in the United States, and indeed more than half of those arrested in the Michael Bianco raid were women.

By 2000 there were as many as 5,000 Mayans in New Bedford. Though they kept their heads down, their presence stirred some ethnic tensions. Many were robbed or vandalized by gang members. "Talk radio stoked ideas that the Guatemalans were taking jobs, ripping off the system," Ken Hartnett explained. "The different ethnic communities avoid each other. But

when there was weekly check cashing, there were attacks on the Guatemalans from the drug neighborhoods."[40] Corinn Williams agrees: "There were
tensions with the Portuguese, but they tend to interact a lot in the fish
houses."[41] One of the remarkable aspects of the Mayans is that they don't
consider themselves Latinos. They instead identify with Native Americans,
and in fact many of them never spoke Spanish at home in the highlands.
One activist I met was wearing a T-shirt depicting Sitting Bull, Geronimo,
and other famous Native Americans on the front; on the back, it bore the
slogan "Homeland Security: Defending Ourselves since 1492." In many
respects, then, the Mayans were more isolated than most immigrants from
south of the border. Solidarity was measured by class—working class, those
who worked as fish cutters and as seamstresses—rather than purely by ethnicity, and while socially the Mayans kept to themselves, they were part of
a larger movement across the hemisphere to keep cultural traditions—language, weaving, ceremonies—alive and useful.

The work in the fish factories was hard, not least because of the decline—
or, more to the point, the breaking—of the unions. Not only were wages
depressed; conditions were horrible, recalling the meat-packing houses
Upton Sinclair had written about in his 1906 novel *The Jungle*. Abuses
included dangerous work practices and lack of adequate safety measures—
the workers were, after all, cutting fish. Unpaid overtime and even substandard wages were commonplace. The managers knew they had a labor force
at their mercy, needing work and unwilling to report abuse. The same was
true of Michael Bianco Inc. The ICE investigation began in part because of
the violations of basic laws governing workplace cleanliness, overtime compensation, and humaneness—workers, for example, would be fined or fired
for taking bathroom breaks of more than two minutes. Some protests of the
working conditions had been staged in New Bedford, and Corinn Williams
speculated that they may have drawn ICE's attention.

The Guatemalans, Salvadorans, and Hondurans at Michael Bianco Inc.
wanted to work (and for a US government contractor), and would work
hard without complaining. Many of them welcomed overtime work, even
though they were denied a higher rate of pay for it. (Insolia had two companies registered, and demanded that workers clock out of one and then clock
into the other, so that he could avoid paying a higher rate for overtime.)
The workers had traveled hundreds of miles in dangerous circumstances,
and had made their way to cold New England to work in the stinking fish

factories or the substandard Michael Bianco plant for scarcely more than the minimum wage.

In New Bedford the Michael Bianco raid may have generated more social capital—extensive community involvement to help the arrested workers and families—than would have been expected, but the effect on the Maya K'iche was jarring. "The Guatemalans were very much a tight-knit community near the north end of town," Father Fallon observed. "New Bedford was a sanctuary from the civil wars." Quite a few of the remaining Central Americans pulled their children out of school and left New Bedford when they were able to, seeking a new life elsewhere. "There's no healing from it," Fallon insisted, citing the 160 deportations. "People ignore the community of Guatemalans. There is still a shadow economy."[42]

"I feel like I'm building a future right on the edge of a cliff," one young man told Tom Juravich, a professor of labor studies at the University of Massachusetts at Amherst who interviewed many members of the Mayan community after the raid. "Every day you get better, but you never know when the future is going to slide down and disappear. We know that can happen any time." He fretted for the well-being of his family. "I'm here for my dream," he said, "but now that dream can disappear any time."[43] This sense of contingency is common to many immigrants, whose anxiety stems from the alien surroundings and culture and rules. But for someone who is subject to sudden detention and deportation, the feelings of vulnerability are acute and unyielding.

Many of the Maya K'iche had migrated north from the highlands because they were one of the primary targets of Guatemalan Army rage—actually, genocide—and they left to escape that wrath and the impoverishment that came with it. They were inclined to keep quiet and keep to their own families, sometimes not even interacting in New Bedford with those from their Guatemalan villages. It was a habit, hard-sown by the military juntas. In Guatemala, some *campesinos* from their villages would be bought off by the government as "village guards"—snitches and intimidators, mostly, and untrustworthy. The Organization of Maya K'iche, a nonprofit group created to serve the sizable Mayan population of southeastern Massachusetts, nurtured the community to be more visible, not least to embrace their cultural traditions and pass them on to their American-born youngsters. But the organization also served a political purpose, both to help with the fundamentals in immigration proceedings—from translators to transportation to court—and to share information about what was possible. Several Mayans who were involved in the ICE raid thought the experience, as horrific as it was in many ways, shook them out of their silence or lethargy and encouraged them to assert and seek rights. Many won those individual battles for a green card or asylum or at least a pause in proceedings; in these cases, the law's delay could help see a child through school.

That some people from Central America managed to thrive in New Bedford, before and after the raid, is all the more remarkable when you listen to their stories. Adrian Ventura is a case in point. Now a leader of the community, he was born and raised in Guatemala's department of El Quiché, but to make a living he moved around frequently within Guatemala and Mexico, making ends meet by selling eggs and similar jobs. He wasn't a political activist in Guatemala, so he was harassed by both the military and guerrillas, but the government forces killed his brother and sister. He finally migrated to Ciudad Juarez, Mexico, and then walked across the border with the help of a "coyote." After landing in New Bedford, he worked for $4 an hour in a recycling plant for three years. Like many other immigrants, he went back to Guatemala only to find the same situation despite the end of the civil war—no jobs, discrimination against the indigenous peoples, few options. A priest told him the military would kill him if he stayed, so he left and again made his way through Mexico and on up to New Bedford.

Ventura had left Michael Bianco Inc. two weeks before the raid. He was nearby during the raid. "I closed my eyes and it sounded like the war in Guatemala," he recalled.[44] "The arms the United States sent to Central America is the cause for people to come here."

He and others found that in the wake of the ICE raid, employers in the fish industry, in landscaping, and in recycling all pointed to what had happened and offered them even lower wages than Michael Bianco Inc. had paid. But those who were deported came back anyway; there was nothing for them in Guatemala.

"For a long time after the raid, the Central Americans weren't going out to work, to doctor's appointments, to school," Corinn Williams recalled. "The collective trauma was enormous. The fear of ICE was enormous. And the economic disruption was severe. MBI was a top-tier employer."[45] A number of firms who knew they had a legally questionable workforce sent many of them home. So there were, all of a sudden, many hundreds of unemployed Central Americans looking for work just as the Bush recession was getting underway. The competition for jobs also drove down wages.

The young Mayan man Juravich interviewed described a post-raid anxiety that kept him inside with his family, partly out of a perception that he could be separated from them. "We don't know how long we're going to be together. Things have changed a lot. It's not just with me but with a lot of my friends."[46]

As happens with so many sudden, harsh jolts in history, the impact of the ICE raid had two different kinds of effects on the immigrants. One was discouragement, further migration, "hiding in place." The second was a new assertion of rights and a strengthening of identity.

As a number of scholars have observed, the identity of immigrants is shaped dramatically by the conditions that impelled them to migrate. In Guatemala and El Salvador, aside from impoverishment and low prospects for a better life, there was political turmoil that intensified that chronic conditions of scarcity, disease, and daily violence. So the Guatemalans in particular arrived in the United States from a place where they were beleaguered not only by poverty but also by institutional racism and violence. They fled from one kind of marginalization to another. Their existence in New Bedford, though not as harsh as life in Guatemala, was arduous. They accepted low wages and low social status, living a subsistence lifestyle in the most run-down neighborhoods. In the small New England city, the social pathologies of crime and disease and dreadful living conditions were a vivid reality. The opprobrium of dominant ethnic groups and talk radio firebrands only added to their sense of oppression. If anything, this hand-to-mouth existence, including job insecurity as well as the ever-present threat of detention and deportation, drove the Guatemalans and other Central Americans toward the "invisible community" status that characterizes so many unauthorized immigrants.

But something else was also happening after the ICE raid. The Mayan community, particularly the women with children, received some attention. All of a sudden, the invisible community not only became visible, but became embattled. Some of the Mayans fled, but many stayed and were helped by public-interest lawyers to fight for legal status. And from the fight came a renewed sense of identity, or an assertion of their Mayan identity, a point of pride and a source of solidarity and belonging.

One of the primary reasons for this assertion was the formation of the Organization of Maya K'iche, a self-help group that had initially, in the first years of the decade, focused on cultural enlivenment, including embracing traditions of the highland *indios* and helping its community learn English. As the decade wore on, the economic and social plight of the Maya K'iche became more central to the organization's mission, and they achieved some tangible gains in terms of city services, police behavior, and worker's rights. The organization went into decline as a source of community cohesion after its founder was convicted of sexual improprieties, but other organizations continued to provide services, advocacy, and comfort to Central Americans generally who were victimized by Francesco Insolia's schemes.

Identity is shaped by the experiences that immigrants had in their home country, but the ways in which they cope with illegal status and uncertain work conditions in the United States are also profoundly influential. For those who saw a long period of residency in the United States as a goal, their behavior and attitudes adjusted accordingly. They tended toward acculturation, rather than assimilation—that is, engagement with the larger community, but not aspirations to become a straight-line American, whatever that might mean to them. Immigrants of all kinds tend to cling to their homeland identities and are wary of assimilation because so many social, cultural, and political barriers are erected against assimilation. The cry of the nativists that immigrants, whether here legally or not, should assimilate—earning legal status and speaking English seem to be the primary manifestations of this standard—is undermined by the high hurdles and hostility that the dominant white culture places in the way, especially the barriers to legalization.

"Over time, [immigrants] encounter a harsh world of work and experience in the indignities of prejudice, discrimination, and blocked opportunities, and most eventually come to see the United States as a place of inequality and racism," write Douglas Massey and Magaly Sánchez R., Princeton University scholars and co-authors of an important 2010 study of immigrant identity. "The dual reality of ongoing engagement and disillusion with the United States suggests a fundamental tension between American and Latino identities and yields a bright categorical boundary that Latin American immigrants must broker in their daily lives."[47]

But many immigrants don't see themselves as Americans, because they don't intend to stay in the United States long. Many come simply to work for a few years and then return to their homelands. Their social attachments are superficial, without roots and without any stake in either acculturation or assimilation. This was the case with some Honduran women I interviewed in New Bedford who had been caught in the Michael Bianco raid and, years later, were still in legal limbo. They had intended to work and return; they had children in Honduras. But one of them had become more attached to the United States than she had expected to, because of her children here (one of whom had special needs), and one of them had completed several years of schooling here and wanted to finish. After the Michael Bianco raid, working was no longer a viable option, so their attachment was based solely on their children's futures. They described the raid as having turned their world upside down, undermining a steady if tenuous existence of work, family, and sending money back to their families in Central America. Church was the one community-defining institution in their lives.

Those who write about migration and exile often refer to "contingent" status. Contingency applies to every aspect of the lives of the Maya K'iche and other Central Americans in New Bedford. If employed in the formal economy, they are employed by exploitative corporations. They have no job security, and they are vulnerable economically. They are legally at risk. Their sense of "home" or "community" is buffeted not only by the migration itself, and sometimes by restless movement within the United States to seek work or avoid detention, but also by oppressive and violent conditions in Central America. It is contingency in spades, and if not for the churches and social-service organizations the contingency would be their undoing. Even their acculturation, their relationship to the mainstream culture, is loose and variable. Assimilation is almost unthinkable under such circumstances.

As Massey and Sanchez R. explain, the Latino immigrant experience is one of "negotiating boundaries" of class and race, dealing with nativist prejudice and discrimination, and contending with an economy in which it is increasingly difficult for lower and middle classes to thrive. Adding the lack of legal status to this challenging mix makes living in the United States for an unauthorized immigrant daunting. Immigrants with papers gradually do assimilate in various ways and at varied rates, and come to identify with American norms and customs. Illicitness renders this all into a vastly more alienating existence, and hence one that has less appeal both in terms of assimilation or identity and in terms of the psychological and emotional investment that rewards immigrants with a new way of seeing themselves and a greater likelihood of acceptance. This is where the raid mentality takes its greatest toll, without addressing the challenges of illegal immigration in a socially and economically constructive way. The threat and fear of home invasion and workplace actions drives immigrants into the shadowy recesses of American society, where they are less, not more, likely to resist assimilation, legalization, and personal commitment to "Americanness."

So in New Bedford and elsewhere, the identity of the migrant is shaped not only by the new circumstances of daily life, of community and work and family, but also by the insecurities of illicitness. Economic and educational opportunity are limited, at least for the migrating generation, and work experiences are broadly abusive. Prejudice from natives, earlier generations of immigrants and their offspring, is sometimes subtle, sometimes not, but ever-present, even in liberal New England. The Guatemalans and others in Massachusetts without legal status don't suffer the institutional hostility from local and state government and news media that is the daily reality for Mexicans in Arizona, but social boundaries, exposure to crime, and the absence of job security are no less real.

It was left to the younger generation of immigrants—those who had been brought to America as children—to challenge this dark void of rights and identity.

4 DREAMING THE DREAM: THE NEXT GENERATION

American history can be depicted as a sweeping struggle to expand rights from the narrow conception of who mattered in the eighteenth century to a gradual recognition that the American polity should not exclude women, racial minorities, some nationalities and religions, people of minority sexuality, the disabled, and others. This now seems a truism, but getting to this recognition—still incomplete—was indeed a struggle against an inflexible, self-righteous dogma about who should be fully vested with political rights. (Economic rights remain even more elusive.) The Civil War, the most violent conflagration in history to that point, was fought over rights—not only the right to freedom for African slaves but the very concept of rights. Nearly 100 years after the Civil War and the bedrock expansion of rights in the Thirteenth, Fourteenth, and Fifteenth Amendments to the Constitution, the rights of blacks to participate fully and freely in political and social life remained constricted, often violently so.

Mexican-Americans and other Latinos were confronted by many of the same barriers and prejudice that African-Americans suffered. But the stories of how Latinos and blacks got to the United States couldn't be more different. Blacks were brought in chains and kept in a system of wicked oppression that persisted long after the Emancipation Proclamation. Tens of thousands of Mexican-Americans became citizens after Mexico's ceding of lands following the US war in the late 1840s. Most of the ranches and farms that Mexicans owned were expropriated by Anglos. The new citizens often ended up as farm laborers on land they once owned or on communally held land. So the indignities visited upon members of these two groups were rooted in different crimes—that most heinous act of American history, the enslavement of millions of Africans and their descendants; and the theft of land from Mexicans and a quickly wrought system of discrimination and even oppression. Only the near-extermination of the indigenous tribes of the continent ranks with these crimes.

Both blacks and Chicanos, in similar ways, sparked and nurtured a rights movement to overturn their respective conditions of being second-class citizens. Those conditions included poor schools that channeled children to futures of domestic service and manual labor, housing that was substandard and confined to certain neighborhoods, "invisibility" in political and social life, economic discrimination of all kinds, and the burden of the past—the "shame" of a parents' having been a sharecropper, a farm worker, a maid, or something more marginal. The Great Migration took blacks from conditions scarcely better than slavery to Northern cities where jobs were more plentiful and rewarding, especially in the 1940s and the 1950s, but the wages were never as high as white workers got, unions were often hostile, housing was in ghettos, and schools were informally segregated. For Mexican-Americans in Los Angeles, Tucson, Houston, and other Southwestern cities and towns, conditions were very similar. The chronic wretchedness of these conditions became intolerable, and revolts began to incubate.

Some of the earliest rumblings took the form of lawsuits. As early as the 1930s there were "Don't Shop Where You Can't Work" boycotts in black neighborhoods, and political organizing became more visible. A civil rights discourse was flowering among black intellectuals that set the stage for a fuller engagement once the Second World War was over and McCarthyism was spent. By the time the Supreme Court ruled against segregation in *Brown v. Board of Education* in 1954, a full-blown black civil rights movement was in the making.

The Chicano movement was slower to emerge (possibly because of the Bracero Program), even as there were important incidents and legal actions in the 1940s and the 1950s. Historians see at least two galvanizing phenomena that propelled the civil rights movement for Latinos.[1] The first was the founding of the United Farm Workers in 1962 by Cesar Chávez, Dolores Huerta, and others. The UFW gave the large numbers of Mexican-Americans working in the agricultural fields of California and Arizona not only a voice but a sense that activism could work for them. Chávez became a national figure who represented the rights agenda and the underclass as only a few other men and women did, most of them African-Americans. He became a potent symbolic figure, was befriended by Robert F. Kennedy and other prominent political leaders, was hailed for his non-violent tactics by his admirers, and was condemned as a rabble rouser by the right wing and especially those linked to the powerful agribusiness lobbies in California and nationally. He was, without a doubt, the foremost role model for young Latinos awakening to political and social activism. In that sense, he was very much in the mold of Martin Luther King Jr.

But the UFW and Chávez, and more militant activists such as Reies López Tijerina in New Mexico (who organized to reclaim land taken from Mexicans after the 1848 war) were mainly interested in land, labor relations, and agricultural workers, even though Chávez himself was a larger symbol of Mexican-American activism and solidarity. In the 1960s and the 1970s, a new urban form of Chicano consciousness arose, most prominently in Los Angeles but also in other Western and Southwestern cities. Denver-based Rodolfo "Corky" Gonzales, who was attuned to the urban and youth potential for a movement, teamed up with Reverend King in the Poor People's Campaign, which forged solidarity between the underclasses on the crucial issue of poverty. . Another important figure was José Ángel Gutiérrez of Texas, who co-founded one of the first groups of the Chicano movement, Mexican American Youth Organization and La Raza Unida (a political organization that fielded slates of candidates in seventeen states and won some local elections).

A high school student movement in East L.A. in 1968 was one of the opening salvos in this new surge of activism. Their walk-out to protest biased teachers and curricula, under-funded schools, and other indignities posed a major challenge to the establishment in California (including Governor Ronald Reagan). They won some important reforms in the school system, and served as a model for other cities. More pointedly, they aroused a generation of Latinos who saw in their grievances, their effort to re-invent history, and their success a model for action more broadly.

The L.A. student "blowout," as they called it, took place in a year of astonishing turmoil in American society, occasioned by a radical turn in the anti-war movement and in the civil rights movement. Non-violent protests had been a longtime tactic of Reverend King and his cohort, and most of the organizations protesting the Vietnam War. Chávez was committed to Gandhian principles of protest as well. But frustration with a resistant political system, despite some very tangible gains for civil rights, fueled more militant tactics. In all social movements, there is a spectrum of action that goes from the cool blues of analysis to lawsuits and public education and mobilization to civil disobedience and, in a very few cases, to the hot reds of violence. The Vietnam War refracted this entire spectrum, as did the civil rights and black liberation movements.

It is often said that the black liberation movement was defeated as a consequence of the assassination of its leaders—Dr. King, Malcolm X, Black Panther leader Fred Hampton. At the same time, the black power movement and the broader civil rights movement threatened the white power structure in the 1960s as few social and political movements ever have. King was the object of irrational obsession by J. Edgar Hoover and his FBI. Malcolm X and the Black Panthers both scared white America with their impassioned and sometimes hostile rhetoric. There were very troubling riots in New York, Los Angeles, Detroit, and dozens of other cities between 1964 and 1968, with thousands of buildings burned and looted and thousands of injuries; the 1967 Detroit riot resulted in 47 deaths. "The whole point of the outbreak in Watts," wrote Bayard Rustin, "was that it marked the first major rebellion of Negroes against their own masochism and was carried on with the express purpose of asserting that they would no longer quietly submit to the deprivation of slum life."[2]

The riots were not an arrow in the quiver of social-movement activists, but violence against property was considered as a useful tactic by the more militant, in part because it was directed against the objects of what they considered to be their oppression—the segregated neighborhoods, the red-lined real estate market, the retail stores that exploited them. Violence was what had been visited upon them within living memory in the Jim Crow South, and was used against blacks and whites in the turbulent South of the 1950s and the 1960s. The macabre memory of 3,400 lynchings in the Deep South in the century following the Civil War was the backdrop to the brutality of everyday life in the South. The Southern Poverty Law Center counts 38 civil rights "martyrs" up to King's death in 1968. Black church burnings came by the dozens year after year. The terrorism and violence that African-Americans were subjected to for decades insinuated itself into their lives. It was, for better or worse, a volatile intersection in the social movement, where the identity forged by violent oppression—and violent origins in the United States—shaped, in some ineffable way, the interactions of protest against that oppression. It was fraught, and it was met throughout the 1950s and the 1960s with an almost unrestrained backlash against their community as a whole by "The Man"—uncivil society and police agencies alike.

The bristling climate of the 1960s never yielded a violent Latino movement (although Tijerina did conduct some "raids" to dramatize his issue of the land grab), but gave rise to many new organizations that sometimes employed sharp-edged rhetoric. Social movements borrow from one another, and so it was with Chicano activism. But, perhaps thanks to Chávez's influence and some concrete victories in a range of campaigns, the Mexican-American movements remained low-key when it came to outright militancy. The blossoming of activist Latino civil society resulted in at least two political parties, legal defense organizations, educational and media NGOs, and hundreds of other organizations—some still at work, such as the National Council of La Raza, which has 300 affiliates. At universities, Chicano and Latino studies grew, and continue to grow. The Chicano movement, later essentially merged into or becoming a broader Latino constituency, followed the familiar pattern of social movements. There were, of course, differences between some groups—for example, between Mexican-Americans, Cuban-Americans, and Puerto Ricans. Some were interested mainly in issues of citizenship, others in poverty, education, and class; Cubans were organizing mainly to defeat Castro; Puerto Ricans lobbied for statehood or independence. But the tactics and strategies were drawn from the same well. This range of actions yielded, over time, to moderating influences, including the institutionalization of the movement into the types of organizations mentioned earlier. Radical action and demands yield to legislative strategies, electoral campaigns, and legal defense funds. The repertoires of "contentious politics" were very similar for blacks and Latinos, women and gays, anti-war protesters and the green movement.

"For Chicanos, the most directly influential component of the African-American fight for social rights was not the Southern organizing of the 1950s, but the Black Power movement of the mid- to late-1960s," the law scholar Ian F. Haney-López notes. "Black Power exercised a direct influence on the Chicano movement because it established racial identity as the principal means of self-conception and group empowerment."[3] The racial or ethnic consciousness that differentiated it from the other significant social movements of the 1960s and the 1970s was appealing to many early Chicano leaders who saw their own oppression as rooted in regressive racial attitudes. Although this was far from a universal opinion among Latinos who regarded themselves as white and assimilationist, for many young activists the parallels between the institutionalized racism afflicting blacks and the discrimination affecting Latinos were too strong to ignore, and called for a similar response.

The Chicano/Latino movements were striking in many respects—the singular, magnetic personality of César Chávez, the nonviolent tactics, the activism of high school students, the attention to recapturing or redefining land and history and culture. Also striking, and bearing some resemblance to African-American activism, was how it brought a largely passive population to engage more widely and seriously in the political process. In many respects, however, passivity and hiddenness remain strong characteristics of Hispanics in the United States, whether citizens, green-card holders, or undocumented.

Passivity is a thorny concept to grasp, because some of the things we see as signs of political passivity (not voting, not raising one's voice, not joining or forming organizations) are intended consequences of dominant groups' actions to suppress minority activism, some are cultural or historically conditioned behaviors conveyed down through generations, and some are elements of a broader pattern of low social capital and networks in communities. Theories of political participation in the United States have long seen Latinos as remarkably non-participatory.[4] In some cases this passivity is largely "structural," attributable to language barriers, lack of citizenship, poverty of resources (not just money, but things like political skills), and the psychological effects that these factors engender. For these structural reasons, the political participation of Latinos—even Latino citizens—is lower than that of African-Americans, and both are lower than that of whites. Education and income levels play strongly into the overall picture, as one would expect—as many studies have shown, low educational achievement and poverty depress political participation.

Although there is variation within Latino communities, higher rates of participation generally come as a result of group identity—often fostered, paradoxically, by pressure from the outside—for instance, from actions by a government that appear to intentionally deny access or resources to Latinos. The growth of mistrust can in this way be a stimulant to activism. As with African-Americans, churches are often an incubator of social concern and participation. Women, especially those with children, are more likely to be energized to act than men. And perhaps most significant, according to Lisa Martinez of the University of Denver, "social ties developed within the context of organizations pull people into social movement activities. Moreover, the organizations need not be political in nature so long as individuals find themselves in a social context where political knowledge and information is shared among members."[5] As Mexican-Americans and Central Americans grew in numbers and permanence, turning inward to their US-based communities, civic associations grew and laid the foundation for more political awareness, articulation of grievance, and repertoires of action. Political activism—something as simple as participating in a protest—also enhances group identity.

The growth of Hispanic civil society in the United States, news media, churches with Spanish services, and other community-building mechanisms meant that greater participation was occurring, but this is difficult to measure politically, because voter turnout—one of the most reliable gauges—has not increased as a percentage of those eligible to vote. Among Hispanic Americans, it was 52 percent in 1992 and 48 percent in 2012.

Among unauthorized immigrants, who cannot vote, measuring participation is a challenge, and indeed participating is a challenge.[6] The three obvious barriers to political involvement are language, educational and income levels, and legitimacy. Of the last, it can safely be said that noncitizens without legal status will not have access to or responsiveness from official institutions and political leaders. Political exclusion in this regard is fairly straightforward. But some political participation occurs all the same. In New Bedford and some other places, the most opportune path for such immigrants is through churches and social-service organizations. The research on this produces mixed results—some findings suggest higher rates of participation than others. Political participation in this realm would include organizing, protest, contacting officials, public education, and the like. But residents with no legal status are political players in a parallel universe that intersects with real politics mainly as others with citizenship enable their access.

It is likely that the "hidden communities" of Tucson, New Bedford, and elsewhere are hidden in nearly every sense. They keep their heads down to escape detection by federal authorities and because keeping one's head down is an ingrained lifestyle in Guatemala, El Salvador, Honduras, and

Mexico. Crime rates for new immigrants is lower than for native-born for the same reason, because drawing attention to oneself may mean deportation. The habits of staying invisible in a political culture that doesn't want to acknowledge that you are there become a tacit agreement of mutual convenience—*You provide us with cheap labor, and receive no benefits and no political enfranchisement, and we let you stay; just don't do anything to expose the deal.* For older immigrants especially—those who came as adults and whose dream it was to succeed by remaining out of the eye of authorities, with all the attendant costs of workplace abuse and housing discrimination—being hidden politically made sense. But not for their children. They dreamed another dream.

In a brilliant film titled *Caché*, Michael Haneke captured the essential reality of the relationship between Algerians and French in Paris. The Algerians are *caché*, meaning "hidden." Their lives are intimately intertwined with those of native French Parisians—a grocer, a gardener, a nanny. They interact in countless ways. Yet they are a hidden community, not visible as equals or fellow citizens. This harsh existence erupts only rarely in civil disturbances in the poor, Arab *banlieues*. In the film, the main French character is confronted by an eruption from a childhood friend who was shunted aside early in life because he was Arab.

The fictional literature of immigration is thin (and written by well-educated English speakers, for the most part, with access to publishing venues), and its central narrative and meaning hinges on the idea of alienation, marginalization, and longing for what is left behind.[7] Those who are in the United States legally have no reason to "hide," but the feelings of separateness and anomie can nonetheless be acute, especially if one is isolated from people of the same nationality, language, or other elements of affinity. When the official threats stemming from illegality are at work, too, then the sense of being a stranger in a strange land, and needing to remain invisible, become compounded and personally compelling.

This contingent status of so many immigrants has been contested from within by other immigrants in at least three ways. First, coping with social isolation through assimilation has been challenged by many of the "new immigrants" (since the immigration law changed in 1965), who have chosen not to integrate or adopt "American" ways so readily as older generations. The multicultural impulse was born in this spirit. Second, the

Chicano movement in particular blazed a path of political activism to demand rights, and forged a non-assimilationist group identity on those grounds. Both of those two reactions—multiculturalism and civil rights demands—are suitable for legal immigrants and their descendants, but not necessarily for those "out-of-status"—that is, undocumented. Adopting multiculturalist practices (or simply sustaining one's Mexican or Guatemalan, etc., cultural shape) or engaging in rights advocacy disrupts the "hiddenness" or "invisibility" of the unauthorized immigrant. But a third expression of overcoming alienation and covertness has emerged, and it is unique to the undocumented: the Dreamers.

The Dreamers are children of people who came to the United States as immigrants without authorization—children who were not born in the United States and thus are not citizens. They are also unauthorized. Since they were brought here as children, they have no culpability for having transgressed immigration rules. They have grown up in the United States going to school, forming friendships and civic attachments, and serving in the military in some cases—being Americans in all but the strictest regulatory sense.

"I think it's fair to say that in a lot of cases, they see themselves as part of the circle of membership in the United States," said Roberto Gonzales, a Harvard professor of education who has studied immigrant children for a decade. "They've had these American experiences and relationships and attachments in ways that give them, I think really, really strong claims to belonging in this country. But the broad question—do they have the right to have rights. Well, that's highly contested and it remains."[8] Gonzales calls them the "invisible victims" of the dysfunctionality of the US immigration system.

One of the poignant aspects of growing up "illegal," Gonzales points out, is that, whereas schools (which such children attend legally, thanks to a Supreme Court decision) are a normal or neutral environment with respect to their legitimacy, their unauthorized status becomes more and more problematic as they approach adulthood. It is difficult to find work, get a driver's license and a car, and pursue the other lifestyle bits that for most people are normal. They become, in effect, increasingly abnormal. Despite their Americanness and their education, they move closer to their parents' contingent status—able to work, for example, only in the subterranean economy. The stigma of this growing "illegality" is like a second border. Teenagers in particular feel suddenly different, left out, isolated. It's a jolt. "As undocumented children make transitions into late adolescence," Gonzales explained, "they move from spaces of belonging to rejection, from inclusion to exclusion, from de facto legal to 'illegal.'"[9]

It is this unique status that eventually sparked the broad participation in the social and political movement that came to be known as the Dreamers. Young Hispanics in the Southwest had been demanding studies relevant to their lives for many years, and had made important inroads into the American education system, particularly through Mexican-American studies curricula. But they were for the most part citizens, and the issue of illegality wasn't centrally at stake. To undocumented young people who had completed high school, college, and to those who had served in the US military, not being accepted in American society was an injustice that had to be openly addressed and remedied.

Around the time George W. Bush became president in 2001, national pro-reform groups saw an opportunity to press for a reform agenda. Bush, having served as governor of Texas, understood the dynamics better than most in his party, as had Ronald Reagan (a former governor of California) before him. One way to grab the attention of a leery public was for the reformers to put their best case forward, and one such case—possibly the best case—was that of the young people who were brought in illegally by their parents and raised "as Americans." It was a natural fit for politics, countering the "alien" meme so prevalent in the right-wing resistance to reform, and relying on American norms of fair play. The "poster children" were high school valedictorians, star athletes, and soldiers. They spoke and acted like your own teenager, and their familiarity was a political asset, a way to win skeptics over.

The Dreamers phenomenon was initiated by several non-governmental organizations in the Washington-centered reform coalition, groups like the National Immigration Law Center and Center for Community Change, which saw an opening for legislation—the DREAM (Development, Relief, and Education for Alien Minors) Act, and hence the name of the movement. But the attacks of September 11, 2001, derailed the early effort. Because the attackers were foreigners who came to the United States on various visas, one major consequence of the attacks was the "securitization" of immigration—that is, a sweeping, militarized clamp-down on immigration authorization and borders. Immigrants, particularly Muslim and other Arabs, were targeted for surveillance, arrest, deportation, or harassment. The right-wing media were vociferous and unrelenting in tagging non-white immigrants as inherently dangerous. Though Latinos had nothing to do with terror attacks or threats, the southern border became an object of obsession, with regular bursts of hysteria about Islamic terrorists crossing in from Mexico, something that knowledgeable officials and observers say is nonsense. But the effort to legitimize the undocumented from Latin America was beaten down by the broad, cultivated fear of terrorists among us.

It took several years before reformers attempted to re-introduce the DREAM Act, and then it was part of the broad reform package offered by President Bush and several leading senators, notably John McCain and Ted Kennedy. But that undertaking—supported by a bipartisan coalition and vast grassroots organizing, peaceful demonstrations, and a largely sympathetic news media—was beaten back, too, undone by the same fears that had long beset reform efforts and inflamed the right-wing opposition. Charges about job losses to and unbearable social-service burdens of "illegals," howls of protest against "amnesty," revived paranoia about terrorism, and a noticeable dose of racism overwhelmed the reform bills in Congress, even with a conservative from a border state in the White House. The DREAM Act went down with the reform ship.

Then something very interesting happened, something that would be familiar to those who study social movements. For nearly 10 years, the Dreamers had largely been led by the national reform groups. These groups were exceptionally image-conscious, displaying the high-achieving dreamers, the ones who had overcome enormous barriers with pluck and smarts and the values their parents taught them—the classic American immigrant story. "The image of the straight-A immigrant student rebuts the stereotype of immigrant youths as deviant and delinquent," Walter Nicholls (an assistant professor of sociology at the University of Amsterdam) writes in the best account of this movement. Nicholls quotes Senator Harry Reid: "The students who earn legal status through the DREAM Act will make our country more competitive economically, spurring job creation, contributing to our tax base, and strengthening communities."[10] And this Little Goody Two-Shoes stratagem was bound up with the broad reform effort in which the Dreamers were merely one part—indeed, a subsidiary part both as strategists and as the leading edge of achieving something concrete in immigration reform. So the young, out-of-status immigrants took over their own movement.

The ownership of the Dreamers movement was, not least, built on the next failure. After the 2006–07 debacle, the reformers thought that the presidency of Barack Obama would open doors. But the economic downturn's severity, the national fight over health care, and the resurgence of right-wing extremism in the form of the Tea Party movement doomed comprehensive reform again in 2010. It was about that time that the Dreamers started to realize that as long as they were in a secondary role, they could be defeated time and again by the hostile anti-immigrant forces. If, however, they broke free from the mainstream efforts enough to push more assertively for their own stand-alone act, just affecting the immigrant youth brought to the United States by their unauthorized parents, they stood a chance of victory.

In part, the change among the Dreamers stemmed from their sense of urgency and entitlement. Just as the black liberation movement sought to break with the white-dominated organizations that strongly influenced (and supported) civil rights in the early years, the Dreamers wanted to guide the movement that bore their name. "Our so-called allies need to realize that they are not undocumented," wrote four activists in the fall of 2010, "and, as such do not have the right to say what undocumented youth need or want. Our progressive allies insist on imposing their paternalistic stand to oppose the DREAM Act and tell us this is not the 'right' choice for us to acquire 'legal' status in this country."[11] It's no wonder that the black activist organization that most strongly appeals to the Dreamers is the Student Nonviolent Coordinating Committee (SNCC), a bold, confrontational group of the 1960s.

Individual groups of youths from various chapters of the new network, United We Dream, began more direct action in 2010—a "Trail of Dreams" trek from Texas to Washington, DC, an occupation of Senator McCain's office, nonviolent challenges at the border, and similar publicity moves. "The Dreamers remind me of the Freedom Riders fifty years ago who, deciding they wouldn't settle for life under Jim Crow, risked jail and racist violence until the Kennedy administration was won to their side, and a political party realignment began," observed Tom Hayden, one of the leaders of the New Left in the 1960s and the 1970s. "The Dreamers have petitioned, engaged in civil disobedience, lobbied for legislation at state and federal levels, and refused to accept defeats along the way. They even were sitting-in at Obama's campaign offices last June when the president issued his 'deferred action' order effectively protecting their status."[12]

It was that striking move by President Obama that validated the Dreamers' strategy of boldly going public. In June 2012, the president issued an executive order that provided a way for Dreamers to remain in the United States without fear of deportation. "They are Americans in their heart, in their minds, in every single way but one—on paper," Obama said at the time. That program, Deferred Action for Childhood Arrivals (DACA), meant that individuals between the ages of 15 and 31, with no arrest records other than for minor misdemeanors, who were in school, had completed high school, or were in or had completed service in the military could earn reprieves. Younger children would be eligible upon turning 15. It was a powerful political move, to be sure, providing Obama with the upper hand among Hispanic voters, some of whom had grown weary of his record pace of deportations and the lack of a viable reform effort in Congress. Qualified immigrants could obtain work permits, Social Security numbers, and eligibility for drivers' licenses and college aid. It toppled their old hidden world and opened up normal space for them. "It's like giving us wings to the people that want to fly," said one immigrant in Los Angeles, and hundreds of thousands like him rushed to secure their new status. By early 2014, about 125,000 had earned the new status in California, which is the home state to the largest contingent of immigrant youth, though the total that did get the new status was less than half of those estimated to be eligible. Nationally, well more than 600,000 had applied—perhaps about half of those eligible—with a small fraction (about 3 percent) denied. "It's a great relief for us," one deferred-action immigrant told a reporter. "Instead of worrying about deportation, we can now focus on our education, for our own benefit and that of this nation. Because we're not leaving the US, this is our country."[13]

DACA wasn't wholly embraced by immigration activists, however. It is a two-year, though renewable, order. Several advocates, while welcoming some relief, noted the fragile nature of the order—that is, it was not the DREAM Act or more comprehensive action for reform. Some argued that the information that the young immigrants had to provide to get their deferred action could be used against them in future deportation proceedings should the DACA program be ended. The practical effect of the program was blocked in some states (notably Arizona, where the governor refused to recognize provisions for drivers' licenses). One immigration-reform advocate noted that Arizona's political climate had "made it especially difficult for deferred-action recipients to get jobs,"[14] not only because of the license ban but also because the state government was blocking DACA's provision for in-state tuition at the state's three universities, as well as access to programs in which a high school equivalency diploma could be earned. Attorney General Tom Horne of Arizona was at the forefront of blocking Dreamers' access to these diplomas, and Arizona was one of only two states (Nebraska was the other) to prohibit them from obtaining drivers' licenses.

There was also some opposition elsewhere. Kris Kobach, the former attorney general of Kansas and the architect of many laws targeting unauthorized immigrants, sued the president on behalf of a few ICE officers; the claim was that the DACA order contravened their duty to uphold the law. "It is imperative that this attack on the rule of law be stopped, one way or another," said Kobach after a judge ruled that the suit was a dispute within the executive branch and not in his bailiwick.[15] No constitutional case could be made against DACA, but the rejectionists nonetheless fought back against something they saw as opening the door to more illegal immigration. The low rate of declined applications indicated to critics that many immigrants with a criminal record were being approved (although the 3 percent rejection rate is more than four times the incarceration rate for foreign-born Hispanics in the United States). But, again, the public supported the Dreamers' case—in one poll, 80 percent approved a pathway to earned citizenship as of February 2014.[16]

The Dreamers have achieved what many social movements set out to do: make visible the hidden, make appeals for justice, plead that the raids and deportations stop, advocate for plausible solutions. Once they found their own voice, surpassing the weak strategies of the parenting NGOs and foundations, they could articulate a case so compelling that only a few diehards stood in their way. They played on cultural ideals—the American Dream, most obviously—that appealed to a broad swath of American society. Their "repertoires of contention," or tactics, such as those of the "Dream 9" (a group that returned to Mexico and then challenged the US government upon returning at a border crossing), have earned some rebukes from pro-reform advocates, much as militant black protesters were rebuked by some of their white supporters in the 1960s.

The Dreamers' goals are relatively modest, finely articulated, convincing, and achievable. Their actions (largely lobbying and publicity seeking) have not been militant. Their message is "We are educating ourselves, serving our country, and ready to be outstanding citizens; let us be." The price of citizenship is so small, so insignificant in terms of the legalities, that virtually everyone agrees that such a longing is appropriate and attainable. Indeed, the Dreamers are successfully embracing the old assimilationist model in their political tactics, saying not merely "Let us be like you" but "We *are* like you." It is this cultural initiative to demonstrably be Americans in every sense of the word that has made them so acceptable and non-threatening. Little about job stealing or crime or other such concerns has surfaced about the Dreamers. It says much about congressional Republicans, the only bastion of resistance to the DREAM Act, that they would block the assimilationist dream at every opportunity.

What the dream gives, the nightmare takes away. The notion of the United States as a dreamscape has a dark side, a nightmare, which can haunt immigrant youth. Ethnic or nationalist gangs, boys and young men mostly, are wreaking violence in East Los Angeles, in Newark, in Miami, in Tucson, in Chicago, in New Bedford, and elsewhere. Their reach is long, and they make trouble frequently. Many of the members, though second-generation, have ties to gangs in the old country. In Tucson, they have names like Barrio Hollywood, the Juggalos, Barrio Libre, Southside Posse Bloods, and Sur 13. In New Bedford, there are the Latin Kings, Monte Park, Bloods, and United Front, franchises with connections to Boston and Providence gangs, some even national. Drug trafficking is their trade. And there are omnipresent rumors that the notorious MS-13 (the largest and deadliest Salvadoran gang, international in scope) and the 18th Street gang (also Salvadoran) are active throughout the United States.

As I note elsewhere, immigrants commit far fewer crimes than native-born Americans, and this applies to gang membership and the trouble they cause. (Most gangs consist of native-born Americans.[17]) Studies show that Latino gang violence is more a stereotype than a reality, but it has a grip on some neighborhoods and it strongly shapes Anglos' perceptions of the "Hispanic threat." In that, it tends to serve as a counterbalance to the Dreamers' story, an entirely different outcome of their common roots in Latin American poverty.

The gangs soak up young men who come from dysfunctional homes, giving them the family they never had, the respect they never got, the in-your-face riposte to being marginalized. "The prestige and respect they get is something they are craving," said a police officer dealing with gangs in Tucson. "When you get them away from the gang element, they are babies, really."[18] There are about 100 gangs, with about 5,000 members, in Tucson; most of the members are Mexican-Americans, and most of those, police estimate, are unauthorized immigrants. In New Bedford, a smaller city, the gangs are a mix of Latino origins, including Puerto Rican and Portuguese, but Salvadorans, Hondurans, and Guatemalans figure prominently in the mix. One ledger of arrests in New Bedford had dozens of gang members taken down for possession and intent to sell, with cocaine the drug of choice.

The violence comes with the drug trade and turf wars. As in the Italian Mafia, the premium on not snitching and the difficulty of exiting from the gang produces executions within the gang. There is doubt about just how much violence originates with the gangs, and the popular image of them as machete-wielding and bloodthirsty are greatly exaggerated, but there certainly is violence—hundreds of murders each year. Gangs are a sizable problem across the country. "Some 33,000 violent street gangs, motorcycle gangs, and prison gangs with about 1.4 million members are criminally active in the US today," according to the FBI. "All use violence to control neighborhoods and boost their illegal money-making activities, which include robbery, drug and gun trafficking, fraud, extortion, and prostitution rings. According to the 2011 National Gang Threat Assessment report, gangs are responsible for an average of 48 percent of violent crime in most jurisdictions, and up to 90 percent in others."[19] A number of gangs are involved in human trafficking, including trafficking of immigrants. In some jurisdictions in Arizona, Colorado, California, Massachusetts, and Texas, 90 percent of crime is attributed to gangs. And they come in all colors: African, Asian, Eurasian, Caribbean, and Middle Eastern: it is not Latino or African-American alone, although by most estimates nearly half are Hispanic and about a third are African-American. If these estimates are correct, that would mean that close to 700,000 Hispanics are in gangs, from a total Hispanic population of 53 million in the United States; if half of gang members are undocumented immigrants, then that is considerably less than 1 percent of the Latino population in the United States.

The Mexican drug trade figures prominently in the Latino gang world, and is identified by the FBI as by far the major threat in this criminal realm. Mexican drug cartels "use street and prison gang members in Mexico, Texas, and California to protect smuggling routes, collect debts, transport illicit goods, including drugs and weapons, and execute rival traffickers," The FBI reports. "Gang members, including Barrio Azteca, MS-13 and Sureños have been intercepted driving with weapons and currency toward Mexico from such states as California, Colorado, Georgia, and Texas." The colossal amount of drug-related violence in Mexico (34,000 murders in the period 2008–2011) invariably affects related gang behavior in the United States. "Gang-related activity and violence has increased along the Southwest border region, as US-based gangs seek to prove their worth to the drug cartels, compete with other gangs for favor, and act as US-based enforcers for cartels which involves home invasions, robbery, kidnapping, and murder," the FBI report notes.[20] In Arizona, the Latin Kings, Sureños, and MS-13 all do local work for the major Mexican drug lords to help satiate America's seemingly bottomless thirst for illegal drugs. Gangs are also committing such "white-collar" crimes as identity theft and mortgage fraud.

The Hispanic gangs and gang membership are a social phenomenon, of course; they aren't a creation of Mexican drug cartels, nor are they political. Gangs stem from the hard conditions of living and how some—very few overall—young men and women opt for the protection and belonging offered by gangs. (As has been noted, the gang world remains dominated by the native-born, not immigrants or their offspring.) It's a predictable and sad story; one study found a high incidence of alcohol abuse in fathers of gang members, for example. In the most insightful study of gangs, *Gangsters Without Borders*, the anthropologist Thomas Ward describes how many future gang members came into the United States illegally and were at a disadvantage in school, since they knew little English and suffered from bullying, some of it violent. "When MS-13 became a traditional street gang," Ward notes, "its members thought of it as a self-defense organization devoted to protecting its members from attacks by other street gang members." (The parallel to militant groups in the Middle East is striking. Interviews with arrested insurgents during the height of the Iraq war in 2004–2008, for example, found that they thought of themselves as protecting their communities.) But "it quickly evolved into a predatory gang, with the accompanying change in objectives: seeking further wealth, power and status."[21]

The link to immigration is irrefutable in many cases. Like the Sicilian Mafia, the Hispanic gangs grew from foreign soil in one way or another. In the case of the most notorious of them—the Mara Salvatrucha or MS-13, a Salvadoran gang mainly linked to Los Angeles but now operating throughout the Western Hemisphere—the formation of the gang occurred as a result of the civil war in El Salvador in the 1970s and the 1980s, a war in which the United States was heavily involved. Thousands of refugees and emigrants flowed out of El Salvador for their own safety and ended up in the United States. Some of the young Salvadorans had been trained in warfare by the US-backed military (and some, though fewer, by the guerrillas), and they brought these skills to the barrios of East L.A. MS-13 was one of the first transnational gangs, as many of them were deported back to El Salvador, where the gang also set down roots, spread to Guatemala and Honduras, and flourished. Now the gangs in Central America are so threatening that they have set off a new wave of northward migration in which children who had been forcibly recruited into the gangs have escaped to the US border. The crisis of the summer of 2014 at the border was a consequence in large part of this phenomenon; about 100,000 children from Central America were estimated to have arrived at the border in 2014. (The flow of such migrants had been high and steady for many months before it gained national attention.) The insecurities of a drug-riddled society (and state), the absence of even-handed justice, the prevalence of corrupt police, and the absence of fair economic development all allowed the criminals to thrive and threaten ordinary folks so severely that they fled, essentially as refugees. With the cessation of the civil wars, the drug trade boomed in the ruined economies and societies of Central America, where weapons were easily available and young men were hardened by the wars' brutal violence. It's one of the legacies of the Reagan Doctrine and the long-standing US policy of the *mano dura*—the mentality of the raid, exported to client states with the weapons needed to apply maximum force. As the researcher Tani Adams elucidated in a 2011 study, the depiction of the violence in Central America as all "gang related" or based on illicit drug trafficking misses the more profound phenomenon of economic dislocation and impoverishment that resulted from the civil wars and neoliberal economic policies.[22] As a result, *mano dura* has failed, both at home and abroad.

Conditions in the United States also foster some criminality. The growth and violent presence of Hispanic gangs (and indeed all gangs) is a symptom of the alienation many young men experience in the marginalized neighborhoods and schools where they have settled. If caught and deported, those who aren't citizens would never be allowed to reside in the United States legally. They are self-marginalizing themselves even more. As one policeman in Tucson put it, there are two ways out of a gang: prison and death.

Paradoxically, the prevalence of gang culture makes the Dreamers' achievements all the more remarkable, but those Dreamers also underscore the poor choices gang members make. In terms of the rights discourse, the gangsters have opted not for "contentious politics"—even of a very militant kind, as did the Black Panthers—but for self-enrichment, misogyny, drug peddling and addiction, and the violence of personal revenge.

Street gangs are a way of life in most cities in the world. They have also been prevalent in African-American communities for years. It is telling that American popular culture romanticizes the Sicilian and Italian Mafias, the Jewish gangs of Meyer Lansky and Bugsy Siegel, and the Irish gangs of Hell's Kitchen, but portrays black and Hispanic gangs as avatars of deadly disorder. The Dreamers have escaped this association entirely, and have burnished a reputation of being avatars of American immigrant aspirations. Turning those aspirations away could be the worst mistake in immigration policy the United States has ever made.

The origins of the gangs and those of the Dreamers are geographically specific, and their statuses are geographically determined. Dreamers are who they are because they are sons and daughters of immigrants fleeing something, mostly in Central America and Mexico—fleeing poverty and joblessness, repression and civil war. And those gang members who are immigrants are part of that same flight, to and fro, burnished by the violent, unforgiving conditions of El Salvador, Guatemala, Honduras, and Mexico, conditions very much a consequence of the American imperium and the ravages of economic globalization.

5 RAIDS GONE GLOBAL: GENOCIDE IN GUATEMALA AND WARS IN MEXICO

Perhaps no country combines breathtaking beauty and ancient culture with brutal politics and repression as does Guatemala.[1] The mountainous, verdant terrain has been home to its indigenous peoples for 18,000 years, but once the Spanish *conquistadores* came to dominate the land in the sixteenth century the Mayans and their once-remarkable civilization of city-states were harshly subjugated. About 750,000 Mayans died during the Spanish conquest. Afterward, a feudal system of servitude called the *encomienda* was enforced coercively by the Spanish. The purpose of the *encomienda* was to Christianize the indigenous peoples while stripping them of their land and culture; the agricultural produce and timber their labor yielded was shipped back to Spain. In this sense the *encomienda* was an early form of globalization. The system morphed several times, but forced labor was always at its core. Independence from Spain in 1821 didn't really end the system—the structure of feudal society with the Mayans at the bottom has persisted.

Large tracts of land that had been expropriated and accumulated by creoles or mestizos over the centuries became plantations on which indigenous peasants worked for subsistence. It became an export economy of sorts, shipping coffee, cocoa, and bananas and other fruits to Europe and the United States, and its success depended on the weather and the market. By the early years of the twentieth century, many of the large haciendas were contractually beholden to the likes of United Fruit Company, the largest of its kind in Central America, and this connection brought the United States into the picture, not only as a consumer but also as a protector of American corporations abroad. United Fruit began meddling in

Guatemalan politics from the beginning, helping to install the strongmen in the president's palace who could rule in the company's interests.

A somewhat unexpected turn toward democratic reform in the 1940s signaled a possible end of the centuries of peonage for the indigenous people. An officers' rebellion against the Nazi-sympathizing president Jorge Ubico—yet another dictator favored by the creole upper class, the US government, and United Fruit—was led by Colonel Jacobo Árbenz Guzmán, among others, who fitfully established a reform government. Árbenz was defense minister in the first reform period of the 1940s, and then ran for president in 1950, winning handily. He vowed land reform for the peasants and a more independent course that would be free from foreign influence.

The US government long suspected Árbenz of having communist sympathies, though in those hysterically anti-communist days anyone with liberal to leftist leanings was suspect. The Truman administration had formulated plans to oust Árbenz, partly at the behest of the Nicaraguan dictator Anastasio Somoza, but the plan was foiled by loyal officers of the Guatemalan military; they faced the constant threat of coups and were vigilant. But the rhetorical attacks on Árbenz escalated. His government was depicted as the "beachhead" of international communism in Latin America. Senator Alexander Wiley (a Republican from Wisconsin), chairman of the Senate Foreign Relations Committee, said "It seems to me that Guatemala is going to be a source of Red infection throughout Central America, and the sooner we help sterilize that source, the better."[2] Newspaper editorials sounded this same alarm. At the height of McCarthyism, Guatemala became the sum of all fears. As in later episodes in Cuba, El Salvador, Nicaragua, and elsewhere, the US government inflated the USSR's influence, convinced itself that a home-grown leftist agenda wasn't feasible, and sought to "sterilize" Moscow's septic contagion.

The intolerable insult in Washington was the taking of land owned by United Fruit, land that was uncultivated and had been acquired over decades through United Fruit's cozy relations with Guatemala's political and landholding elites. Many of Washington's most influential people were involved with the company—the Dulles brothers (John Foster, secretary of state, and Allen, director of the CIA) had previously served on the company's legal team, Tommy Corcoran, a consummate DC insider, was its lobbyist, the powerful Lodge family owned many shares, the propaganda guru Edward Bernays orchestrated the anti-communist fervor, and so on. These relationships paved the way for action against the land reformers. Árbenz paid a fair price for the land he expropriated, and it was to go to the Mayans mainly, whose land it once was. But to US leaders at that time, the principle of expropriation bode ill, and looked too much like Bolshevism. United Fruit had enormous holdings in Central America, and in Guatemala they controlled nearly half the land, virtually all transportation and communications, and the most vital port. It practically owned the country, and it was this stranglehold that Árbenz was breaking, at his own peril. Árbenz's purchase of Czech-made military equipment in the spring of 1954 set a new CIA plan into motion.

In some respects, the plan resembled the CIA action to overthrow the democratically elected Mohammad Mossadeq in Iran less than a year earlier. Mossadeq had also nationalized the Iranian oil industry, then mainly in the hands of British Petroleum; he, too, was falsely accused of being a dangerous leftist. The British and American covert operations built domestic opposition to Mossadeq, including many important Shi'ite clerics, engineered an embargo on Iranian oil, and organized a coup once popular discontent had grown. This "success," according to one history, "elevated the Agency's reputation to unprecedented heights, and the new [Eisenhower] administration gave CIA primary responsibility for the action," which the National Security Council authorized in August 1953, the month of the coup against Iran. According to CIA documents, "the Iranian operation's chief officer found Secretary of State John Foster Dulles 'almost alarmingly enthusiastic' about the outcome" of the coup in Iran.[3]

Not only the circumstances but also the plans bore some resemblance to one another: stir popular doubts about the target, ratchet up American political hyperbole, and assemble a reliable pro-American group to take over when the target quit the scene. In Guatemala, these tactics took the form of boosting a small armed force led by a disgruntled officer, Castillo Armas, and providing training in Nicaragua and Honduras (the latter the victim of a banana company coup in the 1920s). Weapons, airplanes, and other assistance followed from the CIA. The Catholic Church was eager to overthrow Árbenz, but the Church and the landowners alone couldn't dislodge a popular leader. Armas' army, moreover, was quite small; it is likely that no more than a thousand men took part in the initial attack in mid June 1954. So the CIA, already months into a well-orchestrated propaganda effort, inflated Armas' army's size and progress through a massive campaign of disinformation, controlling the news on the front and distorting the facts on the ground—the steady defeat of Armas' band by the Guatemalan army—to make it appear that the government was losing. Some airplane strikes in Guatemala City contributed to a sense of panic in Árbenz, but his downfall was actually the work, again, of the military, which abandoned Árbenz after months of the CIA's propaganda effort. "Árbenz resigned without a fight because the army deserted him," according to one historian, "and the army deserted him because the Church, the plantation owners, and the scared, disoriented populace of Guatemala City were convinced that Árbenz was driving Guatemala into a fatal embrace with communism and a fatal conflict with the United States."[4]

In his resignation speech, Árbenz articulated an analysis that could apply to many episodes in the long and troubled history of the United States in Latin America:

A cruel war against Guatemala has been unleashed. The United Fruit Company and US monopolies, together with US ruling circles are responsible … . Mercenaries have unleashed fire and death, respecting nothing … . In the name of what do they do these things? We all know what. They have blamed their actions on the pretext of Communism. The truth is elsewhere—in financial interests of the United Fruit Company and other US firms that have invested much in Guatemala. Time will show if what they say is true … .[5]

The US ambassador then maneuvered to get Armas appointed as president, fulfilling the goals of the Dulles brothers and restoring the old oligarchy. The land redistribution was reversed, as were the other mildly progressive measures of Árbenz and his immediate predecessor. The country receded to its *encomienda* past in a matter of weeks. And what followed was a downward spiral of repression and corruption as bad as anything ever seen in Latin America, with assassinations, coups, putsches, and dictatorships cascading through the ensuing decades. Armas was murdered by military officers in 1958, and was replaced by Miguel Ydígoras Fuentes, whom Árbenz had soundly defeated in the election of 1950. An unsuccessful coup by young officers in 1960 (Fuentes was ousted by the military in 1963) drove those officers into a revolutionary movement that commenced a civil war that would last 36 years.

The civil war was brutal. An estimated 200,000 people died, and large numbers of peasants were dislocated when their villages were burned or devastated in other ways. Much of the killing by the military and police came during the presidency of General Efraín Ríos Montt in the early 1980s in a bloodbath that took tens of thousands of lives. "State violence in Guatemala was distinguished by how deliberate it was and how long it lasted," according to a study published in 1999 by the American Association for the Advancement of Science. "Over time, the armed conflict shifted from the city to the country to the city and back to the country again. State terror took different forms, from paramilitary death squads that murdered their victims one at a time, to massacres directed against entire rural villages."[6]

Many of the victims were political activists and labor leaders. Many were "disappeared" as a tactic of intimidation to silence their colleagues. With Ríos Montt, however, the war escalated—perhaps in reaction to the rebel Sandinistas' triumph next door in Nicaragua in 1979—and was taken aggressively to the countryside. Fifteen thousand troops were deployed to the highlands, including El Quiché, to devastating effect. Sweeps of villages, burnings, lootings, sexual violence, and summary executions characterized the military campaign. Death squads targeted individuals they considered undesirable. (Later, the death squad diaries of the killers were found and published.) Amnesty International reported that the Guatemalan soldiers were "beheading their victims or burning them alive, and smashing the heads of children against rocks." Victims of torture were burned alive or thrown out of helicopters.[7]

The US government was heavily involved in aiding the succession of *juntas* and *genocidaires*. Tens of millions of dollars in military aid were given to Guatemala, even as President Jimmy Carter tried to impose human-rights conditions on such aid. (The *caudillos* refused to accept conditions.) The CIA appears to have known the extent of the war crimes and to have occasionally helped the military in its dirty war. President Ronald Reagan infamously praised Ríos Montt and held him up as an exemplar of democratic values.

The violence subsided between Ríos Montt's ouster (in August 1983) and the signing of a peace accord in 1996, though there were some gruesome episodes of village destruction in the 1990s. But the war's ruinous impact went well beyond the grim mortality figures. Agriculture, markets, transportation, education—virtually everything was affected. In rural communities, which were mainly Mayan, any disruption or destruction of infrastructure was a heavy blow to people's chances of recovering livelihoods. So during and after the civil war, emigration—especially by peasants—increased quickly. There was no work, and the violent climate of fear and repression was stultifying. Even after the peace accord, the deep racism of the ruling elites toward the *indios* persisted. And everyday violence, the chronic violence of criminal gangs in particular, rose sharply as a consequence of the wars throughout Central America and the burgeoning drug trade, which catered to Americans' desire for marijuana and cocaine.

About 400,000 Guatemalans departed during the civil war, but more than twice as many left afterward, a clear indication of how disrupted the countryside was. The United States was stingy with its grants of asylum, much more so than for Cubans or Nicaraguans, so a large number of the refugee migrants entered the United States illegally. From about the end of the civil war, increasing numbers of women emigrated, indicating that rural poverty in particular was so severe that mothers would leave their children in Guatemala with an elder relative and seek work in the United States. (Incidences of sexual violence and "femicide" remained high as well.) By the mid 2000s, one-third of all Guatemalans were receiving remittances from relatives in the United States, where about a million of them resided. Those cash transfers amounted to 10 percent of Guatemala's economy.

Today Guatemala, though politically more stable and with less state terror imposed on the usual targets, remains a chronically poor country with a very low Human Development Index rating (133rd in the world, worst in Latin America). More than half of all Guatemalans are poor, and in the rural areas 80 percent of the people are living in poverty. The governments there have done little to alleviate poverty and stimulate sustainable growth. And poverty is increasingly structural, an outcome of how the economic system works. Because of their experience with the United Fruit Company, Guatemalans recognize how the system works, even as it has new permutations—that is, the globalized economy, in which foreign companies come to dominate poor countries that have valuable resources. In the case of Guatemala, that resource is its agriculture. Multinational companies, many of them American-based, purchase or lease land, employ agricultural workers at below subsistence levels, and sell the harvest in global markets for several times its cost. Some farming, such that of biofuels, is diverting fertile land from food production, but the principal problem is distribution. According to a 2011 report in *The Guardian*, "Aida Pesquera, Oxfam director for Guatemala, says: 'The food is here but the main problem is distribution. Land is concentrated in very few hands. The big companies pay very little tax. Labour conditions on plantations are appalling. It's a classic case of how a very productive country with high rates of exclusion, especially among the indigenous population, cannot feed its own people.'"[8] Half of the children in Guatemala are malnourished, one of the highest rates in the world, and it isn't hard to see why: the prices of staples have doubled or worse in a short time due to agribusiness dominance of the arable land, pushing out subsistence farming.

The reforms since the end of the civil war have been typical "neoliberal" measures: privatizing state assets, financial and trade reform to provide easy access for multinational corporations, easing of regulations. Guatemala's public debt is high (a chronic and often destabilizing phenomenon in Latin America), but its tax base is low. This classic embrace of the dark side of globalization keeps the poor in poverty and the wealthy untouched by public obligations.

The impact of such neoliberal policies has been hotly debated for 30 years. No doubt in some economies that once were top-heavy with state cronyism and inefficiency they have freed up entrepreneurial energy and initiative. In many developing countries, however, the selling off of state assets has been accompanied by a reduction in state budgets for education and health care, among other services, and these cuts have affected the rural populations most directly. Very few children complete secondary school, for reasons that mainly hinge on public financing. According to the US Agency for International Development, "these and other low indicators are largely due to deficiencies in the education quality related to poor teacher training, a lack of pertinent learning methodologies for rural and indigenous children, and insufficient financial, material and technical resources."[9] Poor nutrition (indeed near starvation), poorly funded education, pressure on fertile land, and health-care access and outcomes that are among the worst in Latin America all indicate a profound failure of economic globalization as an instrument of fair and equitable development. And much of this can be attributed to the United States—by far Guatemala's major trading partner and the aggressive promoter of the very globalization policies that are keeping Guatemala in ruins.

Chronic poverty and the increasing difficulty of rural life have led, as one would expect, to an increase in emigration. As the data reproduced here in table 5.1 show, many more people left after the end of the civil war. So although the war did provoke a steadily increasing outflow of people (about 380,000 between 1980 and 1995), the numbers since then are substantially greater. As of 2010, there were an estimated 1.1 million Guatemalans living in the United States, up from 280,000 in 1990.

The war's part in the emigration story should not be discounted, however. Not only did it spur the large migration, but it left the country in shambles, especially the devastated countryside where Ríos Montt's genocide occurred and where underdevelopment was centuries old. The turn to neoliberal policies, when the state was too weak to maintain order (or remained a source of state terrorism through paramilitaries) and was too poor to improve education, health care, and agriculture, was the final blow for many *campesinos*. To escape their deplorable conditions, they would emigrate to the north.

Peering out of a church where he was taken during a horrifying attack three decades ago, Ramiro Osorio watched armed men take small children from his Guatemalan village and bash them into a tree before tossing their bodies into a well.

He was 5 years old. Osorio and his siblings grabbed onto their mother's legs, but she was seized from them and taken to the well pleading for her life.

"I heard my mom screaming for help and 'Please, don't kill my kids. They don't know nothing. We don't know nothing,'" Osorio told an American jury Friday in the trial of a former Guatemalan soldier charged with lying about the massacre on his U.S. citizenship application. Osorio's parents and six siblings all died in the attack, which virtually wiped out the village.

Amy Taxin, "Survivor tells of Guatemalan massacre at US trial," Associated Press, September 27, 2013

Osario was a witness for the prosecution in an immigration-court proceeding the purpose of which was to strip Jorge Sosa, a lieutenant in the Guatemalan army in 1982 when the atrocities occurred, of his US citizenship, which he had gained by lying about his crimes.

Many of the million Guatemalans living in the United States have stories of this kind, if not as gruesome. Adrian Ventura, the New Bedford organizer, is an example. "My father didn't go to school and didn't read or write, but he fought against the forced labor of indigenous peoples at the hands of the ladinos and the government," he recalled. "I grew up taking tortillas and tamales to the farmers, who worked like slaves for no pay to widen the highways around Totonicapán, Xela, and the north of K'iché. It had a huge impact on me."[10]

Table 5.1

Emigration from Guatemala, 1960s through 2005.

	Number of emigrants
1960s	6,700
1970s	56,843
1981–85	84,897
1986–90	159,809
1991–94	141,755
1995–00	558,776
Total (through 2005)	1,364,546

source: International Organization for Migration, Guatemala

In Guatemala, Ventura (who has headed both the Organization Maya K'iché in New Bedford and the workers' rights group Centro Comunitario de Trabajadores) had been on a path to labor organizing, a dangerous profession. He recalled that phase of his life as follows: "In the 70s began a period of severe government repression and my whole family was ordered to be killed. They lit our house on fire and burned some of our LIO Campesino[11] documents, along with the emergency funds collected to help workers who were hungry and thirsty. We fled to my brother's house, but they found us and burned the house and some of the surrounding forest. The military unloaded all their weaponry against us. They tortured me and tortured my mother in front of me. I was able to escape to southern Mexico along with many others also fleeing the violence."

In Mexico, Ventura worked as a street vendor. Many Guatemalans flee to Mexico, but there is little support for them there. "When I returned to Guatemala in search of my family," he recounted, "I found my parents still alive. With the support of the elderly in the village, I began to work again with LIO Campesino and we grew stronger. A few years later, I was forcibly recruited into the military. They beat me all over. If you were Catholic, they killed you. Under the command of General and President Ríos Montt, they forced us to accept the word of God as Evangelical Christians. Part of our training as soldiers was learning to destroy churches marked with a cross— the Catholic churches—and let be those without marking—the Evangelical churches. We patrolled all day long with no pay. They tortured people in the schools in front of us. I couldn't stand it and after a month I fled to Escuintla. I went to the coast to work and organized a worker's union."

Ventura also worked for the Recovering Historical Memory Project, a remarkable collection of testimony by those ravaged by the civil war and repressive governments, an effort organized by Bishop Juan José Gerardi and far surpassing the government's truth and reconciliation document. Ventura took testimonies from Mayan farmers and translated them for the project. After some land-reform work following the end of the civil war, he continued to receive death threats from Ríos Montt's gang. He left for New Bedford.

Adrian Ventura's story is hardly unique, as the Recovery of Historical Memory Project makes clear. The project documented 422 massacres from 1960 to 1994. It estimated a total death count of 200,000. There was large-scale sexual violence, disappearances, and kidnappings. About 200,000 children were orphaned. The project's four-volume report (titled *Nunca Mas!*) contains page after page of descriptions of torture, mass killings, and intimidation, almost all by the Guatemalan army and paramilitaries. Rape was used as an instrument of war, and according to one entry "women were frequently assaulted in front of their families." "The army would bring down to the zone big native girls with fat braids in their hair and earrings made of wool thread," stated another entry. "They brought them because they said they were guerrillas. They would rape them and disappear them." Another story is from a daughter whose father was interrogated, was tortured, and died in custody; the police riddled his face with bullets so he couldn't be identified, then dumped him in a mass grave. Others tell of going from morgue to morgue, looking for loved ones, and seeing mutilated corpses, often burned beyond recognition. The testimony is often elegiac. "The ones who died there rotted. There they remained. No one collected them. No one buried them," one Mayan woman recalled from a massacre in 1982. "Because they had said that anyone who picked them up or went to see them would be killed right there. Whoever buried them was one of them. Even now I don't know what happened to them—if some animal or dog ate them. I don't know. That is the violence that my mother and father suffered. There is a constant ache in my heart, and I always think about the violence they endured."[12]

Thousands of stories like these emerged. When the Catholic Church and the office of the archbishop released the testimony in 1998, it sent shock waves through Guatemala. Many such stories had been aired before in various ways, usually from safe havens. One especially striking eyewitness account was given by Dianna Ortiz, a Catholic nun who had worked in Guatemala in 1988 and 1989. "I was abducted and brutally tortured by Guatemalan security agents," see told a congressional panel. "My back was burned over 100 times with cigarettes. I was gang-raped repeatedly. I was beaten, and I was tortured psychologically, as well—I was lowered into a pit where injured women, children, and men writhed and moaned, and the dead decayed, under swarms of rats. Finally, I was forced to stab another human being."[13] She said she believed an American was running the operation, and later revelations confirmed that the CIA had cooperated with the Guatemalan state on a range of illegal activities in the name of anti-communism.

The truth tellers pay a price when confronting entrenched state power. Dianna Ortiz faced stonewalling by the government and even attempts to discredit her by celebrity journalists. Bishop Gerardi, the ultimate truth seeker in Guatemala, was murdered by the military two days after the release of his landmark report, beaten to death in his church chambers.

It was the violence of the army, the police, and the criminals; it was the violence of rural poverty, disease, malnutrition; it was the violence of ethnic division, racism, and hatred. As one immigrant said, the dream isn't about having a better life in the United States. It's about living a better life in Guatemala. But it has to start in the United States, that dream, because that is the only way to make enough money. So migration launches with the idea that it is bounded temporally, that they will return after they have earned enough to build a house and pay for life's necessities.

What was not part of the dream was a return hastened by deportation. In the small village of Xicalcal, in the highlands of El Quiché, several families told a reporter for the New Bedford *Standard-Times* of the wrenching decision to make their way back to the beautiful but economically barren province. One couple that had been split up by the ICE raid, with the husband in a detention prison in Texas and the wife not allowed to work, decided that the wife should return to Guatemala because they had no work, and if she did work, she later told an interviewer, "I was afraid I would lose my son if they caught me again."[14] The husband returned, too, after his release, but couldn't find work in Xicalcal.

There were several other stories almost identical in shape—the detention, the release of the mothers to care for their children, their return to El Quiché because staying in New Bedford held too many perils, and the hardscrabble life that awaited them and their children in Guatemala. Without returning to the United States, with all the attendant perils and costs of that journey, there was no hope for the better life they all yearned for in Guatemala. As one man said upon being deported for the third time, there were just two choices for a young man in Guatemala who wanted to make money: the "narcos" and the United States. Even a legal job, as scarce as they are, would pay just enough to get by: not the stuff that dreams are made of.

The American experience in Mexico is more intimate, more consequential, and more complex than the relatively minor sideshow of Guatemala.[15] Mexico and Mexicans are intertwined with American history, particularly that of the nineteenth century, when Americans pushed out from what was a mix of territories and sixteen states all east of the Mississippi River to fill what eventually became the 48 contiguous states. That enormous area of expansion west of the Mississippi was mainly territories of France and Spain. The first became the Louisiana Purchase, Thomas Jefferson's nifty bargain from a cash-strapped Napoleon Bonaparte; the second became Mexico when it won independence from the Spanish crown in 1821 after a decade-long struggle supported by the poor and indigenous peoples, who had been, not surprisingly, horrendously abused by the Spanish colonists. What ensued from independence wasn't pretty—decades of civil strife, assassinations, dictatorships (particularly the harsh, 35-year rule of Porfirio Díaz), and revolution—and the loss of half its territory to the United States through the wars in Texas and what we call the Mexican-American War and Mexicans call *la invasión norteamericana*. Over that history of reformers and despots, the dreadful conditions of the peasantry scarcely improved. A system of oppression of the indigenous and poor mestizos kept them in debt bondage. Mexico, despite considerable natural wealth, remained a stratified society, with wealth and power in the hands of a small number of elites, however shifting that group was as politics brought one clique or another to power.

Díaz was a modernizer of sorts. After he opened Mexico to foreign direct investment, American money poured in to buy up oil fields, mineral mines, and land for farming, and to set up factories where goods for export could be produced more cheaply than in the United States. Many of the elements of globalization were at work late in the nineteenth century and early in the twentieth, and Mexico was a convenient laboratory. This was "dollar diplomacy," using political muscle and military threats—and frequent intervention in Latin America and the Caribbean—to protect US economic interests, such as oil fields owned by the Rockefellers in Mexico. During the bloody and tumultuous revolution that unseated Díaz, President Woodrow Wilson kept gunboats off the coast to protect those interests, a show of the flag that led to a six-month occupation of the seaport city of Veracruz in 1914. Just before that, the US ambassador was implicated in a coup that brought another ruthless dictator to power. These events among others have fed subsequent generations of Mexicans with a deep distrust of US meddling and intentions in their affairs, even as later presidents, most famously Franklin D. Roosevelt, sought to implement a "good neighbor" policy that would lower the American profile.

Among the elements of distrust—or at least mixed emotions—is how America has brought in and sometimes expelled Mexican immigrants. The border was virtually nonexistent for many decades, and Mexican labor, especially for agriculture, was pivotal in the American Southwest. As was noted earlier, this labor tended to be seasonal, and the Mexicans would return home after harvesting. This was the more or less routine pattern for more than 100 years. There were periods of disruption and tragedy. In the 1930s, prompted by the Great Depression, at least 400,000 Mexicans working in the United States were suddenly and often brutally expelled; recent scholarship suggests it may be closer to a million. According to a recent report, "in a June 1931 memo to superiors, Walter Carr, Los Angeles district director of immigration, said 'thousands upon thousands of Mexican aliens' have been 'literally scared out of Southern California.'"[16] Many of the children were US citizens. But many of the adults were in the country legally, some of them citizens, and they became targets, too, in the desperation of the economic catastrophe. "The slogan has gone out over the city (Los Angeles) and is being adhered to—'Employ no Mexican while a white man is unemployed,'" a Chamber of Commerce executive was quoted as having said. "It is a question of pigment, not a question of citizenship or right." The expulsion jarred the Mexican-American community much as the raids and deportations of recent years have, throwing into question the identity of those who had settled in, and were authorized to be in, the United States.

Then things changed suddenly once more. The Second World War drained away the field hands who could be drafted or who volunteered for military service. Once again, Mexican workers were needed, but this time a guest-worker program was enacted. The Bracero program aimed to recruit and assign hundreds of thousands of workers annually to ranches and farms throughout the West. The program continued into 1964. It was popular with American employers, and about 5 million Mexicans were recruited in those 22 years. The weight of opinion about the Bracero program is that it was fairly effective. However, abuses were common (workers could be dismissed and deported for little cause), labor conditions were dodgy, and, as it turned out, the program didn't prevent about an equal number of Mexicans from entering and staying without authorization in those years. Many of the Bracero veterans stayed, too, as did their children, who had been socialized into the Bracero life.[17] Just after the program was ended, the immigration reform of 1965 altered the relatively cozy migration patterns for Mexicans (and other Latinos), making it more difficult to enter the country, yet another abrupt reversal of the longtime relationship.

Within Mexico, US influence was growing after the war. But throughout the postwar period, the United States' expanding scope as a regional and global power sprang more from economic rather than military power. Apart from three catastrophic wars and several smaller ones, the preferred mode of shaping political choices in other countries has been through economic leverage, exercised in part through the World Bank and the International Monetary Fund, bilateral and multilateral trade agreements, and the sheer clout of major American corporations. William Appleman Williams, Richard Barnett, Noam Chomsky, and many others have chronicled and dissected this "neoliberal" agenda in great, convincing detail.[18] It is *neoliberal* because it stresses freedom of action: free markets, free (non-union) labor, free entry (no tariffs or other trade barriers), and free movement of capital. As was noted earlier, the results have been troubling for many developing economies, because all this freedom tends to facilitate the dictates of foreign investors and to privilege local elites while disrupting traditional livelihoods and many middle-class jobs. Crippling debt obligations often came with the "reform."

The results of neoliberal policies for Mexico are mixed, as they are for most countries, but several statistics are troubling. According to the World Bank, as of 2012 about half of Mexico's households were living in poverty, roughly the same as at the time of the enactment of the North American Free Trade Agreement (a quintessentially neo-liberal policy) in 1994. Rural poverty was even higher—60 percent. About 10 percent of the country's 120 million people were living in "extreme poverty." School enrollments were well below the regional average. Access to health care was spotty. Food security—having reliable access to sufficient amounts of affordable, nutritious food—remained acute for one-fourth of all Mexicans. Without a doubt, the Mexican economy has improved since the 1990s and again after the Bush economic collapse of 2007–2009, when extreme poverty rates were two to three times worse and the poor's access to education and health care was deplorable. Some of this is due to better management of economic development programs, less corruption, and a public that mobilized against the inept and self-serving political party that long dominated Mexican politics.

Still, economic growth in the last 20 years has been very modest overall (1.2 percent per year), distribution is as usual concentrated at the top, unemployment remains high, and real wages for most workers have sagged. Whatever the benefits of "marketization," the downsides for a majority of workers and families can be severe. Because of Mexico's proximity to the United States, the effects are almost all derived from that relationship; 90 percent of Mexico's exports go to the United States. After NAFTA was enacted, US firms invested heavily in Mexican manufacturing, continuing and escalating a longtime trend. The multinational firms were lured by low wages, lack of environmental and safety regulation, ample natural resources, and the sizable Mexican market for goods.

Another consequence of the trade pact was the dumping on the Mexican market of American products (especially corn and other things that are heavily subsidized in the United States). That widespread practice has undercut Mexican farmers and manufacturers. Food prices have risen as small farmers have given up farming and moved to Mexican cities or to the United States.

Meager economic growth, rising food prices, and the scarcity of arable land have made life difficult for tens of millions of people in Mexico. Whether or not this would have happened anyway is arguable. Not every ill in a developing country can be blamed on neoliberal policies. But ever since the debt crisis of the early 1980s, which was the beginning of neoliberal policies, Latin America and Mexico particularly have performed poorly. According to the economist Mark Weisbrot, "Mexico, like the rest of the region, began a long period of neoliberal policy changes that, beginning with its handling of the early 1980s' debt crisis, got rid of industrial and development policies, gave a bigger role to de-regulated international trade and investment, and prioritized tighter fiscal and monetary policies (sometimes even in recessions). These policies put an end to the prior period of growth and development. The region as a whole grew just 6% per capita from 1980–2000; and Mexico grew by 16%—a far cry from the 99% of the previous 20 years."[19] Mexico had doubled its economic output from 1960 to 1980 using "import substitution" policies that many development experts regarded as a success. That is, it protected industries from foreign, predatory practices and resisted privatization. Whether this model could have sustained such growth is debatable. But there is new respect among economists for the old ways, particularly given how disappointing neoliberal policies have been.

"If, in too many instances, the benefits of globalization have been less than its advocates claim, the price paid has been greater, as the environment has been destroyed, as political processes have been corrupted, and as the rapid pace of change has not allowed countries time for cultural adaptation," wrote the eminent economist Joseph Stiglitz. "The crises that have brought in their wake massive unemployment have, in turn, been followed by longer term problems of social dissolution—from urban violence in Latin America to ethnic conflict in other parts of the world."[20] This can be seen in Mexico (and Guatemala and much of Central America) in the drug trade and the brutal violence that inevitably accompanies it. Murders by firearms in Mexico have risen sharply since the 1990s; most are attributable to the drug economy.

Phenomena that rip the social fabric are difficult for social scientists to measure, but they are no less important than, and go hand in hand with, economic disruption and decline. One of the highly symbolic "reforms" pursued in the neoliberal whirl of the 1980s and the 1990s was the selling off of common lands used by many small farmers for grazing, an ancient tradition. Almost in exact replica of the evidence used in Karl Polanyi's brilliant argument in *The Great Transformation*, the closing of the commons was a "necessary" and quite radical change, a thoroughgoing disruption of social and economic relations during the Industrial Revolution in Britain and the continent, yielding low-wage labor for the new factories. In Mexico, the great transformation was so disruptive that it produced an enormous swell of people, small farmers mostly, who had few options. Many of them felt compelled to turn north, to the United States, to take care of their families.

David Bacon has chronicled this phenomenon with stories of Mexican workers who were ravaged by the new realities of a globalized economy. In his 2013 book *The Right to Stay Home: How U.S. Policy Drives Mexican Migration*, Bacon follows several Mexicans in a valley near Veracruz that became, almost overnight, the center of a huge pig-farming operation of the American company Smithfield Foods. A million pigs were raised for slaughter each year to feed American and Mexican consumers. The effects were immediate. The water table became contaminated. The air "smells like rotten meat, and the wind "has a chemical smell," according to one small farmer in the valley. The stench attracted flies. Wild dogs would dig up pig carcasses.[21] Swine flu erupted. "With 30 percent of the area's residents now infected with the virulent flu bug," the website *Grist* reported, "people are demanding that state and federal authorities inspect hog operations there. So far, reports [the Mexican newspaper] *La Marcha*, the response has been: *nada.*"[22] (Smithfield Foods denied the allegations.) Smithfield brought subsidized corn feed from the United States for the hogs, so the disruption to farming was nearly complete—about 4,000 hog farms owned by Mexicans closed, and the corn feed sold by Mexican farmers dropped in price. Efforts to remedy the many negative impacts of the Smithfield operation were met with hostility and intimidation by Mexican authorities.

The consequences were not difficult to see. Poverty rose sharply in Mexico in the 1990s, and so did emigration. As Bacon notes, the number of Mexicans living in the United States doubled in the 1990s, from 4.5 million in 1990 to 9.75 million in 2000, and continued to rise until the financial crisis of 2008. One young man near Veracruz grew up on a small farm that depended on common land, and his family gradually lost out to paltry farm prices. "We couldn't sell what we were growing," he told Bacon. "The free trade agreement was the cause of our problems. They were just paying as little farmers as they could ... . After the crisis, we couldn't pay for electricity—we'd just use candles at home. But when you see that your parents don't have any money, that's when you decide to come [to the United States], to help them."

In a survey conducted by Douglas Massey and Magaly Sánchez R., the principal motivation for immigration to the United States from Latin America is for economic reasons—20 percent say "economic conditions at origin," another 20 percent say "opportunities at destination"—and other motives probably have similar elements (family ties, social networks). About 44 percent intend to return to their country of origin; 34 percent intend to stay in the United States. The survey underscores both misperceptions about immigrants (that they all intend to stay) and reinforces the belief that economics is the primary cause of migration. A 2004 survey by the Pew organization in which 5,000 Mexicans were questioned showed somewhat similar results. About 60 percent said they would like to remain in the United States as long as possible; 35 percent intended to return to Mexico. About two-thirds of those wanting to stay indefinitely also said they would take part in a temporary-worker program that would enable them to travel back and forth between Mexico and the United States. Family ties in the United States were prevalent and work in the United States was relatively easy to find.[23]

The number of visas available to Mexicans to enable them to work in the United States isn't adequate to meet the demand for them from Mexicans and from American employers. Between 2000 and 2010, from 35,000 to 90,000 immigrant visas were issued to Mexicans per year, according to the Department of Homeland Security. Only 84,000 employment visas were issued during the same period. As of the beginning of October 2013, 1.3 million Mexicans were on the waiting list for work visas.[24]

The Mexican drug cartels affect every aspect of Mexican life. Although their coercive power over Mexicans' perceptions of life in Mexico and Mexicans' motivations to emigrate rarely figures in discussions of foreign policy or immigration,[25] the drug cartels (which are far more dangerous than their southern counterparts) have created an atmosphere of sheer terror, especially in the north and in Mexico City. In the years 2005–2013, about 86,000 Mexicans were murdered or went missing, many of them presumably as a result of the cartels' internecine wars for control and profit. Anyone who complains about the cartels is in danger. In May 2013, ten farmers were executed in Michoacán by the gang Los Caballeros Templarios because they complained about extortion. Vigilantes have formed militias to combat the narcotraffickers. Social media are used to warn ordinary people of danger, and to recruit "soldiers" to fight the cartels. The cartels engage in human trafficking and coerce migrants to carry drugs.

The vast majority of the unauthorized immigrants in the United States (perhaps 7 million) were born in Mexico. Although significant numbers of Mexicans return to their country of origin, there is still a sizable northward flow, and most experts agree that it will continue and that it is increasing again as the US economy strengthens. The proximity, the kinship networks, the pathways from their home towns, the lure of the American economy and culture, and—most profoundly—the persistent poverty and stratification of Mexican society will ensure an increase in migration. Even though Mexican-born workers in the United States earn only slightly more than half the average of all immigrants, and unemployment in the United States is above the national average for all workers, the prospects in El Norte are vastly preferable to the prospects in Mexico.

The Great Migration was driven by economics, too, and the parallels to Mexican and Central American movement north are apparent. The systems of sharecropping in the American South and the *encomienda* system of Spanish and post-Spanish America virtually guaranteed permanent indebtedness for the small, peasant farmers and agricultural laborers. As late as 1910, for example, only 13 percent of black farmers in Georgia owned their own land; across the old Confederacy, 75 percent of all blacks were sharecroppers as of 1900. Shortly after the First World War, in the Mississippi Delta, where the concentration of blacks was high (about 80 percent or more), they still owned only 2 percent of the farms. As tenant farmers, they owed too much in rent to the white owners to sustain their families in near-dire poverty. It was hard not to see the north and its factories as infinitely preferable, even if that promised land didn't turn out to be as advertised. Some blacks migrated temporarily to earn more money than they ever could in the South. Some returned. Most stayed.

Economics wasn't the only motivating factor of the Great Migration, of course. Black-white social relations and political disenfranchisement also were proximate causes. As the historian Leon Litwak points out, for the South's plantation owners the end of the Civil War meant the end of slavery but yielded an enormous reserve of docile, low-skilled, scarcely educated blacks ready to buy into a dream of being independent farmers, a dream that was simply an illusion. The Supreme Court's 1896 decision in

Plessy v. Ferguson, which provided a legal basis for "separate but equal" segregation, underscored the subservient position of blacks in all things, a system braced by extraordinary white-on-black violence. Education, marriage, transportation, health care—indeed, every aspect of daily life—was defined by segregation, which was a system of separate but decidedly not equal.[26]

The system of "Jim Crow" was nourished, root and branch, by racism. The colonial and postcolonial experience in Guatemala and Mexico were similarly racist in origin and practice. Both countries still have large populations of indigenous peoples—*indios*—who are, if not held in the utter contempt that blacks were in the South, not faring much better. The immigration flows demonstrate this. It isn't the Creoles that migrate; it's the indigenous peoples and the *mestizos*, and this correlates to income levels. The pogroms unleashed by Ríos Montt and other dictators in Guatemala were aimed at the Mayans. I recall a dinner with some Guatemalan businessmen in the capital in the 1990s during which one Creole said bitterly of the Mayans "They beat their wives. We cannot beat our wives." Apart from the troubling connotations of this statement (and others like it) for gender relations in a country where domestic violence and rape are rampant, it conformed with a view that the indigenous people were lazy, drunkards, abusive to their wives and children, unreliable, and endlessly complaining. These depictions closely mirror the caricatures of blacks in the American South.

Both in the old Confederacy and in the old Spanish colonial precincts of Mexico, Guatemala, and the rest of Central America, an economic, social, and political structure was built that discriminated, often harshly, against the indigenous and the dark-skinned. Which of those attitudes, laws, and practices drive emigration isn't easy to say, as they are in effect constituted as a system of oppression (whether intended or not) and reinforce each other. The long-standing *encomienda* and sharecropping core of economic life made even subsistence living a challenge, and social institutions such as good schools as well as political power were denied to people of color in both regions. When the chains came off a little with modernity, and the siren call of another system—the factories of the north—was audible, they went.

It is important to recognize in the cases of Mexico and Central America that migration, labor migration especially, can be seen as a component of globalization, not just an unintended consequence but very much intertwined with its logic. The Princeton sociologist Douglas Massey, a leading migration theorist, has put this well, and is worth quoting at length:

International migration originates in the social, economic, cultural and political transformations that accompany the penetration of capitalists markets into non-market and premarket societies … . In the context of a globalizing economy, the entry of markets and capital-intensive production technologies into peripheral regions disrupts existing social and economic arrangements and brings about a displacement of people from customary livelihoods, creating a mobile population of workers who actively search for new ways of achieving economic sustenance. International migrants tend not to come from poor, isolated places that are disconnected from world markets, but from regions and nations that are undergoing rapid change and development as a result of their incorporation into global trade, information, and production networks. In the short run, therefore, international migration does not stem from a lack of economic development, but from development itself.[27]

Though one probably can't say with complete assurance that the neoliberal policies and the emerging system of the global economy are the main reasons for this migration, the large number of immigrants into the United States since the neoliberal era began speaks for itself, as do the immigrants themselves. Migration can even be seen as a "safety valve" for the sending countries, potentially reducing the political turmoil that can be roiled by rapid economic disruptions—much as the capacious frontier in the United States provided a safety valve from labor unrest and shanty towns in the industrial East Coast, an acknowledgment of class struggle centrally involving another set of immigrants, those from Eastern and Southern Europe. Hispanic migrants from south of the border provide cheap labor in the United States, as African-Americans did (and do). To the extent that migration's role in globalized capitalism can be described as a coherent system, the steady movement of people—including unauthorized migration—fits with the needs of the governments and corporations that are profiting from it. In this sense, then, the *problem* of illegal immigration is the *solution* of globalization.

6 THE ROCKY ROAD OF REFORM

The notion that the economic policies of the United States in Central America and Mexico have anything to do with illegal immigration, or that, consequently, immigration reform should take these policies into account, is completely alien to the Washington mind. It isn't just that immigration reform has a fairly disreputable history in the United States. It's that even while admitting a problem exists, it is unforgiveable to attribute that problem to the sturdy tenets of the American frontier mythology.

Instead, reform has focused resolutely on the racial characteristics of those seeking entry. Most legislation of this nation of immigrants has sought to exclude new ones, or at least ones of racial and ethnic characteristics (and class) out-of-favor with political elites. The Chinese Exclusion Act and other prohibitory legislation was the hallmark of American governance on this matter until well after the Second World War, when there was governance at all. Since the Magnuson Act in 1943, reform has generally opened the gates wider to a more diverse immigrant population, although for Latin Americans—who were free to immigrate before the 1965 reform— it became much more restrictive. The contentiousness of reform, however, remains as fractious as ever.

After the presidential election of 2012, in which Barack Obama garnered 70 percent of the Hispanic vote, new hopes for immigration reform blossomed. Republicans, it was said, could no longer resist the tide of Latino political power, now apparent in many more places than the border states alone, and the preferences of this new voting bloc included immigration reform that would, in effect, legalize the 11 million unauthorized immigrants in the United States, 90 percent of whom are from Latin America. It was an article of conventional wisdom within days of the election that immigration reform was inevitable and would be shaped along the lines of the 2006 attempt by President George W. Bush and Senate sponsors John McCain and Ted Kennedy.

And so it continued to look through the following spring, when the so-called Gang of Eight senators filed a bill that did indeed win their chamber's approval, and by a vote of 68–32. The Gang of Eight was a bipartisan group in a Congress infamous for its inability to work together—Democrats Charles Schumer of New York, Michael Bennett of Colorado, Dick Durbin of Illinois, and Robert Menendez of New Jersey and Republicans Jeff Flake and John McCain of Arizona, Lindsay Graham of South Carolina, and Marco Rubio of Florida. All apart from Graham represented states with large numbers of undocumented immigrants. (Though the bill was often depicted as bipartisan, which it was in sponsorship, Republican senators voted against it 32–14.)

The Senate bill laid out a legalization strategy that included a path to citizenship (long and arduous), and would grant green cards to Dreamers in five years, along with major investments in border security (20,000 more Border Patrol agents and 700 miles of new fence along the Mexican border) and employment verification. In most observers' reckoning, it was the best feasible compromise—enhanced security and employer sanctions in exchange for legalization and citizenship.

The Gang of Eight's triumph was short-lived, however. Like the efforts of the previous decade, the legislation withered on the House vine. It was starved of support by the Republican leadership, which vowed immediately that there would not be a vote on the Senate bill, and by the Tea Party radicals who wanted no reform—no "amnesty"—at all. In a paradox worthy of an Evelyn Waugh satire, the right wing huffed and puffed about "illegal aliens" but stoutly refused to engage in the legislative process meant to remedy the problem. Their idea of a solution was to deport every single person not authorized to reside in the United States, including the Dreamers. Legislative action—apart from action to enhance the capacity of police to raid more energetically—was not to be pursued. This was true in 2006 and with equal fervor in 2013 and 2014. What accounted for the resistance?

The stubborn refusal in the House Republican caucus to even consider reform could obviously not be based on politics: the political winds were all against the Tea Partiers, especially after 2012. True, the the Tea Party movement and the Republican leadership both wanted to deny Obama any sort of political victory as the guiding hand of comprehensive immigration reform, but that was their strategy with all White House initiatives from the beginning of the Obama presidency, so it doesn't distinguish their resistance to the Gang of Eight's bill. In the end, that still may have been the best explanation.

Economic arguments were occasionally voiced in the months of House languor. A weak bow to the "stealing jobs" meme was made, but few took that seriously by then; there was simply too much evidence that the new immigrants worked where Americans wouldn't and enhanced overall economic growth. The one area where the new immigrants might harm US workers—low-skilled blacks—wasn't something that normally would bother the Tea Partiers. The Heritage Foundation, a right-wing think tank in Washington, tried to block reform by claiming it would be exorbitantly costly. "The conservative think tank released a new study warning that the immigration bill by the Senate Gang of Eight would cost taxpayers $6.3 trillion in new spending on entitlements and social programs," *Politico* explained. "It's an update of a 2007 Heritage study that helped derail the last immigration reform bill that year." But the claims were so politically biased that even "high-profile Republicans and conservative thinkers were telling the rest of the GOP not to listen to Heritage."[1] Economic arguments about reform never got traction, even in the chronically weak economy, signaling perhaps the end of that line of argument.

The nativist resistance was instead anchored in cultural warfare. "In a pre-Tea Party world, the Senate immigration bill would have been welcomed by House Republicans," Senator Schumer, one of the Gang of Eight's most vocal proponents, explained in early 2014. "However, the Tea Party rank and file knows it's a different America. It looks different; it prays different; it works different. This is unsettling and angering to some."[2]

Race is always a loaded issue in American politics, as Senator Schumer knows, and it is complicated in the case of Latinos because "Latino" or "Hispanic" is not a race but an ethnicity. Hispanics range from very white to very darks. (In the 2010 US census, 53 percent of Hispanics self-identified as "White," 37 percent said "some other race," 6 percent marked more than one racial category, and 3 percent said "Black.") In the political and social discourse about immigrants, and especially illegal immigration, race is one of the frames of perception. One detailed academic study of Arizona during the rise of fierce anti-immigrant sentiment in the late 1990s found that "Arizona [anti-immigrant] activists demonized Hispanic residents of all legal statuses while lauding the contributions of White citizens."[3] An editorial comment in the *Arizona Republic*, the state's largest daily, stated "If you are not Hispanic or black, getting help (from social services)[,] even when you need it desperately, is almost impossible. The whole system is so unfair to Anglos."[4] The rhetorical attack on all Latinos (the tirades didn't distinguish between those with authorization and those without) pivoted on the familiar and largely false narrative about welfare fraud. It was a "race frame" because for at least three decades it had been used against blacks, and could still prompt anti-immigrant mobilization even though the welfare system had been reformed and unauthorized immigrants were not eligible for most benefits in any case.

Notably, the bill of indictment by conservatives against the Gang of Eight reform in 2013 included several references to welfare fraud or similar code words. The bill, S. 744, "is bloated and unwieldy along the lines of Obamacare," said one broadside signed by many prominent Tea Party activists. The Senate bill further "threatens to bankrupt our already strained entitlement system,"[5] even though the newly legal immigrants would have access to very few federal benefits. In fact, according to the National Immigration Law Center, "People with [newly legal] status will not be eligible for subsidies available under the Affordable Care Act that would help make health insurance more affordable. Nor will they be eligible for Medicaid, the public health insurance program for low-income people. Nor will they be eligible for safety-net programs like food stamps and welfare."[6] But the assumption among conservatives is that these immigrants will cheat the system—a throwback to Reagan's welfare queen.

In January 2013, the right-wing blogger Michelle Malkin put this case succinctly: "Among the many self-deluded promises that GOP illegal alien amnesty promoters are making, this one is especially snort-worthy: Those who have obtained probationary legal status would not be allowed to access federal benefits. Oh, yeah? How, pray tell, do these capitulationist Republicans propose to ensure that shamnesty beneficiaries don't get access to federal benefits later when they can't do anything to prevent the Obama administration from sabotaging existing federal prohibitions on welfare for immigrants *now*?"[7] (There was no such sabotage, of course.) There are some programs that immigrants are entitled to, such as food stamps, but rates of use among immigrants is no higher than among native-born Americans, even though first-generation immigrants tend to be poorer. That massive misuse of benefits is underway is a myth. For example, when unauthorized immigrant families get food stamps, it is for American-born children, who are entitled to that assistance. The actual misallocation of benefits is minuscule in comparison with the costs of the programs. But the conflation of welfare fraud with illegal immigration is one of the sturdiest tropes of the right-wing resistance.

The Senate bill, according to the above-mentioned letter from Tea Party conservatives, "rewards law breakers and punishes law enforcement, further undermining the constitutional rule of law." As I explained earlier, unauthorized entry into the United States is a misdemeanor, but the discourse of criminality is exceptionally intense among the nativists. Nor is there any provision in the Constitution about immigration. The "reward" of legalization comes with fines and back taxes for those who qualify; someone who committed a felony, for example, would be ineligible. But the opposition to S.744 took up the earlier resentments of overlooking the criminal behavior of these undocumented immigrants. That is, the very act of crossing the border without authorization or overstaying a visa makes them criminals, and criminals should not be granted blanket "amnesty." They should, instead, be treated as criminals, arrested at any opportunity, and deported.

I take up some arguments about the contingent meaning of "legality" in chapter 7, but it is interesting to regard the way this has been used in the current debate about reform, and the similar debate in 2005–2007. One of the favorite tactics in this for the right wing is to recount stories of heinous crimes committed by unauthorized immigrants. Because the crime rate for all immigrants is lower than that for natives, these anecdotes serve to distract from the essential law-abiding lifestyles of immigrants, who naturally don't seek attention. It isn't criminal activities per se that are at issue (though they are never far from view); it's the essential quality of these immigrants as law-breakers. "Do we reward bank robbers who steal what doesn't belong to them? Do we reward thieves who rob a gas station? Illegal aliens are no different," one columnist wrote in 2013. "They lie and cheat their way into this country. They steal people's identities ruining their credit and lives. They steal the fruits of our labor to pay for their illegal babies, education and the massive cost of clogging our judicial system with their crimes. And now we're going to reward them?"[8]

This gnawing sense that illegal aliens would take what wasn't theirs, whether loot or welfare, was all the more enraging to conservatives because they "cheat their way into this country." The resentment boils over to scald Washington, and especially Obama, for allowing—even encouraging— this cheating, for keeping the borders open and then proposing amnesty. It didn't matter that Obama was spending more on border security and deporting many more immigrants than his predecessors, because those policies didn't jibe with the resentment narrative. The president and *both* political parties, one columnist wrote in early 2014, "will finally betray the nation and pass some form of illegal-immigrant amnesty."[9]

This general sense of not rewarding law-breakers was apparent in a statement of principles issued by Republicans in the House of Representatives in early 2014: "Our national and economic security depend on requiring people who are living and working here illegally to come forward and get right with the law … . These persons could live legally and without fear in the US, but only if they were willing to admit their culpability, pass rigorous background checks, pay significant fines and back taxes, develop proficiency in English and American civics, and be able to support themselves and their families (without access to public benefits)."[10] So the familiar list of anti-immigrant, cultural grievances was articulated: acknowledge your guilt and pay up, learn English and American "civics," and don't even think about federal benefits.

Most important, as it turned out, was the insistence that the reform package in the House not include a path to citizenship, as the one in the Senate did. "There will be no special path to citizenship for individuals who broke our nation's immigration laws," The House Republicans declared, for "that would be unfair to those immigrants who have played by the rules and harmful to promoting the rule of law."

Citizenship thus became the hot potato of the 2013–14 immigration-reform fracas. The website Red State offered a vivid summation of the conservative view: "Those millions upon millions who have violated our nation's laws in one way or another don't deserve to be rewarded with a pathway to citizenship. What they deserve is a boot to the ass as they are kicked out of this country."[11] The Republican caucus on the Hill could just about accept the main provisions of S.744, but not the "pathway to citizenship." The sacredness of citizenship could not be bestowed upon people who had committed a … misdemeanor.

And so it was depicted. The sanctifying of citizenship became the bulwark against the illegal alien "invasion." The solutions proffered by the Gang of Eight in 2013 and by Republican (and conservative) President George W. Bush in 2006, altogether about as practical as one could imagine, had been carefully crafted to deal with the 11 million and discourage further illegal entry. The reason the two reform bills were so similar is that there weren't many alternatives, at least not policy remedies within the acceptable parameters of Washington politics, and it was understood that the compromises were inelegant but might be functional. That's why the 2013 version gained fourteen Republican votes in the Senate. So in order to bring a halt to this progress, the Tea Party activists used the last arrow in their quiver, that of citizenship, to lance S.744 and bring it down, perhaps for good.

The objections came in several shapes and sizes. One was the conjecture that enacting a citizenship provision would spark new surges of illegal entry. "Any time you offer a pathway to citizenship—which in this case will be amnesty—will only encourage millions more, like it did in 1986," said Representative Lou Barletta, a Republican from Pennsylvania. "You're encouraging them by offering the benefits of American citizenship at a time when our when our borders remain open. We have no way of stopping people from coming here illegally right now."[12]

The trend lines don't show an increase right after the 1986 "amnesty," which is understood in right-wing circles as a catastrophic cave-in to the "open borders" lobby (Hispanics, big business, and of course liberals); in fact, one comprehensive analysis shows a net decrease in border apprehensions through 2000, despite beefed up border security.[13] The effects of the nearly 30-year-old measure are fairly well understood, however, and, contrary to the anti-immigrant narrative, it was reasonably successful. At least one study of the economic impact of the 2.6 million people who gained legal status shows that they produced a net boon for the economy and fed entitlements accounts like Social Security.[14] Notably, only about half of those newly eligible later became citizens, indicating that citizenship is not a much-cherished goal. "At some point in time, you have to do something," Alan Simpson (who as a Republican senator from Wyoming had co-authored the bill) recently said, "unless you want to go hunt people. And who wants to be part of a country who goes hunting people to get 'em out? That's nuts. You have to give them some kind of status."[15] Still, the 1986 bill, strongly associated with President Reagan and largely successful on its own terms, remains to the right wing a touchstone for what *not* to do.

The citizenship provision of the 2007 effort was one reason it was sunk. But more important was the politics at the time, the fissures in the Republican Party that allowed outright opposition to the failing Bush presidency and the ambiguous legacy of Reagan on immigration issues—that is, conservatives, always quick to embrace Reagan, saw the 1986 law as the beginning of the problem of illegal immigration and would not repeat it. It is probable that the many high-profile ICE raids at the time, including in New Bedford, were occasioned by the administration needing to look tough on enforcement in order to gain an edge in the tumult of the immigration debate. The Iraq war, moreover, then at its height in deadliness, created a new sense of panic about security—fed by conservative talk radio and blogs—and this displaced anxiety was red meat in the immigration debate. The raid mentality was fully charged. All "aliens" were suspect, especially illegal aliens. The sheer emotionalism of the attacks on "open borders" doomed the reform package almost immediately, more so than any concerns about citizenship. For the most part, the 2013–14 version of this debate was more restrained and focused on the "undeserving" quality of the immigrants: their illegal acts shouldn't be rewarded, they shouldn't be able to jump the line in front of normal applicants, they should never have the full benefits of citizenship, and so on. It was in some respects a debate that didn't account for the views of the subjects, the unauthorized immigrants themselves, who seemed mostly eager to be granted some legal status and were less concerned with actual citizenship, as the consequences of the 1986 policy seemed to show. A pro-immigrant critique also emerged, which both insisted on the citizenship provision as a *sine qua non* of their support—a foolish red line, as it turned out—and decried the long path to citizenship, which was typically pegged at 13 years but easily could have been longer. A more worrisome provision in S.744 was the requirement for income and employment that seemed punitive, e.g., unemployment for any 60-day period could disqualify an applicant, and analysts estimated that could disenfranchise 40 percent of all such immigrants, or 4–5 million people. As a result, citizenship could be foiled by poverty or recession or just the luck of the draw in getting and keeping jobs. That's not only a high bar, but one entirely contingent on one's economic status, rather than any concept of civic virtue that typically should be the only criterion for becoming a citizen or being legal.

Something else was occurring that changed the tenor of the reform discussion, and that was a determined reassessment of the Fourteenth Amendment granting birthright citizenship. The Fourteenth Amendment, one of the great achievements of the post-Civil War era of trying to rectify the horrors of slavery, was meant to provide a grant of citizenship to former slaves who were born in the United States. It had always been interpreted by the courts to include anyone who was born on American soil. But it has been for a number of years the subject of a robust debate among legal scholars over the exact meaning of the amendment's language: "All persons born or naturalized in the United States, and subject to the jurisdiction thereof, are citizens of the United States and of the state wherein they reside." The tricky phrase "subject to the jurisdiction" may have been meant to exclude "accidental citizenship" of foreign-born parents who happen to be in the United States when their child is born; they are subject to the jurisdiction of another nation. Some argument about the amendment's framers may support that idea—in effect, an exclusion based on the citizenship of the parents. But the phrase about jurisdiction could also have been intended to apply only to those not consenting to citizenship, such as diplomats' children. In any case, the Supreme Court ruled in 1898 that the Fourteenth Amendment did indeed include broad birthright citizenship, and that has never been overturned.

The issue has returned, however, not only because of the legal scholars' discourse, but because the nativists adopted the most extreme interpretation of this argument to lambaste "anchor babies" and even "birth tourism" (the incidence of which is unspecified but clearly quite low). On the basis of 2010 US Census, according to the Pew Research Center, the number of babies born in the United States to unauthorized immigrants is estimated at 80 percent of all such immigrant children, or about 4 million. Thirty-seven percent of unauthorized immigrants are parents of US citizens, which further complicates notions of belonging—questions of who is an American in so many mixed families. The citizenship of children has also led to leniency for the parents in situations, such as the New Bedford raid, in which expulsion of the unauthorized parents would seem to violate the rights of the citizen-child.

These numbers have led many to insist that the Fourteenth Amendment had to be repealed in order to correct this mistake of birthright citizenship. The public is against such a change, according to recent surveys. But what was once a quirky, nativist sideshow has become a core belief of conservatives on immigration: to them, reform affecting citizenship is about restricting the long-established constitutional *jus soli* (right of the soil). It is notable that the shining achievement of the Fourteenth Amendment, one of the post-slavery measures granting citizenship rights and "legality" to black Americans and that made possible the Great Migration, has also enabled the second great migration and raised the ire of those who would oppose both.

A central feature of the reform discourse since the Bush reform effort got underway is "securitization"—the promise to tighten the borders as a *quid pro quo* for legalization. The stated insistence of every Republican lawmaker has been to "secure the borders" before granting legalization. The Senate bill proposed to double the number of border police, to nearly 40,000, mainly on the southern border. The Immigration Policy Center explains:

At least 700 miles of fencing, including double fencing; increasing mobile surveillance; deploying aircraft and radio communications; constructing additional Border Patrol stations and operating bases; hiring additional prosecutors, judges, and staff; providing additional training to border officers; and increasing prosecutions of illegal border crossings. The bill specifies mandatory area-specific technology and infrastructure that includes watch towers, camera systems, mobile surveillance systems, ground sensors, fiber-optic tank inspection scopes, portable contraband detectors, radiation isotope identification devices, mobile automated targeting systems, unmanned aircraft, radar systems, helicopters, and marine vessels, among other minimum requirements.[16]

Internal enforcement of visas would also be increased. The cost would reach $30 billion for the additional Border Patrol agents for ten years, $8 billion for the fence, and other items for a total of $46 billion, adding to what is already the most expensive security operation of the US government apart from the military.

For anyone who has actually spent time on the border, it is surprising to hear politicians talk of "open borders" or lack of enforcement. The border areas I have witnessed in Arizona had ample resources applied by US agents, including high-tech watch towers with night vision, regular helicopter and SUV patrols, and checkpoints. Doubling the number of agents and enhancing technology will, no doubt, make the border more difficult to cross. Federal budget commitments reflect that. Between 2003 and 2013, the budget of Customs and Border Protection doubled, and that of ICE rose 73 percent. (The Border Patrol's budget has increased tenfold since 1993.) In that light, the numbers of apprehensions by border patrol tell an interesting story.[17] In 2005, there were almost 1.2 million apprehensions, and it had been above 1 million for nearly twenty years. That number declined steadily until 2011, when it was just over a quarter of that 2005 figure. Nearly everyone attributes that decline to the Bush recession, which began in 2007. But even with the economic recovery that began in 2010, the numbers of apprehensions remains a fraction of what it was a decade ago: in 2013, they totaled 420,000. What that likely means is that border enforcement is much more effective than it was not long ago. Apprehensions are down in part because the border is more difficult to cross.

That "effectiveness" includes growing concern about the use of deadly force by the Border Patrol, however, possibly a result of the rapid expansion of the patrol and consequently lowered standards and quality control. Cross-border shootings and alleged human-rights abuses are more common now than ever, according to investigations, so border enforcement cannot be accused of a light touch.[18] New guidelines for the use of deadly force issued in early 2014 by DHS were necessary because fatal shootings without cause had become more frequent.

The "enforcement first" advocates see this as a glass half empty, and their insistence on "securing the border" before remedial action on the 11 million undocumented immigrants now inside the United States is an unrealistic standard. As long as the US economy is so much stronger than those in Mexico and Central America, as long as those countries suffer the atrocities of drug-gang violence, the immigrants will come, and they will find a way. In the area of Arizona where I spent several days on three different occasions, one could see the detritus of crossings (rope ladders, empty water bottles, clothes abandoned in the desert) close by a major Border Patrol station. No matter how well policed, they will come.

It may be, of course, that doubling the number of Border Patrol officers and building more fence would reduce the numbers of illegal entrants even more than they have been reduced in recent years. The Congressional Budget Office estimated that only 44 percent of the southern border is under control, although the feds have focused on the most obvious crossing

Table 6.1
Apprehension and deportation figures (in thousands).

	Total apprehensions	Apprehensions at SW border[a]	Deportations	ICE and CBP budgets[b]
2003	1046	905	211	9.2
2004	1264	1139	241	9.7
2005	1291	1171	246	9.4
2006	1206	1072	281	11.0
2007	961	859	319	12.4
2008	1044	705	360	14.4
2009	870	541	392	17.3
2010	752	448	383	17.0
2011	642	328	388	17.6
2012	643	356	419	17.6

a. Southwest border includes California, Arizona, New Mexico, and Texas.

b. ICE: Immigration and Custom Enforcement. CBP: Customs and Border Patrol. Budgets in billions of dollars.

sources: 2012 Department of Homeland Security Yearbook; Center for Immigration Studies

points. Internally, better monitoring of visa holders and raids on employers who hire unauthorized workers would yield more apprehensions, too.

What does it mean, however, to "secure the border," and what is the threshold for implementing the legalization of immigrants already here? The border hawks demur on that crucial point because to acknowledge that border policing will never be 100 percent effective would upset the nativist base, and to specify a threshold would also mean that legalization could, at some point, proceed. The Republican leadership added another barrier in early 2014: their deep distrust of President Obama's willingness to enforce border security—distrust that was based on his granting of extensions for health-care enrollment. If that sounds like a flimsy, mercurial excuse, it's because it was. Making the Affordable Care Act work had virtually nothing to do with border and visa enforcement, in which Obama had shown himself to be more than a willing enforcer of the law.

The Democrats pushing immigration reform have gone along with the boost in spending and manpower as a necessary compromise to gain a foothold toward legalization and citizenship. The added funds for immigration enforcement, very much reminiscent of military spending (and in many cases the same defense contractors), is pork-barrel spending in a period of budget austerity, so it hasn't been too difficult for anyone to swallow this added spending, though it is worth noting that since 1993, when a tighter border-enforcement strategy was implemented, nearly $200 billion has been spent on the project—a hefty sum even by Washington standards.

As the Immigration Policy Center concludes, "Enforcement first" is just more of the same; more of the same enforcement-without-reform approach to unauthorized immigration that has consistently failed to work for 27 years and counting. Trying to enforce a dysfunctional immigration system as a prerequisite for reforming that system is a fool's errand." It is almost certainly the case that more of a policy that is already in effect—enforcement first, high deportation rates, increased spending—and has already proved to be inadequate will not satisfy many. But this argument also implicitly concedes one of the conservatives' major points—that S.744 doesn't discourage more immigrants from coming illegally. What happens to those who enter after the bill's enactment?

The insistence on enforcement first is fully consistent with the increasing militarization of American life and the application of force and surveillance to problems that are not truly amenable to such approaches. The idea that raising the threat of force or more efficiently watching the border or surveilling immigrants will end the problem of illegal immigration is no more valid than the idea that the use of force could tame insurgents in Iraq or Afghanistan or the idea that the "war on drugs" would stop the consumption of cocaine and marijuana in the United States. The mania about the border is in fact a deep well of insecurity. That insecurity generally has become *the* emotional pivot of our politics and society may be due to 9/11 or Iraq or climate change or an aging elite, but whatever its source it is thoroughly gripping. When it comes to immigration, that insecurity plays out vividly on the border, the heavily armed and closely watched border whose alleged porousness stirs howls of alarm from conservatives. Enforcement first is the raid mentality incarnate, around the clock, and at a high price. The cost is not just in the dollars poured into militarization budgets but also in the fact that making it so difficult to enter means that, once Mexican and Central American workers are here, they will stay—a paradox of enforcement that will continue to vex the enforcement-firsters and sustain the insecurity anxieties.

And enforcement first is an occasion to embrace the grievance narrative in its fullest. When Speaker of the House John Boehner (a Republican from Ohio) walked back his attempt to pursue a House bill because the Tea Party caucus refused to go along, his excuse was that President Obama wasn't trustworthy, and therefore the Republicans could not go forward in good faith. "There's widespread doubt about whether this administration can be trusted to enforce our laws. And it's going to be difficult to move any immigration legislation until that changes," Boehner said in February 2014.

The lack of trust in the president was intensified by the "border kids" crisis of mid 2014. The Border Patrol and other federal agencies seemed to be overwhelmed by unaccompanied youngsters from Central America requesting asylum. Mothers with small children also showed up (particularly in Texas), seeking protection from the gangs and corrupt police of Guatemala, Honduras, and El Salvador. Though this had actually been underway for more than a two years,[19] it suddenly caught the attention of the national news media and became a cause célèbre for both advocates and opponents of immigration reform. The latter tried to demonize the children, accusing them of freeloading and bringing disease and drugs into the United States, and the surge stirred a new eruption of paranoia about the possibility that Iraqi terrorists would enter the country among the children. None of those allegations were true, but the alarms grew to the point where President Obama's handling of the crisis earned low marks in opinion surveys, and he backed off a promise to use executive authority to shield more unauthorized immigrants from deportation. Anything like reform was, at that point, beyond resuscitation.

So, in the midst of a congressional session in which immigration reform was all but guaranteed by the Washington opinion elite, the collapsing consensus came back to the cultural bugaboos of the issue: who should belong in society, who can be trusted, and who should be sent home. Obama's executive order of late 2014 dealt with only about half those already in the country, not with root causes. That there isn't even a bow to the causes of migration—as literally embodied in the border kids and their desperate pleas—says as much as all the militant posturing. Not even the palliative of reform as envisioned by the Gang of Eight was feasible, because the cultural backlash was so fierce and unyielding. The dream of reaching a consensus on reform had died again.

7 LEGALITY AND LANGUAGE AS CULTURAL WEAPONS

A few years ago in Everett and Somerville, two hard-bitten cities adjacent to Boston, surveys were conducted to ask about unauthorized immigrants. What was it they found objectionable about these migrants? Two answers stood out: illegality and the use of Spanish. It wasn't about stealing jobs or crime or other threatening behavior in towns that had their share of all those ills. It was legality and language.[1]

These attitudes are, at root, cultural in nature. They frame the issues of immigration as matters of opprobrium and alienation. They have little to do with economics or politics, although both involve political mechanisms. In different ways, they enable the mentality of the raid: the status of illegality in the narrow, technical sense (ICE raids triggered by the presence of unauthorized immigrants), and the alienness of language and culture, of otherness, the trigger for identifying the people who are to be rounded up, arrested, detained, and deported. Even for those not caught up in the deportation process, the strictures imposed by the norms of legality and language keep many Latino immigrants marginalized in all dimensions of daily life.

Of all aspects of the immigration debate, the most fraught is the meaning and use of the concept of legality. The fiercest opponents of reform default to the familiar taunt "What part of illegal don't you understand?" The entire immigration matter is reduced to a simplistic formula: either you're here legally or not. If not, get out. It's a useful formula for them, because it avoids the complexities of immigrant status, the legal as well as moral questions in which immigration is entangled. Well-meaning people also rely on this formula, welcoming legal immigrants but chary of "illegals." Like most public policy issues, it isn't so cut and dried.

Even the use of the word 'illegal' is controversial. Some activists (Jose Antonio Vargas among them) insist that describing unauthorized immigrants as "illegal" is insulting, that no person is illegal. The right wing likes to call such people "illegal aliens," an even more provocative phrasing, as if the immigrants are from another planet. Making them as different as possible, and illegal as well, is a political device to sharpen the perception of "the other," with all its ramifications. Most policy professionals simply refer to undocumented, unauthorized, irregular, or out-of-status immigrants.

Beyond the battle over what to call these border-crossing people are more consequential issues having to do with the law and how people who are not in compliance are treated. Over more than 100 years, the laws have changed profoundly, altering who can enter and stay legally. Much of this history is shaped by racist attitudes—the exclusion of Asians, for example, was an explicit policy enacted by Congress and upheld by the courts for decades. Though this exclusion was particularly acute with regard to Chinese, it also barred Indians, Japanese, and Filipinos, among others; the exclusion of Filipinos is especially poignant given the United States' takeover of the Philippines in 1898. At that time, in a replay of the Mexican-American War, the absorption of the Philippines was rejected in part because of fears of racial mingling. The exclusionary laws began to come down in 1943 with the Magnuson Act, but quotas based on nationality—with visas granted on the basis of a particular nationality's current presence in the United States—were continued until the 1965 Immigration and Nationality Act. It is noteworthy that the immigration reform to eliminate racial and ethnic preferences came around the same time as the great civil rights legislation led through Congress by President Lyndon B. Johnson, and this immigration reform was a conscious undertaking to signal a broad adoption of equality and fairness.

Even if intended to be fair, the 1965 action, which was good for Asian immigrants, had a deleterious effect on Mexican and Latino aspirants. Immigration from the Western Hemisphere was much more lightly regulated beforehand, and the numbers of Mexican guest-worker and residence visas changed dramatically—from 450,000 guest workers and unlimited residence visas to no guest workers and merely 20,000 residence visas.[2] So in one swipe of legislative action, the long-standing traditions of Mexican immigration were disrupted. The need for farm labor didn't abate, of course, and so the era of illegal immigration—much of it the circular migration of seasonal workers—commenced in earnest. The wink-and-a-nod border enforcement allowed much of the unauthorized border crossings without much of a hitch for the ensuing two decades.

This largely laissez-faire approach was apparent in Ronald Reagan's 1986 immigration reform. In a presidential debate in 1984, Reagan expressed support for a comprehensive overhaul of immigration law: "I believe in the idea of amnesty for those who have put down roots and who have lived here even though some time back they may have entered illegally." He later reinforced that sentiment in an interview, saying "we need protection for people who are in this country and who have not become citizens, for example, that they are protected and legitimized and given permanent residency here."[3] The 1986 law did grant amnesty to those who had been resident for five years or more. The light enforcement mechanisms and the robust economy of the 1990s brought in millions more unauthorized immigrants from Latin America, and pushed the issue to the fore again.

By 2001 (the year of the 9/11 attacks and the new "securitization" of migration), Latinos seeking to enter had to cope for 35 years with a radically changing legal environment. Largely unmolested before 1965, severely restricted afterward, but only occasionally challenged at the border or within the United States, then granted amnesty and broadly welcomed, if quietly, to fill the jobs of a booming economy—this was the topsy-turvy world of law and custom, often at odds, that a Mexican farm laborer had to sort through. It is what one scholar calls the "production of illegality."[4] No wonder that the taunt of "what part of illegal don't you understand" was meaningless. Social norms and rapidly changing laws said otherwise.

Those who have analyzed this knot of contradictions critically arrive at one or more of three conclusions. One is to place the migration/legality conundrum in a broader context of social acceptance and civil rights. A second is to parse the legal rulings affecting immigrants to see what 'legal' and 'illegal' mean in jurisprudence. A third is the common-sense approach of regarding illegal immigration as a net benefit, and placing it in the context of how society treats other comparable forms of illegal behavior.

A number of critical theorists lambaste the nation-state not only for its inconsistency but also for its assumption that it can define the terms of legal residence and citizenship. Leaving aside the peculiar complaint that defining citizenship is up to someone else beside the state, and acknowledging inconsistency, we still have a broad field of custom to consider. There is a widely held notion that immigrants who have been in the United States for many years, who have worked and paid taxes, who perhaps have children who are citizens or at least have grown up in the country, and who haven't committed crimes should not be shipped off to a detention center for deportation and possibly some criminal charge that would preclude them from re-entering legally. Civil rights apply. One is protected from others and to some degree from arbitrary action by the state. Several constitutional guarantees apply to all in the country, regardless of status. According to the legal scholar Christina M. Rodríguez, a broader formula may also exist: that of incorporation in "the people," a slippery concept but one worth examining. "The process of incorporation requires taking into account the preferences and prerogatives of the existing members of the body politic, thus implicating a reciprocal relationship between the noncitizen and the polity," Rodríguez wrote in 2013.[5] Differentiating between civil rights protections stemming from respect for "personhood" ("a basic legal regime") and being incorporated into the people, she described as "civil rights as an ongoing social struggle."

More specifically, Rodríguez cited Supreme Court decisions that "articulated a concept of 'the people' that entails earned membership but that does not necessarily map onto formal legal status, a concept the legal scholar Hiroshi Motomura has called 'immigration as affiliation.'"[6] The Supreme Court's language cited by Rodriguez seems to deny *legal* presence in the United States, but the notion of membership, one that becomes more persuasive with time, is nonetheless worth considering (and seems to be what Reagan had in mind for amnesty). Fulfilling social obligations to contribute to society like citizens is, in this formulation, more important than a strict adherence to the immigration laws. As Rodriguez argued persuasively, on many occasions the courts have implied as much.

There is also a strain of critical thinking that sees the entire set of legal interventions by the US government as a means to discipline labor and to provide an exceptionally cheap alternative—Mexicans and other Latinos who will work in substandard conditions for low pay, as happened at the Michael Bianco Inc. plant in New Bedford. That is, the wink-and-nod border practices, until 9/11, were for the benefit of the ranchers and other farmers, factory owners, and others who wanted cheap labor. It wasn't constructed as a system, but its features were unmistakable (and likely one reason why Reagan could easily be convinced of illegal immigration's value). It both provided cheap labor and undercut, potentially, the farm labor unions and others trying to establish a living wage for these workers, underscoring the long-standing enmity of unions toward unregulated immigration. As we have seen, moreover, the entire experience with undocumented labor has been racially charged, which adds a powerful cultural element to this economic mixture—the brown people need not be paid as much as the white, barely speak English, and are largely temporary in any case, all of which makes it easier to exploit them. Most prominent as an intimidating instrument is not racial attitude, however, but the simple fact that they can be deported on a moment's notice. As the scholar Nicholas De Genova put it, "the legal production of 'illegality' provides an apparatus for sustaining Mexican migrants' vulnerability and tractability—as workers—whose labor-power, inasmuch as it is deportable, becomes an eminently disposable commodity."[7]

This perspective, then, sees the "legal" as mere exploitation, a consistently tighter set of laws that "produces illegality." It's an arrow in the quiver of global capitalism, as useful as the *maquiladora* factories on the Mexican side of the border or the factory hog farms near Veracruz. Workers' demands are tamed by the legalities. Law is thus not about sustaining some pure Americanness or keeping the aspiring hordes in check at the border, as advertised, but about regulating labor and enhancing profit.

This quasi-Marxist interpretation of migration was more convincing before 9/11. That is, the securitization of the border, the raids, and the large-scale deportations don't fit well with the labor-exploitation narrative. This is not to say it has no value, and it does shine a light on the fact that the porous laws and borders did benefit certain businesses above all other players. The "production of illegality" is an important concept when considering the quality and depth of what 'legal' and 'illegal' mean in regard to immigration. It reflects brightly through the economic lens, but also the cultural, as unauthorized immigration became associated with the anti-terrorist campaign after the al Qaeda attacks in 2001. The vague but powerful sense of threat fostered by the news media and many politicians regarding all immigrants particularly applied to "illegals" and the long, vulnerable border. Illegality then took on a new meaning, a more menacing meaning, in that the unauthorized immigrants might not just be interested in taking jobs and welfare checks, but something far more sinister. So what was a pesky issue of job security and overburdened schools and hospitals along the border became a panic-stricken emergency, and "legality" defined its character.

This, too, was "racialized" in the sense that the panic focused on the southern border and demonized the Latinos as new security threats. (Few Muslims crossed, and this made it difficult to sustain the argument that they were using the porous border to gain entry.) One Republican congressman wanted more border security because, he said, Arab terrorists could mingle with Mexicans and no one would know the difference. Another insisted that Iran had an enormous operation to recruit Latinos to infiltrate the United States. Baseless charges of this kind use old stereotypes of anti-American Latinos and conflate Arabs and Hispanics.

The first approach toward dissecting "illegality," then, relies both on a positive interpretation of what could constitute a new understanding of immigrant incorporation (including those in the United States without authorization) and on a negative interpretation of how "illegality" has been manipulated, inconsistently applied, and even "terrorized"—that is, made an integral part of the terrorism discourse. Coming to terms with the latter, negative history makes the social incorporation argument all the more persuasive.

I submit that the real conundrum for unauthorized immigrants is not only the way the capitalist economy has marginalized them in the United States, however important that is, but what one scholar calls their "legal nonexistence," from which their status and economic problems stem. Legal nonexistence "is characterized by being physically present and socially active, but lacking legal recognition." While this doesn't prevent social participation and political activism, "legal nonexistence is a state of subjugation that results in vulnerability to deportation, confinement to low-wage jobs, and the denial of basic human needs, such as access to decent housing, education, food, and health care."[8] So the question of marginalization, then, does pivot on legal grounds.

Here the second approach to parsing 'legal' and 'illegal' in regard to immigration is helpful, being purely one of jurisprudence. The courts have opened the door a little to give standing to unauthorized immigrants, and these openings are significant in themselves and suggest a broader application as well. Rodríguez mentioned one aspect of this with respect to civil rights protections under, for example, the Fourth Amendment, which outlaws unlawful searches and seizures—that is, that unauthorized immigrants have the same rights as citizens under this amendment. But the constitutional footing may actually be broader.

One oft-mentioned Supreme Court decision concerns schoolchildren. A 1975 Texas statute barred children who were not authorized to be in the country from attending public schools. A challenge made its way to the Supreme Court, which ruled in 1982 that Texas could not deny these children an education. The decision, *Plyler v. Doe*, was somewhat narrow in construction, saying that the Texas statute applied only to schoolchildren, but was rooted in constitutional law. According to the legal scholar Hiroshi Motomura, "the Court started with the proposition that the Constitution—in particular, the Due Process and Equal Protection clauses of the Fourteenth Amendment—applies to all persons in the United States, regardless of lawful or unlawful presence. The dissent agreed with this proposition."[9] As several knowledgeable commentators have pointed out, *Plyler* has not yet been used to expand rights for unauthorized immigrants; the special case of children in the country for reasons not of their own doing was its sole concern. That does raise the possibility of a constitutional footing for the Dreamers, of course, beyond the confines of K–12 education.

As Motomura points out, another Supreme Court decision opened the door a little wider: the 1971 decision in *Graham v. Richardson*, which held that lawfully present non-citizens had rights to government benefits. What is interesting about the decision's argument, even though the specific action didn't apply to unauthorized immigrants, was how it included all "aliens" in discussing rights: "Classifications based on alienage, like those based on nationality or race, are inherently suspect and subject to close judicial scrutiny," said the Court.[10]

Neither *Plyler* nor *Graham* has been used to further expand the legal status of unauthorized immigrants. The courts have, however, upheld such immigrants' rights to be included in collective bargaining—a recognition of personhood in the sense of Rodríguez's discussion of civil rights. There is also the matter of discretion. The federal practice of deporting some unauthorized immigrants but not others suggests that "illegality" is not an absolute value. The frequently used discretion to permit unauthorized immigrant parents of citizen children to remain in the United States nearly constitutes a standard practice, for example, and carves out a quasi-authorized status for those relatives.

Unauthorized immigrants have constitutional protections against discrimination. They have the right to due process. Even under conditions of deportation, they have the right to a hearing. In some states, the undocumented have the right to compensation if injured while working. In several states, out-of-status college students may receive "in-state" tuition discounts. In California, attorneys who are unauthorized immigrants may be certified to practice law.

The sum of these rulings is fragile but nonetheless clear: "Legality" is, even in jurisprudence, a patchwork. It is evolving, and it is moving in the direction of what one scholar calls "liminal legality." The status of the Dreamers is one illustration of liminal legality: They are not being deported, but they are not on a path to citizenship. Parents of citizen children remain in this in-between zone, too. A single immigrant's status, if he or she is in the United States for a number of years, can change because the rules change, and because longevity of membership in a polity or community confers some added legitimacy. This contingency is difficult in the daily life of unauthorized immigrants, but it indicates that the categories of legal and illegal are not static.

A third approach to viewing this, which might be called a common-sense approach, is less reliant on concepts of "the people" or on jurisprudence than on a basic sense of fairness. This approach begins with the simple observation that unauthorized entry is a civil offense, not a crime. Criminalization of unauthorized migrants is typically a result of an employers' demanding a Social Security number and a migrant's procuring one illegally. In New Bedford and many other places, Social Security fraud has been widely used as a reason for arresting and deporting unauthorized workers. The journalist David Bacon correlates Social Security fraud with union busting and other anti-labor practices. The coincidence of labor organizing with the sudden use of Social Security letters from the federal government seeking information on irregularities (even though the feds in these cases warn employers not to use these letters as a cause of dismissal) is noteworthy. In New Bedford, Corinn Williams thought the 2007 raid was spurred by a demonstration by workers, many of them Guatemalans, several months before. The logic of globalization holds that cheap labor, whether south of the border or north and illegal, should not be unionized. (The demonization of unions is very much a part of this logic.) The paradox here is that courts have recognized these labor rights for the undocumented, one of the areas in which the rights enjoyed by undocumented individuals are much the same as those enjoyed by citizens.

As Bacon argues, the basis for anti-immigrant raids and deportation is as often the crime of identity theft as the civil misdemeanor of illicit entry. "Using someone else's Social Security number to get a job is hardly the same as using someone else's credit card to purchase expensive stereo equipment," he writes. "There is no evidence to suggest that the genuine holder of a Social Security number is harmed when someone else uses that number on the job."[11] In the Postville raid and in the New Bedford raid, such identity theft was the basis of criminalizing workers who had committed no other crimes.

The well-understood need for unauthorized workers, which economists calculate is a net plus for the US economy, provides another common-sense example of how "legality" can be usefully considered. We acknowledge in the macroeconomic sense not only that this is happening but also that it is a positive national good. As the migration theorist Douglas Massey concludes from the empirical literature, "Within receiving societies, once immigrants have been recruited into particular occupations in significant numbers, those jobs become culturally labeled as 'immigrant jobs' and native workers are reluctant to fill them, reinforcing the structural demand for immigrants. Immigration changes the social definition of work, causing a certain class of jobs to be defined as stigmatizing and viewed as culturally inappropriate for native worker."[12] That the economy as a whole prospers more as a consequence of illegal immigration, and the economy is even organized in response to the availability of these migrants, raises the question of legality in a different way: Doesn't the fact that the formal, "legal" economy (and we citizens, as its constituents) benefit from unauthorized immigration vitiate the "illegality" of this recruited and condoned labor?

Similar questions run through all discussions of legality, not least because of the imbalance between the minor infraction of illegal entry or overstaying a visa and the economy's signaling that labor is needed and because of the imbalance between being out of status and being a longtime member of an American community. That these glaring imbalances aren't considered much in the debate about immigration indicates an excessive and exclusive reliance on an exaggerated conception of "illegal," precisely what the nativists want and need to make the misdemeanor of unauthorized entry seem ghastly and threatening.

Throughout the immigration debate, however, we have generally failed to recognize that all the references to legality are culturally and socially formed. Laws are not given by a deity or somehow inscribed in our DNA. They are human-made, and, as we have seen in the history of immigration, quite changeable, sometimes turned inside-out, and always fabricated to meet the exigencies of particular times and to respond to specific configurations of power. In this sense, legal norms are cultural and social norms. Not permanent, universal fixtures in the political firmament, they conform, more or less, to such "soft" norms. There is no specific constitutional principle guiding the immigration laws, and the one most fixed—the Fourteenth Amendment of birthright citizenship—is the one the immigration foes are keenest to upend.

The black experience in the United States, unlike the Latino experience, is easily divided into two distinct epochs: the time before Emancipation and the Thirteenth, Fourteenth, and Fifteenth Amendments to the Constitution, and everything after. (Some might argue that the Hispanic experience is similarly divided, into the time before the wars in Texas and Mexico and the time after.) And for African-Americans, citizenship per se was not at issue after 1868, when the Fourteenth Amendment established their rights of citizenship. In this, the difference with unauthorized immigrants, regardless of origin, is distinct. But the actual practice of citizenship, or, one should say, how blacks were treated as citizens, is a much more muddled picture.

That treatment is vividly illustrated by the history of Jim Crow. Citizenship was the right of the former slaves and their descendants, but denial of full citizenship was the norm, particularly, but not exclusively, in the South. It was denied by voting laws that were designed specifically to exclude blacks, despite the unambiguous language of the Fifteenth Amendment. It was denied by discrimination in the quality of education. It was denied by discrimination in housing, lending, hiring, and labor rights, and in where one could sit and where one could eat. There was not only a nearly complete denial of political rights, but even more pervasively, of social rights—intermarriage, most obviously, but intermingling of all kinds. And much of these daily acts of discrimination and exclusion were embodied in law, and in law that was not merely a product of the reactionary South, but of the Supreme Court (in the 1896 *Plessy v. Ferguson*, which upheld "separate

but equal" laws until struck down by *Brown v. Board of Education* in 1954).
So, indeed, the "legality"—in the sense of legitimacy—of black citizenship
was contested by the dominant culture and political elites of the country
for 100 years or more after the Emancipation. The recent spate of voting
restrictions and the Supreme Court gutting the Voting Rights Act merely
reaffirms that disgraceful history.

We don't often think of black disenfranchisement during Jim Crow as
a legal issue in the same way that jurisprudence deals with unauthorized
immigration. But the basis of discrimination against blacks was the denial
of their humanity—their personhood, if you will, their membership in
the body politic we call "the people." That blacks were very specifically
excluded is central to the history of Jim Crow until the civil rights laws of
the mid 1960s. It was not merely discrimination in all aspects of daily life,
but "invisibility," as several black writers have noted. The African-Americans, north, south, east, and west, were often the hidden people—housemaids, gardeners, factory workers, garbage men, farm workers, and so on,
doing the jobs that undocumented Latinos would also come to do. Treated
unequally in salary, in job choice, in school choice and housing, and so
treated without a thought of these inequities. Their exclusion from political life, from the middle and upper classes of work and stature, were readily accepted for decades, even by many blacks themselves who didn't want
to rock the boat. Tellingly, the grip of exclusion from full citizenship was
broken in part by African-Americans acting "illegally"—that is, through the
civil rights movement's civil disobedience, disruption, and implicit threat
of outright rebellion.

So the black experience very much mirrors, or presages, the Latino
experience, whether legal or illegal. The pervasiveness of social inequality throughout the United States even as postwar legal equality was being
established reflects the "production of illegality" phenomenon for Latinos, in that a production of illicitness for African-Americans was commonplace—that is, the white assumption that many blacks were criminals,
delinquents, sexual predators (male and female), drug dealers, drug users,
indolent, welfare queens, brooding, angry, and virulently anti-white. This
is not just a thing of the bad old days. Attitudes remain stubbornly fixed in
many realms of social and legal life: opinion surveys reveal that blacks are
more than likely to describe racism in their daily encounters, for example,
and see this as a permanent feature of American society. The harsh reality of

legal discrimination remains, moreover, as blacks are likely to be sentenced to longer prison terms than whites for the same crimes, for example, and harassment by law enforcement is high—the "driving while black" phenomenon. Wage differentials remain present; a white worker will earn 20 percent more than a black worker in the same job.[13]

The sum of this is not merely to remark upon the similarities between African-American and Hispanic experiences, but to underscore the dodgy nature of "legality" *even when speaking about citizens*. And frequently this was and is done through the denial of equality in relationships, in an intentional denial of the very existence of a wholly enfranchised African-American. After the Civil War, "it is astonishing how quickly and purposefully whites realized that striking at relationality was the surest way to perpetuate the slave system's denial of blacks' personhood," the cultural theorist Nick Bromell observes. Since blacks "could claim to be free and equal, those crucial criteria of democratic life had to be robbed of all meaning. And the surest way to do so had already been learned and practiced within the slavery system: do everything possible to destroy and deny their sense of their own dignity. Relationships between blacks and whites thus became a terrain of intense struggle over the very possibility of meaningful black democratic citizenship."[14] The denial of fully functioning citizenship was a *cultural* assault, backed by the legal and law enforcement system, in addition to an economic system that fostered dependency. It brings to mind the continuing disrespect of black culture, including, at one violent end, the many instances of burning black churches throughout the old Confederacy even today—disrespecting in extreme acts the most culturally sacred and enduring dimension of African-American life.

Bromell makes a strong case for "dignity" as an indispensable constituent of democratic values, and that membership in The People is a conveyance or embrace of mutual respect. This he identifies from black writers and philosophers in his 2013 book *The Time is Always Now: Black Thought and the Transformation of US Democracy*. The withholding of respect, the denial of dignity, is a stratagem of denial of personhood and a fully enfranchised citizen. It is worth considering the parallel in unauthorized immigrants, most of who are subjected to racist attitudes and discrimination. Where their social contributions have been established, however—gainfully employed, tax-paying, responsible parenting, long residence in the community—an unmistakable quality of respect is conveyed even from some of the least expected sources, such as President Reagan or the Supreme Court. And these very qualities were the ones that opened the possibility of a firmer footing for inclusion in The People and a candidacy for belonging, if not outright citizenship.

In the reform effort underway since the beginning of President Obama's second term, one of the most contentious issues is the "path to citizenship," that is, that unauthorized immigrants could earn citizenship eventually if they met certain criteria. The path as envisioned in the Senate version of the bill passed in 2013 was a long one, and would take about thirteen years. Among the many objections to this path was the possibility that these immigrants would "jump the line" of Mexicans and others waiting for visas—a backlog of about a million in Mexico alone. But more frequently, the route to citizenship was blocked by outrage at accepting these "illegals" as equals, that it constituted amnesty and should not be a reward for committing the "crime" of illegal entry. It was perhaps the most contentious issue in the reform package. (Never mind that many Latinos don't aspire to be citizens.) Some of the opposition—clearly a small minority view, according to most polls—was predicated on the belief that the grateful Latinos would vote Democratic. But the more convincing case is that granting citizenship, even in this long and laborious route, was extending membership, and this, for cultural reasons, was too much for the right wing.

Legality and all its centrifugal reverberations is not a hardy principle from which we can guide public policy and action. Legal norms, shaped and subverted and reborn through social and cultural forces and political opportunism, are malleable, enormously elastic even if laws don't change. The suspension of deportations for various reasons, the openly uneven application of laws and regulations, the friction between state and federal laws, the use of law as a hammer to prove toughness, the fundamental unfairness of insisting on legality for immigrants but forgiveness for Wall Street hucksters or torture perpetrators or tax evaders—these among other manifestations of the law's unsuitability as the North Star of immigration practice reveal "illegality" to be an unreliable and biased tool of cultural preferences. It is the brittle ideology of the raid. That is, to answer the common taunt, what we *do* understand about the word 'illegal'.

If the objection to unauthorized immigrants becoming citizens isn't economics and jobs, or legality, what is it? I have argued that the principal barrier to acceptance of the reality of immigration from Mexico and Central America is cultural. The illicit entry into the United States of millions of migrants is driven by economics in the sending country, and is ensnared in the national security state in the United States, but neither economics nor legality is truly at the core of the vociferous opposition to sensible reform.

The cultural anxiety that besets about a third of the American population that consistently opposes reform combines a grab bag of traumas, paranoia, and misperceptions. Some of this anxiety is rooted in the economic doldrums that beset the middle class in the 1970s and has not eased up. Some is rooted in simple racism toward Hispanics. Both of these common and abiding sentiments bear similarities to the "white flight" syndrome that emptied out many Northern cities in the late 1960s and the 1970s. The civil rights activism of the 1960s and the "race riots" that occurred in many cities in that decade struck fear into large portions of the white middle class, who quickly abandoned cities and politically resisted any more "giveaways" to African-Americans. There was a geography to this fear, just as there is a geography or territoriality to the fear of the Hispanic "invasion"—oftentimes the same language of "them" coming to inhabit "our" neighborhood is used. (This was for many years enforced by a kind of customary law—the redlining of neighborhoods to prevent black residency.) But it was more than geography; it was the sense of lost entitlement, the "giveaways" of welfare, the decline of schools, the contamination of language, music, and sexuality—in short, an entire universe of cultural values were under siege, or perceived to be.

Fast forward slightly to the 1990s and the 2000s. Black-white integration increasingly becomes accepted, at least outside the old Confederacy, and to some extent cities are repopulated by whites as the suburbs look less appealing. But a new "invasion" is apparent, and not just along the southern border. Dispersion of immigrants is nationwide. What was once a localized set of issues regarding how to handle seasonal influxes of immigrants is a national problem of permanent settling in states as far-flung from the border as Minnesota, Idaho, and New Jersey. The Second Great Migration is in full swing, spurred by the Reagan amnesty of 1986 and the Clinton economic boom of the 1990s. While this migration did raise alarms, it tended to be discussed in terms of jobs, the costs of bilingualism, and the burden on social services. That is, it was so discussed until September 11, 2001. The Al Qaeda attacks changed the discourse to one stressing the otherness of immigrants, their danger not just to the economy but to our "way of life," and in words that signaled this was no ordinary political skirmish but another phase of the "twilight struggle." So it should not have come as a complete surprise when manifestos began appearing after 9/11 warning of the perils of the brown people—Arabs and Latinos, particularly—stealthily slithering across our borders to do us harm.

Of all the books and articles and blog tirades launched after 9/11, the one intellectually serious effort to argue against immigration from Latin America came from one of America's most distinguished academics, Samuel P. Huntington, a longtime Harvard professor who had made major contributions to the theory of international relations. In an article in the journal *Foreign Policy* and in a book, he described "the Hispanic challenge" as a dire threat to American identity. It wasn't the first time Huntington stirred controversy. Ten years earlier, in a book titled *The Clash of Civilizations and the Remaking of World Order*, he had posited a deadly confrontation between the West and Islam, and he had demonstrated a penchant for contrarian thinking long before that (including the assertion that apartheid South Africa was a "satisfied society"). *Who Are We?*, his 2004 book on the Hispanic challenge, was far and away the most articulate statement of cultural opposition to the enormous flows of legal and illegal immigration from south of the border.

The basic argument Huntington forwarded is spare and unsparing: The United States was founded on principles that define its culture and character, a winning combination that has not only served the European settlers of the continent well, but has been a magnet for millions of immigrants eager to adopt those same values, which he calls "the creed," a term coined by Gunnar Myrdal. "The creed," he states at the outset of the *Foreign Policy* article, "was the product of the distinct Anglo-Protestant culture of the founding settlers. Key elements of that culture include the English language; Christianity; religious commitment; English concepts of the rule of law, including the responsibility of rulers and the rights of individuals; and dissenting Protestant values of individualism, the work ethic, and the belief that humans have the ability and the duty to try to create a heaven on earth, a 'city on a hill.'"[15] One could pick apart these sentiments on their own terms, as the cultural theorist Richard Slotkin has done in his trilogy on the frontier myth. But, be that as it may, the self-image of most Americans is approximately as Huntington describes.

Huntington relies on a kind of determinism that is remarkable in its starkness. If French Catholics had settled America, it would be immensely different, he avers, and we would have many fewer of the distinctive American triumphs we have long accepted as the norm in economic dynamism, political openness, and so on. Yet there was immigration and lots of it, of course, bringing Catholics, Jews, and Orthodox Christians—the kind of immigrants who came from Europe, particularly in the great waves of the late nineteenth century and the early twentieth, and who understood the creed, adopted it as their own, and enriched it. But the new immigration (particularly since 1965) is different, and particularly so with respect to the influx of Mexicans. "The extent and nature of this immigration differ fundamentally from those of previous immigration, and the assimilation successes of the past are unlikely to be duplicated with the contemporary flood of immigrants from Latin America," Huntington predicted. "This reality poses a fundamental question: Will the United States remain a country with a single national language and a core Anglo-Protestant culture? By ignoring this question, Americans acquiesce to their eventual transformation into two peoples with two cultures (Anglo and Hispanic) and two languages (English and Spanish)."[16]

That is the crux of it—two cultures, two languages. Huntington reflected the American Anglo anxiety by casting a spotlight on the matter of language, which is the major manifestation of difference and the galling assault on Americanness in many natives' ears. My grandmother, born and raised in Hungary, forbade the use of Hungarian in the household, and my father and his brothers learned nary a word of it. We're Americans, we speak English—and this is a prevailing view so embedded in political and social culture that a violation of it, even for incoming immigrants, is a serious breach of civility.

The crux of culture in this argument, however, is not only language but the willingness to embrace the creed, and especially the Protestant work ethic. Huntington is right to underscore how powerful the work ethic is in American society, although he fails to argue persuasively that the adoption of this ethic is essential to national success. (*Who Are We?* includes a chart that shows attitudes about "a job well done," in which Americans and British score very high, but Germans—residents of the most successful economy in Europe, the birthplace of Protestantism and its work ethic—score low.) Huntington is scathing about Latino work habits, the *mañana* culture, the "mistrust of people outside the family; lack of initiative, self-reliance, and ambition; low priority for education; acceptance of poverty as a virtue necessary for entry into heaven." He includes in this indictment the differing attitudes and institutions regarding the reduction of inequality. And immigration from Mexico is fueling the strengthening of Mexican values in the Mexican-American subculture of the United States. "The high level of immigration from Mexico sustains and reinforces among Mexican-Americans the Mexican values which are the primary source of their lagging educational and economic progress and slow assimilation into American society."[17]

Most of Huntington's arguments about language and the work ethic have been debunked empirically, but perhaps the more pernicious aspect of his presentation is how detached they are from the realities of immigrant life in the United States. As we saw in the Tucson curriculum case, the educational attainment of Latinos has been structurally and intentionally hindered by a lack of resources and commitment in public education. This decades-old dereliction of duty by Anglo school administrators, which have stereotyped Hispanics as non-achieving laggards bound for low-end jobs, has been a self-fulfilling prophecy. When a few educators devised a way to raise performance by emphasizing ethnic pride as a motivator, it was crushed. This is just one of many examples of how an underclass is kept down; the same could be said in many respects for African-Americans, who have few if any of the liabilities attributed by Huntington to Mexican immigrants and their progeny. How to explain their underperformance? It's a complicated question, of course, and one that isn't addressed in the arguments about the unique handicaps brought to the United States by Latinos.

A similar point is noteworthy with respect to inequality and the lack of opportunity for all people who are in the bottom half of the economy. Economic mobility in the United States is static and has been for decades, far below mobility in European countries and Canada. It is partly a matter of education, another reason the curriculum issue is significant. But the fact that most Americans who are already poor or lower middle class cannot move up says much more about the structure and persistence of inequality in this enormously wealthy country than it does about whether Mexicans have sufficiently adopted the Protestant work ethic. One even might suspect that all the talk about work habits and attitudes masks the harder reality of growing inequality and stagnant mobility.

At root, Huntington's ideas are entangled with garden-variety distaste for multiculturalism. He repeatedly makes the claim that Mexican-American identification with their own subculture and especially that their clinging to Spanish will create Quebec-like situation in the United States (without exactly saying why this is so lamentable, even if true). The multicultural-ists, he writes,

encouraged immigrants to maintain their birth country cultures, granted them legal privileges denied to native-born Americans, and denounced the idea of Americaniza-tion as un-American. They pushed the re-writing of history syllabi and textbooks so as to refer to the "peoples" of the United States in place of the single people of the Constitution. They urged supplementing or substituting for national history the his-tory of subnational groups. They downgraded the centrality of English in American life and pushed bilingual education and linguistic diversity. They advocated legal recognition of group rights and racial preferences over the individual rights central to the American Creed. They justified their actions by theories of multiculturalism and the idea that diversity rather than unity or community should be America's overriding value. The combined effect of these efforts was to promote the decon-struction of the American identity that had been gradually created over three centu-ries and the ascendance of subnational identities.[18]

All of this, to be sure, is a cultural critique. But it stretches credulity to believe that the United States has in some fundamental sense been torn apart or degraded by multiculturalists. To introduce into the national nar-rative the forgotten people of the United States—many if not most of who have been here for decades or centuries—and call it diversity is scarcely a sin against the creed of hard work. Moreover, ten years after Hunting-ton's analysis, nothing suggests that what he feared or even predicted is any closer to becoming reality.

Yet Huntington's admonitions about migration from the south remains the most articulate and compelling case for nativism, as it embodies nearly every argument anti-reform forces use. For that alone, it deserves to be examined, and examined it was. One of the advantages of having earned the reputation of being a creative thinker is that people pay attention to what you say, and Huntington's book earned enormous attention.

The main critique of his conjectures were based on extensive use of census data and surveys (as he himself did) to demonstrate that Hispanics were adapting to American life much as other immigrants had for genera-tions. One such quantitative study published by the American Political Sci-ence Association sought to sort out the language issue particularly—were

Latinos hanging onto Spanish in such a way that it impeded their adoption of English? Was there something different about these immigrants—as Huntington insisted—compared with migrants from other countries and continents?

What the authors found[19] was a high level of consistency between Latinos and other immigrants in use of language: the first (migrating) generation retained Spanish as their primary tongue; the second generation who were living with their parents were far more likely to use English as their day-to-day language; and "all others" (second generation not living with parents, and third generation, etc.) were considerably more English-friendly, using English as their primary language in the home and outside it. This corresponded reasonably well with migrants from Asia and Europe. And it is particularly striking that adoption of English by Latinos increased markedly between the 1980 census and the 2000 census in all three categories, and in the third category—second generation not living with parents and third, fourth, etc., generations—the use of English was very nearly identical with all other immigrants. This increasing adoption has continued, according to the census taken in 2010.

This pattern is evident in other, related issues: preferences for bilingual education diminish sharply toward the third generation, which favors English-only; retention of Spanish fluency drops dramatically by the third generation; and self-identity as an "American" (rather than, for example, "Mexican" or "Latino") strongly correlates with language use. By the third generation, about two-thirds of Hispanics say they are "American" alone.

As the Pew Research Center reports, moreover, there are many other indicators of acceptance of "American values" and "normalcy" by Latinos living in the United States. In May 2013 the Center noted that the rate of college enrollment for Latinos right out of high school was for the first time higher than for white children. Over the decade of the 2000s, Latino high school students cut their dropout rate by half. Hispanic teen pregnancies have decreased sharply since the mid 1990s to a level much closer to all teenagers in the country. Hispanics in first and second generations who see themselves as "typical Americans" are almost precisely the same as those among Asian-Americans who see themselves as typical Americans, according to 2011 data. And as to the work ethic, while this is difficult to measure conclusively, surveys of employers have found that they believe Latinos to be good, dedicated workers, no different from European-origin Americans.[20]

Not all the statistics are good: poverty remains stubbornly high compared with the whole population, home ownership is lower than for most groups (Latinos took a disproportionate hit from the 2007–2009 recession), and so on, but considering the enormous influx of Latinos into the United States— almost all of them with poor educational levels and few resources—the group as a whole has held on remarkably well and has improved in some areas.

The Huntington thesis of an increasingly segregated Latino population, constantly nourished by Mexican values and identity, dependent on government handouts and low-skilled jobs (taken away from low-income Americans), insistent on speaking Spanish rather than the "language of the Declaration and the Constitution," and dismissive or unmindful of the Protestant work ethic that would critically weaken American identity, patriotism, values, and strength, has simply not come to pass, and doesn't show any signs of doing so in the foreseeable future.

Despite the nearly complete debunking of Huntington's analysis, the points he asserts remain the bedrock of the opponents of Latino immigration. Much of this focuses on the language issue. There are quite a few organizations dedicated to making English the official national language (and indeed 31 states have done so, up from three in 1980). Opinion polling shows majoritarian support for this, although the salience of this issue— how important it is to respondents—is questionable. Without much doubt, it is the growing presence of Hispanics in the United States that has stirred this backlash, although, strangely, several conservatives blame the left-wing professoriate for degrading English. (Said one: "In an irony that surpasses comprehension, the Modern Language Association, an organization of English teachers, is the leader of the politically correct movement to bring down English."[21]) The public stance of many English-only proponents is that such measures would bring national unity, which is a highly dubious claim. There is also concern about the costs of translation, said to be about $2 billion annually (equal to about 0.002 percent of an average citizen's tax burden). The pro-English motivations clearly stem more from resentment about a growing population of non-English speakers, and while other "values" can't easily be legislated, use of language in schools and other government institutions can be regulated. The English-only impulse has become a standard trope of the "culture wars" that have been waged over sexuality, racial preferences, censorship, and other matters, and divides fairly clearly along right-left fissures on those issues.

Among the most telling aspects of this debate is the willingness of the English-only forces to favor a monolingual country—with no clear or compelling benefits to being so—at the expense of ensuring the political franchise is broad. In many states and localities, ballots and government services are increasingly offered not only in Spanish but also in Chinese, Hindi, Korean, Portuguese, and other languages. The reasons for doing so are obvious and admirable: many citizens who don't speak English well would be disenfranchised without such a service. Isn't the expansion (or maintenance) of democratic choice preferable to a symbolic adherence to a single language? "For most citizens," a group of scholars wrote in 1990, "English proficiency is a highly resonant symbol of American nationality. The evidence strongly suggests that an important reason for the popularity of 'official English' is the pervasive public desire to reaffirm an attachment to a traditional image of Americanism that now seems vulnerable."[22] The authors cite 1988 survey data indicating that more than 60 percent of Californians believe in denying voting rights for non-English speakers and that 70 percent oppose bilingual education. If anything, the sense of vulnerability of the national identity has risen sharply in the ensuing quarter-century, and polling data indicates that most Americans support English-only measures.

One of the most interesting Latino philosophers in the United States, Jorge Gracia, has grappled at length with the issue of language and states as well as anyone the psychological underpinnings of the English-only impulse. "The English-first principle might be surreptitiously intended— although most likely some supporters of it are not conscious of it—to do more work than it is explicitly acknowledged by those who favor it," he wrote in his 2008 book *Latinos in America: Philosophy and Social Identity.* "I suspect that behind its use there is a commitment to English-only supported by a misguided sense of American nationality in which the United States is identified necessarily as an English-speaking country and those who are not proficient in English are not quite, or truly, considered American citizens." This, Gracia asserted, is a "dangerous notion," because the polity, the political construct of the nation "is transformed into a cultural one, in which language is one of its distinguishing features. It is dangerous because it excludes many, typically those who have already been oppressed, and provides a veneer of normalization to that oppression."[23] It is not mere convenience to have one language, or a brace of some fantasy of national identity, but an instrument used however unwittingly to marginalize large numbers of citizens and others in the country.

And, yes, it happens with blacks. While the language dimension of black-white relations and how African-Americans are viewed as a challenge to American identity differ from Latino-Anglo encounters, the comparative dynamics are no less revealing. Explorations of black dialect, sometimes called Ebonics, bear remarkably similar contours to Latinos' use of Spanish in the United States, especially among the young, because the costs of consciously being outside the mainstream are not as apparent. Ebonics provides group identity and cohesion. In its starkest form, it is consciously a language of resistance to the dominant white culture, a "latent, yet ongoing, subversive war of Black identity maintenance," according to one anthropologist studying high school students in Washington, D.C. She describes a "commitment to a Black identity [that] that is centrally embedded in their linguistic repertoire, compelling them to 'diss' 'the standard' dialect by only leasing it rather than internalizing it from nine to three."[24] The "standard" English is more than the language use per se; it is the attitudes that are associated with it, including the denigration of Ebonics. "The standard, understood in this broad sense, might be resisted by African-Americans because its definitions of caste, which stigmatize black speech, extend easily to other practices associated with black people."[25] Language, again, is a central, distinguishing cultural characteristic.

It is certainly true that we arrive at this point of similarity between African-Americans and Latinos in the United States from dissimilar starting points. (Although many would say they both begin with similar forms of oppression.) But the use of non-standard English or any English by both groups puts them on a track of low achievement and low-paying employment, and reinforces the language difference in subsequent generations. Difficulty with standard English and literacy after the Emancipation was used to legally disenfranchise African-Americans, just as the insistence on English-only ballots, green card applications, and government services is aimed to disenfranchise Latinos: here again is "legality" as a cultural weapon.

The fevered maintenance of a particular kind of American identity by the white Anglo cultural guardians involves much more than English-first guardianship, restrictive immigration policies and practices, hyper-patriotic educational curricula, and the like. For the diehards of this view—perhaps 30 percent or so of the American public—their attitudes follow a pattern of racial bias and accepted discrimination, seeking militant solutions to complex social problems, and dismissing the deeper structural issues (income inequality, the ravages of globalization) that lay at the base of so many social, economic, and political problems. It's the same group of people who are quick to go to war abroad in Iraq and elsewhere and who then ignore the consequences, quick to disparage scientific findings like climate change and who then ignore the consequences, and quick to demand special favors for themselves like tax cuts and then ignore the consequences. It is all of a piece, really: the same ideological construct that results in so many destructive policies has been at work like an infectious disease on the immigration issue as well.

The embrace of marketization at home and abroad is one example of this malady. The anti-union policies especially prevalent in the old Confederacy but increasingly apparent throughout the United States created a labor market that in many respects conveys advantages to unauthorized immigrants over native (and especially unionized) workers. Abroad, and especially in Mexico, new and largely unregulated factories, typically owned by American corporations, soaked up local resources, supplanted traditional livelihoods, disrupted social and natural ecosystems, and created new armies of the dispossessed and unemployed, who then headed north. The rationale for this, the market ideology, was that business should be free to act as it wishes. Prices and supply were kept to satisfy consumers. But the consequences were to impoverish Mexicans at one end and harass them at the other. Don't want to pay the economic and political costs of unionized labor? Undercut it and attract low-paid Latinos. Then complain about Spanish being spoken and laws being transgressed and a culture under siege.

In the same vein, the "solution" to the problems or occurrences of Latino immigration is either militancy or ignorance. The presence of so many Mexicans and Latin Americans in the United States is, in this ideology, purely a failure of policing and border security. Policing, in the form of raids and arrests and detentions and deportation, is at an all-time high. Border security continues to cost more than any other form of security apart from the US military itself. The border is heavily militarized and has been for years: it is a stationary raid. That this is the problem-solving apotheosis of the nativists' ideology is starkly revealing. The social and economic factors at work in fueling immigration are essentially ignored, and measures to address such factors are ignored or dismissed as well.

This toxic mix of militancy and ignorance necessitates a moral or cultural underpinning, and the cacophony over illegal aliens and Spanish and cultural invasions and such becomes, in this reckoning, just such a cultural maneuver—hardly deft, but effectively playing the heartstrings of a diminishing and once-dominant group. The hollowing out of the American middle class and the increasing diversity of American society have embittered a sizable segment of the population that is ready to blame immigrants and Spanish speaking for the gradual erosion of all that they believe once made the United States great. The *emotional* dimension of the immigration debate spins on this cultural axis, even if the issue itself is wrought by structural—mainly economic—causes, namely, corporate capitalism's restless global search for cheap labor and resources.

8 HOPE FOR THE DREAM CHASERS

While so much of the immigration debate seems hopelessly stuck, with no movement toward a solution seeming to be politically feasible, it may also be true that some cultural and political change is stirring. Earlier I cited some polling figures that suggest a considerable softening of American attitudes about a path to citizenship, for example, and broad acceptance of the Dreamers' case—about 70–80 percent approving, in both cases. It may be that slowly, gradually, cautiously, the majority of Americans are recognizing that rigidity on "legality" is not a problem-solving attitude.

Some of that flexibility is simply the human element. People see that with the Dreamers, but it's also true that they tend to be "just like us"—our children's friends, the high school standout—so it's relatively easy to accept that their lot is unfair. The bigger challenge is to see the same story in the gardener, the maid, the guys hanging around the 7-Eleven store waiting for a day job. They may be a little darker skinned, may not speak English, may have no formal education. In other words, a tough sell. But even that might be changing as we know more about the root causes of the poverty that drove them north, or simply come into contact with them as Latinos stream out across the country.

This sliver of hope brightened when I came across an essay by Anthony Bourdain, the CNN television host of a show about food and culture. I found the essay remarkable because it comes from someone who isn't associated with politics or immigration issues.

"We demand that Mexicans cook a large percentage of the food we eat, grow the ingredients we need to make that food, clean our houses, mow our lawns, wash our dishes, and look after our children," Bourdain said in the introduction to a spring 2014 show on Mexico. "As any chef will tell you, our entire service economy—the restaurant business as we know it—in most American cities, would collapse overnight without Mexican workers. Some, of course, like to claim that Mexicans are 'stealing American jobs.' But in two decades as a chef and employer, I never had *one* American kid walk in my door and apply for a dishwashing job, a porter's position—or even a job as prep cook. Mexicans do much of the work in this country that Americans, provably, simply won't do."

Bourdain went on to speak of how Mexicans know our dark desires for being entertained, particularly illicit drugs. Drugs have imposed high costs on ordinary Mexicans as a consequence of the US war on drugs and the Mexican drug gangs—80,000 dead over the past few years. And then, a memorable phrase: "Mexico. Our brother from another mother. A country, with whom, like it or not, we are inexorably, deeply involved, in a close but often uncomfortable embrace."[1]

One of the many wrinkles in the immigration controversy is that the nativists, in their unrelenting and voluble resistance to Latino culture, have drawn attention to it from others who perhaps weren't paying attention before. The "hiddenness" of illegal immigration is now diminished. Bourdain's essay reflects that quite elegantly. Hollywood is paying attention. Now there are popular television series (e.g. *The Bridge*) that portray immigrants sympathetically, even while focusing on the drug cartels, well-regarded films that depict real-life dilemmas for the unauthorized (e.g. *A Better Life*), and a constant flow of documentaries. The short film *Inocente* won an Academy Award in 2013. The art world is paying attention: Valerie James's "memorial" sculpture in Arizona using found objects of clothing in the desert left by immigrants crossing illegally, is particularly striking, as are many works by immigrant artists. In 2014 the Smithsonian Institution mounted an enormous exhibition titled "Our America: The Latino Presence in American Art." And then there are the new media, probably the real path-breaker in this fresh view of immigrants. The journalist and advocate Jose Antonio Vargas is a constant presence on Twitter and other social media. Pharrell Williams has a YouTube channel—iamOther, with a million subscribers—that has shown bold pieces about artists making music, paintings, posters, and films about immigration policy and the culture of nativism. Favianna Rodriguez, an artist and activist, has worked with Williams,

Vargas, and others to showcase the artists and connect to the political issues in a YouTube series, "Voice of Art." Aloe Blacc's song "Wake Me Up," subtitled on some versions of his music video "based on 11 million true stories," where he takes up a saga of unauthorized immigrants in story telling visuals; his several music videos with this song have been viewed 450 million times in less than a year on YouTube.

The expanding uses of art and film and television and social media signal the normalization of the immigration discourse, a conversation—no matter how imagined or represented—that takes up the issues of inclusiveness and justice for the undocumented. It differs fundamentally from the discussion of the nativists in that it is filled with the real lives of immigrants, the flavors of diversity, the bright colors of cultures and their adaptations in America. It is also angry and tragic, imbued with the loss of homeland and the arduous journey north, and occasionally the brutality of the ICE raids, the border patrol, the grandstanding politicians. Above all else, it is a universe of expression about longing and place—very much the idiom of all immigrants the world over, throughout human history. The growing acceptance of the unauthorized immigrant, however fragile, is reflected through and prompted by these images, words, sounds, and social connectedness.

This may be an instance of what political scientists call a "norm cascade," a concept pioneered by Martha Finnemore and Katherine Sikkink in an international context.[2] It denotes a change in attitudes and behavior based on what people perceive is morally right and practically achievable. Finnemore and Sikkink describe different stages—emergence, cascade, internalization—and how different motivations and actors stimulate and coalesce these stages. This scheme is wholly applicable to the immigration debate, although one would "domesticate" the actors more fully. I expect that with respect to the illegal immigration debate, we are somewhere between Stage 1 and Stage 2. The Dreamers, for example could be considered norm entrepreneurs—proposing ideas involving empathy and working by persuasion. Non-governmental organizations, academics, and artists would also be considered as such. The "cascade," the most important stage, is realized as the state (that is, the US government) legitimizes the emergent norm through legislation (Senate bill in 2013) or executive action (DACA in 2012), as do other institutions. With passage of immigration reform and economic development remedies in Mexico and Latin America, the cascade would move toward internalization.

I would not belabor this model too much, but it's useful as a way to see how an emergent norm about belonging and citizenship in particular is forming. Before the passage of the Senate bill proposed by the Gang of Eight, citizenship for unauthorized immigrants was far less plausible. It remains elusive legislatively, but the strong public opinion in favor of a path to citizenship was stirred in part by the Senate bill itself—namely, the discussions and attention it prompted.

While the politics of immigration remain stuck in Washington, stuck in precisely those cultural tropes this book has surveyed, the hinterlands have to a remarkable extent taken it upon themselves to convey a different message, one wholly in keeping with—an expression of—the norm cascade. Among the actions many states and cities have adopted are sanctuary status for unauthorized immigrants—notably, that the status of immigrants here without authorization should not be reported by public employees. Even in Utah, a conservative state, the legislature passed a law in 2011 allowing unauthorized immigrants to work and live in the state. San Francisco, Maine, New York City, San Diego, Oakland, Houston, Chicago, Miami, and about sixty other places are sanctuary cities or states, typically meaning that the immigrant's status alone is not a reason for reporting, though status is in play if the immigrant is arrested for a criminal act. It is mainly symbolic, but also a little defiant.

More remarkable has been a more recent "welcome" movement in cities and towns. The *New York Times* columnist David Bornstein, whose beat is social entrepreneurship, highlighted these efforts early in 2014. He pointed to Nashville, Tennessee, a city long riven by ethnic tension that turned a rejectionist stance into a much more embracing attitude toward immigrants. He relayed a story in which one woman said her husband was angry about the changes in his old neighborhood and voted for an English-only ordinance. "The issue here is not economics," wrote Bornstein. "It's what happens when people feel they are losing their sense of belonging and continuity with the past." An activist named David Lubell decided to begin a new organization called Welcoming Tennessee, which took the insights of Robert Putnam and other social scientists to heart and tried to connect people on a personal level, not just analytically or politically, but face to face. "They organized community dinners, gatherings at churches, talks at Rotary clubs. They trained hundreds of community ambassadors to bring people together across racial and ethnic lines. They worked with media

Table 8.1
The norm "life cycle."

	Stage 1: Norm emergence	Stage 2: Norm cascade	Stage 3: Internalization
Actors	Norm entrepreneurs with organizational platforms	States, international organizations, networks	Law, professions, bureaucracy
Motives	Altruism, empathy, ideational, commitment	Legitimacy, reputation, esteem	Conformity
Dominant mechanisms	Persuasion	Socialization, institutionalization, demonstration	Habit, institutionalization

and put up billboards with positive messages about immigrants," Bornstein reported. "'People were only hearing negative things,' Lubell recalled. 'But most of the immigrant population were there to make their families' lives better. They wanted to contribute to the community.' And many were struggling themselves with the loss of a sense of belonging."[3]

The results were remarkable. Over a fairly short time, Nashville's attitudes toward immigrants began to change; for example, it rejected an English-only referendum by 57–43 percent. Other NGOs joined in with Lubell's effort. The city created new programs to connect immigrant communities with old Nashvillans. And, most tellingly, the "welcome" movement has grown. Now there is a Welcome America, with 30 cities affiliated, including Los Angeles, Pittsburgh, Denver, Hartford, Indianapolis, St. Louis, and others large and small. Something like 50,000 people have participated in 1,000 events in these cities. Many of the affiliates are very active, training their welcomers and building out with new ideas. A few local polls show changes in attitudes toward immigrants, some of which almost certainly is due to the welcome movement. Several cities and state officials have promoted their programs. As of mid 2014 it was continuing to grow.

Whether or not the welcome movement can change the cultural attitudes that undergird cultural resistance to immigration reform is at this
point an open question. That there is such a movement and it seems to be
thriving is astonishing in itself. What seems clear is that they are addressing
precisely the root of the resistance, and doing so in a conciliatory way. Cultural change occurs in such situations mainly by diffusion, by introducing
cultural icons, practices, beliefs, and so on through direct contact—in this
case, demonstrating that the several Hispanic cultures now living around
the United States bring values that are not threatening to traditional Anglo
culture. As one rigorous study of attitudes toward unauthorized immigrants
noted, "efforts that aim to reduce misinformation regarding threats, negative stereotypes, and intergroup anxiety may, in turn, reduce prejudicial
attitudes and intergroup hostilities."[4] It is particularly important, I contend,
to overcome the decrepit notion that immigrants must assimilate in order
to "belong" to the American community. They do assimilate eventually,
in fact, adopting the English language and "American" beliefs such as the
value of hard work, but it's hardly necessary to consider that a prerequisite
for legalization or citizenship.

That same 2012 survey reported something else that may change the
nature of the culture and politics equation: older Americans are much more
likely to perceive threats from and express prejudiced sentiments toward
immigrants (legal or not) than younger, college-age people. Like issues of
gay marriage or climate change, these generational differences could prove
profound and alter the political landscape very soon. The changes in same-
sex marriage laws were remarkably sudden after a long period of rejection,
and some of that had to do with generational politics and familiarity (as
sons and daughters "came out," they prompted parents and other relatives
to change attitudes—again, personal contact drove the change). Younger
Americans are also far more likely to know unauthorized immigrants from
school than older people would, enhancing that familiarity effect in the
classroom and the playground.

All of these trends suggest that the dour climate of rejection may change
sooner than we think. Even the diehards in the Republican House caucus
may feel the need to be more flexible. Cultural accommodation, though
hard, is clearly something that Americans are getting accustomed to.

We can see this, too, in the reactions to the border kids who have
arrived at the US-Mexico border from Central America. The eruption of the

right-wing media and some angry protestors in places where the children and some young mothers were bused for processing made it seem that these "illegals" were not wanted here. President Obama felt pressure to deport them, lest tens of thousands more got the message that the United States would grant them asylum. Across America, there were many pockets of voluble opposition, much of it from worried officials saying they couldn't afford to place the children in their crowded classrooms. But another spirit became evident if one looked closely. Thousands of volunteers went to the border and organized in receiving towns and cities to accommodate these refugees. After more than a month of the controversy, a poll showed that 70 percent of the American public said that the children should be treated as refugees, not as unauthorized immigrants. Another poll came to similar findings, including the expressed belief that the government should allow the children (with 69 percent in favor and 28 percent opposed) to join their families already in the United States.[5] Reminiscent of the aftermath of the raid in New Bedford, churches led the relief efforts for the children and volunteer lawyers represented them in asylum cases. Yet the attention to the Tea Party opposition and the difficulties of resettling the children lent the impression of widespread resistance to their presence, and this was reinforced by ingrained habits in Washington's polarized politics—the black and white of the kids' being "legal" or "illegal." Remarkably, however, there was only a smattering of media attention, and virtually none in Washington politics, to the economic and social conditions in Central America that prompts this extraordinary flow of migrants.

The neoliberal economic policies that drive migration from Mexico and Central America are very difficult to change because they involve such high stakes for American corporations and the politicians who accept the dogma of "free trade." Neoliberalism—free markets, free movement of capital, direct foreign investment, and so on—has disrupted traditional ways of life with such force and suddenness that many tens of thousands leave each country every year to emigrate to the United States. This continuing great migration is cultural and economic, cultural because so much of the movement of people is prompted by drug cartels and gangs who are waging internecine war to control the American drug habit. The children who walked across Mexico to the Texas border—100,000 each year—were escaping the drug gangs. The drug criminals control so much of the political establishment that American drug consumption and the politics of Latin

America are intimately intertwined, and migration is one consequence. One of neoliberalism's enduring legacies is to weaken states—to end cronyism, diminish state-owned enterprise, lower taxes, and so on. This has meant that fewer young people are being educated, fewer incorruptible police are combating the drug traffickers, and fewer people have viable options for making a living. The culture of drug trafficking and violence fills these gaps.

President Obama's executive order in November 2014 expanding deferred action on deportation to 5 million unauthorized immigrants disrupted the political logjam in Washington, although Republicans vowed revenge. But it was striking how the reaction to Obama's order focused on the process of excluding Congress rather than on the substance of deferred action—oddly enough, another hopeful, if limited, sign. Thus, while hope is warranted in the pockets of acceptance and welcoming in the United States, it is strongly conditioned by the abrupt changes economic globalization has wrought. Immigration reform may come, but it will not stop the migrants as long as the economies of the global South are a shambles. Without that reform—sensible economic justice—unauthorized immigration and the resistance to it will continue to roil American politics.

NOTES

CHAPTER 1

1. "Immigration Restriction League," Harvard University Library Open Collections Program (http://ocp.hul.harvard.edu).

2. I use the words 'Latino' and 'Hispanic' more or less interchangeably in this book. There are debates about which is preferable—or if either is useful as a substitute for specific nationalities—but I find that both words impart approximately the same meaning, remain neutral, and are useful to designate Spanish-speaking people whose family origins are in Latin America and the Caribbean. The K'iche of Guatemala, as I note later, object to being included with these designations, for three reasons: their tribe predates the Spanish conquest of Central America, they are not native Spanish speakers, and they identify with indigenous peoples first and foremost.

3. Ira Berlin, *The Making of African America: The Four Great Migrations* (Penguin, 2010), chapter 4.

4. Isabel Wilkerson, *The Warmth of Other Suns: The Epic Story of America's Great Migration* (Random House, 2010), 216.

5. Ibid., 217.

6. Ibid., 260.

7. Malcolm X, quoted in the PBS television documentary *Eyes on the Prize*.

8. Gustavo Valdes, "Georgia governor to sign law targeting illegal immigration," CNN (http://www.cnn.com), April 15, 2011.

9. I use 'unauthorized' most often to denote someone who has entered the US without the proper papers, or someone who is overstaying a visa. I accept Jose Antonio

Vargas' insistence that no person is illegal and therefore we should not use the term "illegal immigrant." But I also challenge the entire legal/illegal dyad, in part because 'illegal' connotes a criminal offense, something that crossing the border without authorization is not.

10. Aaron Couch, "State illegal immigration laws: What have they accomplished?" *Christian Science Monitor*, March 23, 2011.

11. Quoted in Elias Isquith, "Laura Ingraham: Justice Sotomayor's 'allegiance' is to 'her immigrant family background' and not the Constitution," *Salon* (http://www.salon.com), February 4, 2014.

12. "Mexican jingoism," quoted in "Laura Ingraham: English language 'is in decline,' 'a sign of jingoism,'" Media Matters for America (http://mediamatters.org), January 30, 2014.

13. Michelle Malkin, "Joey Vento: Assimilation warrior," The Front Page (http://www.frontpagemag.com), August 29, 2011.

14. Michelle Malkin, "DREAM Act nightmare: 2.1 million future Democrat voter recruitment drive," michellemalkin.com, November 19, 2010.

15. Michelle Malkin, "Assimilation, not amnesty," michellemalkin.com, November 12, 2012.

16. Michelle Malkin, "Muslims for open borders," michellemalkin.com, April 10, 2006.

17. "Laura Ingraham uses Boston bombing to stoke fears about immigration reform," Media Matters for America (http://mediamatters.org), April 16, 2013.

18. Erica Ritz, "Ann Coulter says 'zero immigrants should be collecting welfare assistance,'" The Blaze (http://www.theblaze.com), May 1, 2013.

19. Source: Quinnipiac University poll, April 25–29, 2013 (http://www.pollingreport.com/immigration.htm).

20. "Laura Ingraham: Horrible crimes committed by illegal immigrants," *The O'Reilly Factor*, July 26, 2013.

21. On the economic impacts of immigration see Gordon H. Hanson, *The Economic Logic of Illegal Immigration*, CSR 26 (Council on Foreign Relations, April 2007); George J. Borjas, ed., *Issues in the Economics of Immigration* (University of Chicago Press, 2008); Patricia Cortes, "The Effect of Low-Skilled Immigration on U.S. Prices: Evidence from CPI Data," *Journal of Political Economy* 116, no. 3 (2008): 381–422; Giovanni Peri, The Effect of Immigration on Productivity: Evidence from US States, National Bureau of Economic Research Working Paper 15507, 2009; Gianmarco I. P. Ottaviano and Giovanni Peri, Rethinking the Effects of Immigration on Wages, National Bureau for Economic Research Working Paper 12497, 2006; Frédéric Doc-

quier, Çağlar Özden, and Giovanni Peri, The Wage Effects of Immigration and Emigration, National Bureau of Economic Research Working Paper 16646, 2010.

CHAPTER 2

1. Eric Sagara, "TUSD chastised for Huerta speech," *Tucson Citizen*, April 21, 2006.

2. Nadine Zylberberg, "Justice Scalia dissents," *The New Yorker*, June 25, 2012.

3. Kerry Fehr-Snyder, "New Arizona schools chief John Huppenthal tackles tough issues," *Arizona Republic*, January 8, 2011.

4. Gabriel Matthew Chivone, "US district judge orders TUSD to reinstate 'culturally relevant courses,'" *The Nation*, February 12, 2013.

5. Richard Slotkin, *The Fatal Environment: The Myth of the Frontier in the Age of Industrialization, 1800–1890* (Atheneum, 1985), 191. See also *Gunfighter Nation: The Myth of the Frontier in Twentieth-Century America* (University of Oklahoma Press, 1998).

6. Mike Wilson, interview by John Tirman, April 15, 2013.

7. Patrick J. Buchanan, *State of Emergency: The Third World Invasion and Conquest of America* (St. Martin's Press, 2006), 136.

8. Quoted by Michael Krenn, *Race and U.S. Foreign Policy in the Ages of Territorial and Market Expansion, 1840 to 1900* (Taylor & Francis, 1998), 7.

9. Eric Meeks, *Border Citizens: The Making of Indians, Mexicans, and Anglos in Arizona* (University of Texas Press, 2010), 37.

10. Bárbara Cruz, "Don Juan and rebels under palm trees: Depictions of Latin Americans in US history textbooks," *Critique of Anthropology* 22, no. 3 (2002): 323–342, at 335.

11. Angela Valenzuela, *Subtractive Schooling: U.S.-Mexican Youth and the Politics of Caring* (SUNY Press, 1999), 3.

12. Sean Arce, interview by John Tirman, April 17, 2013.

13. Quoted by Al Letson, "A year without Mexican-American studies in Tucson," Weekend Edition, NPR, June 24, 2012 (http://www.npr.org/2012/06/24/155644119/first-year-without-controversial-class-in-ariz-ends). The speaker was Lorenzo Lopez.

14. Paulo Freire, *Pedagogy of the Oppressed*, tr. Myra Bergman Ramos (Continuum, 1970, 2005), 48.

15. Arizona Department of Education, Office of John Huppenthal, "Superintendent of Public Instruction John Huppenthal Statement of Finding Regarding Tucson Unified School District's Violation of A.R.S. §15-112" (n.d.), 1.

16. Ibid., 2.

17. Asiya Mir and Ryan Velasquez, "Youth coalition rejects Huppenthal ruling on TUSD program," *Arizona Daily Star*, June 17, 2011.

18. *Curriculum Audit of the Mexican American Studies Department Tucson Unified School District* (Cambium Learning, 2011; available at http://www.tucsonweekly.com, 31.

19. Gary Grado, "Huppenthal to avoid witness stand in TUSD hearing," *Arizona Capitol Times*, August 26, 2011.

20. Mir and Velasquez, "Youth coalition rejects Huppenthal ruling on TUSD program."

21. Mark Stegeman, interview by John Tirman, April 17, 2013.

22. Eliza Mesa, interview with David Dougherty, "Tucson students occupy school board meeting to defend ethnic studies," therealnews.com, May 3, 2011.

23. Mother Mags, "Tucson students take over school board meeting. Update: AZ Republic's Take," www.dailykos.com, April 27, 2011.

24. Jim Hoft, "La Raza student mob shuts down Tucson school board meeting (video) ... Update: Rep. Grijalva's daughter cheers on mob," thegatewaypundit.com, April 30, 2011.

25. Stegeman, interview.

26. Nicholas Lundholm, "Administrative law judge finds TUSD's Mexican American Studies program illegal under Arizona's Ethnic Studies Law, questions remain about how broadly the law should be interpreted," http://www.arizonalawreview. org/2012/syllabus/administrative-law-judge-finds-tusds-mexican-american.

27. On multiculturalism, see Charles Taylor, *Multiculturalism: Examining the Politics of Recognition* (Princeton University Press, 1994); Tariq Modood, *Multiculturalism* ((Wiley, 2013); Brian Barry, *Culture and Equality: An Egalitarian Critique of Multiculturalism* (Harvard University Press, 2002); Monica Mookherjee, *Women's Rights as Multicultural Claims: Reconfiguring Gender and Diversity in Political Philosophy* (University of Edinburgh Press, 2009); Paul Kelly, *Multiculturalism Reconsidered: 'Culture and Equality' and Its Critics* (Wiley, 2002).

28. On economics and ethnic diversity, see Jose G. Montalvo and Marta Reynal-Queros, "Ethnic diversity and economic development," *Journal of Development Economics* 76, no. 2 (2005): 293–323; James Habyarimana, Macartan Humphreys, Daniel N. Posner, and Jeremy M. Weinstein, "Why does ethnic diversity undermine public goods provision?" *American Political Science Review*, November 2007: 709–722; Alberto Alesina and Eliana La Ferrara, Ethnic Diversity and Economic Performance, National Bureau of Economic Research Working Paper 10313, 2004; Paul Collier, "Ethnicity, politics and economic performance," *Economics and Politics* 12, no. 3

(2000): 225–245; Kate Baldwin and John Huber, "Economic versus cultural differences: Forms of ethnic diversity and public goods provision," *American Political Science Review* 104, no. 4 (2010): 644–662.

29. On ethnic stereotypes and the contact hypothesis, see Peter Burns and James G. Gimpel, "Economic insecurity, prejudicial stereotypes, and public opinion on immigration policy," *Political Science Quarterly* 115, no. 2 (2000): 201–225; Gerardo Marín, "Stereotyping Hispanics: The differential effect of research method, label, and degree of contact," *International Journal of Intercultural Relations* 8, no. 1 (1984): 17–27; Thomas F. Pettigrew, "Intergroup contact theory," *Annual Review of Psychology* 49 (1998): 65–85; C. G. Ellison, H. Shin, and D. L. Heal, "The contact hypothesis and attitudes toward Latinos in the United States," *Social Science Quarterly* 92, no. 4 (2011): 938–958.

30. Stegeman, interview.

31. Arce, interview.

32. Curtis Acosta, "Empowering young people to be critical thinkers: The Mexican American Studies program in Tucson," *VUE: Voices in Urban Education*, no. 34 (2012): 15–26.

33. Nolan L. Cabrera, Jeffrey F. Milem, and Ronald W. Marx, An Empirical Analysis of the Effects of Mexican American Studies Participation on Student Achievement within Tucson Unified School District. Report to Special Master Dr. Willis D. Hawley on the Tucson Unified School District Desegregation Case.

34. Liam Julien, "Come study La Raza," National Review Online (http://www.nationalreview.com), July 2, 2008.

35. Quoted in "Mexican American Studies: Bad Ban Or Bad Class?" National Public Radio (January 18, 2012); http://www.npr.org/2012/01/18/145397005/mexican-american-studies-bad-ban-or-bad-class.

36. Al Letson, "A Year Without Mexican-American Studies In Tucson," National; Public Radio (June 24, 2012); http://www.npr.org/2012/06/24/155644119/first-year-without-controversial-class-in-ariz-ends.

37. Richard Martinez, *Curtis Acosta et al. v. John Huppenthal et al.*, Motion for Summary Judgment, US District Court for the State of Arizona, May 25, 2011, 25–26.

38. Sources of statistics on Arizona's Hispanic population: Tom R. Rex, The Latino Population in Arizona—Growth, Characteristics, and Outlook—with a Focus on Latino Education, W. P. Carey School of Business, Arizona State University, 2011; Demographic Profile of Hispanics in Arizona, 2011, Pew Hispanic Center; US Census Bureau (http://quickfacts.census.gov).

39. Adelita Grijalva, interview by John Tirman, April 16, 2013.

40. Richard Martinez, interview by John Tirman, April 15, 2013.

41. Barack Obama, Statement by the President on the Supreme Court's Ruling on *Arizona v. the United States*, June 25, 2012.

42. Minutemen's problems: David Holthouse, "Jim Gilchrist Fired By Minuteman Project," Intelligence Report 126, Southern Poverty Law Center, summer 2007 (http://www.splcenter.org/get-informed/intelligence-report/browse-all-issues/2007/summer/minute-mess); Steve Lemons, "Chris Simcox's Life Arc Mirrors the Nativist Movement's Demise," *Phoenix New Time*, September 5, 2013); http://www.phoenixnewtimes.com/2013-09-05/news/chris-simcox-demise-of-nativist-movement; "T. J. Ready," Southern Poverty Law Center (n.d.); http://www.splcenter.org/get-informed/intelligence-files/profiles/jt-ready; Stephen Lemons, "Minuteman CEO Carmen Mercer Named in Arizona Attorney General Lawsuit Over Property Tax Scam," *Phoenix New Times* (August 17, 2009); http://blogs.phoenixnewtimes.com/bastard/2009/08/minuteman_ceo_carmen_mercer_na.php.

43. David Neiwert, *And Hell Followed With Her: Crossing the Dark Side of the American Border* (Nation Books, 2013), excerpted in *Salon* (http://www.salon.com), March 23, 2013.

44. David Holthouse, Minutemen, Other Anti-Immigrant Militia Groups Stake Out Arizona Border, Intelligence Report 118, Southern Poverty Law Center, 2005.

45. "Extremists declare 'open season' on immigrants: Hispanics target of incitement and violence" (n.d.), Anti-Defamation League archives (http://63.146.172.78/NR/exeres/D7BECD3A-D17C-48ED-9BA6-5A109D1125FA,DB7611A2-02CD-43AF-8147-649E26813571,frameless.htm).

46. Quoted in "Fact-checking the claims about 'anchor babies' and whether illegal immigrants 'drop and leave,'" PolitiFact.com (n.d.).

47. Brady McCombs, "Border watch group draws to close," *Arizona Daily Star*, March 25, 2010.

48. Devin Dwyer, "Tea Party senators target birthright citizenship for immigrant children," ABC News (http://abcnews.go.com), April 6, 2011.

49. Bob Key, "Guest contributor: Bob Kee, writing on the work of the Tucson Samaritans," roygermano.com, February 5, 2011.

50. "Derechos Opposes Hoeven-Corker Amendment: New Immigration Bill is a Step Backward for Border Communities and Many Immigrant Families," Coalición de Derechos Humanos, June 26, 2013 (http://www.derechoshumanosaz.net/page/2).

51. Ananda Rose, *Showdown in the Sonoran Desert: Religion, Law, and the Immigration Controversy* (Oxford University Press, 2012), 29.

52. Michelle Malkin, "Open Borders and the Catholic Elite," michellemalkin.com, April 18, 2008.

CHAPTER 3

1. The events of the raid on New Bedford's Michael Bianco plant on March 6, 2007 are retold from newspaper accounts (mainly in the New Bedford *Standard-Times* and on its website, SouthCoastToday.com, and the *Boston Globe*), from interviews (cited below), from videos of events, from interviews with New Bedford residents (on You-Tube in particular), and from some broader treatments in books and magazines (cited below).

2. Source of statistics on detentions and deportations in 2011: John Simanski and Lesley M. Sapp, "Immigration enforcement actions: 2011," in Annual Report of Office of Immigration Statistics, Department of Homeland Security, 2012, 1.

3. Quoted by Eric Jay Dolin, *Leviathan: The History of Whaling in America* (Norton, 2008): 213.

4. Herman Melville, *Moby-Dick* (New American Library, 1892), 36.

5. Zephaniah W. Pease, ed., *History of New Bedford*, volume 1 (Lewis Historical Publishing, 1918), 217.

6. On Portuguese migration, see Benjamin Bailey, History and Description of Portuguese Immigration and the East Providence/SE New England Portuguese Community (available at http://works.bepress.com); Jerry R. Williams, *In Pursuit of Their Dreams: A History of Azorean Immigration to the United States*, second edition (Tagus, 2007); Kimberly DaCosta Holton and Andrea Klimt, eds., *Community, Culture and The Makings of Identity: Portuguese-Americans along the Eastern Seaboard* (Tagus, 2009).

7. Source of 2010 census data for New Bedford: http://quickfacts.census.gov.

8. "New Bedford Detainee Testimony," March 13, 2007 (https://www.youtube.com/watch?v=a-8ke8gd60g).

9. "New Bedford detainee testimony," April 10, 2007 (https://www.youtube.com/watch?v=2qG6FZbr9rM).

10. Bianca Vázquez Toness, WBUR radio, May 10, 2010 (http://www.wbur.org/2010/05/10/invisible-communities-i).

11. "New Bedford detainee testimony."

12. Corinn Williams, interview by John Tirman, July 20, 2011.

13. Bethany Touré, correspondence with John Tirman, May 21, 2014.

14. Marc Fallon, interview by John Tirman (April 11, 2011).

15. Becky W. Evans, "Deported after raid, 20-year-old makes the best of it in Guatemala," New Bedford *Standard-Times*, March 6, 2008.

16. Corinn Williams, interview by Tirman, July 20, 2011; Ken Hartnett, interview by Tirman, July 19, 2011.

17. David Kibbe, "Governor defends state response to rid," New Bedford *Standard-Times*, March 15, 2007.

18. Richard Wilson, interview by John Tirman, April 11, 2014.

19. Yvonne Abraham and Brian R. Ballou, "350 are held in immigration raid," *Boston Globe*, March 7, 2007.

20. Corinn Williams, interview by Tirman.

21. "New Bedford immigration raid separates families but unites legal community response," *Lawyers Journal* (http://www.massbar.org/publications/lawyers-journal), March 2007.

22. Pam Belluck, "Lawyers say U.S. acted in bad faith after immigrant raid in Massachusetts," *New York Times*, March 22, 2007. The speaker was the attorney Bernard J. Bonn III.

23. Eva Millona of Massachusetts Immigrant Rights Association, interview by John Tirman, May 13, 2011.

24. Debbie Schlussel, "Desperate ICE-Wives: Who is Julie Myers?" debbieschlussel.com, September 21, 2005.

25. Esther Yu-His Lee, "How The Postville immigration raid has changed deportation proceedings," Think Progress (http://thinkprogress.org), May 10, 2013.

26. Jennifer Bennett, "Operation Return to Sender," *Slate* (http://www.slate.com), May 30, 2008.

27. For reports of detainees' being beaten by ICE officers, see Sunita Patel and Tom Jawetz, "Conditions of confinement in immigration detention facilities" (n.d.) (https://www.aclu.org/files/pdfs/prison/unsr_briefing_materials.pdf).

28. Lindsay Kee, "We Don't Need a Warrant, We're ICE," Blog of Rights (https://www.aclu.org/blog), October 21, 2011). On the $1 million settlement for abusive home searches, see "ICE settles home invasion lawsuit for $1 million," http://www.lexisnexis.com, April 5, 2013.

29. Julie Myers Wood, interview by John Tirman, November 14, 2012.

30. Bruce M. Foucart, "Immigration raid went by the book," SouthCoastTimes.com, March 6, 2008.

31. Yvonne Abraham, "DSS chief raps immigration agency over detainees," *Boston Globe*, March 13, 2007.

32. Erik Camayd-Freixas, "Interpreting the Largest ICE Raid in U.S. History: A Personal Account," New America Media (http://news.newamericamedia.org), July 11, 2008. Camayd-Freixas has since published a book: *US Immigration Reform and Its Global Impact: Lessons from the Postville Raid* (Palgrave Macmillan, 2013).

33. Aarti Kohli, Peter L. Markowitz, and Lisa Chavez, "Secure Communities by the Numbers: An Analysis of Demographics and Due Process," School of Law, University of California, Berkeley, October 2011 (https://www.law.berkeley.edu/files/Secure_Communities_by_the_Numbers.pdf).

34. An interactive map of ICE detention centers in the United States is available at http://www.detentionwatchnetwork.org/dwnmap.

35. "Immigration Detention" (n.d.) (https://www.aclu.org/immigrants-rights/immigration-detention). Several useful reports and maps are available at this website.

36. Dana Priest and Amy Goldstein, "As tighter immigration policies strain federal agencies, the detainees in their care often pay a heavy cost," *Washington Post*, May 11, 2008.

37. "Lost in Detention," *Frontline*, PBS television, October 18, 2011 (http://www.pbs.org/wgbh/pages/frontline/lost-in-detention).

38. Charles Bowden, "We bring fear," *Mother Jones*, August 2009.

39. Ahilan T. Arulanantham, Written Statement of the American Civil Liberties Union, Senate Judiciary Committee, March 20, 2013 (https://www.aclu.org/files/assets/testimony_of_ahilan_arulanantham_for_3_20_13_senate_judiciary_committee_....pdf).

40. Ken Hartnett, interview by Tirman.

41. Corinn Williams, interview by Tirman.

42. Marc Fallon, interview by Tirman.

43. Tom Juravich, *At the Altar of the Bottom Line: The Degradation of Work in the 21st Century* (University of Massachusetts Press, 2009), 93.

44. Adrian Ventura, interview by John Tirman (July 20, 2011).

45. Corinn Williams, interview by Tirman.

46. Juravich, *At the Altar of the Bottom Line*, 95.

47. Douglass Massey and Magaly Sanchez R., *Brokered Boundaries: Immigrant Identity in Anti-Immigrant Times* (Russell Sage, 2010), 21.

CHAPTER 4

1. On Chicano-rights movement see Carlos Muñoz, *Youth, Identity, Power: The Chicano Movement* (Verso, 1989); Armando Navarro, *Mexican American Youth Organization: Avant-Garde of the Chicano Movement in Texas* (University of Texas Press, 1995); Marguerite V. Marin, *Social Protest in an Urban Barrio: A Study of the Chicano Movement, 1966–1974* (University Press of America, 1991); F. Arturo Rosales, *Chicano! The History of the Mexican American Civil Rights Movement*, revised edition (Arte Publico, 1997); Mario T. Garcia, ed., *The Chicano Movement: Perspectives from the Twenty-First Century* (Routledge, 2005).

2. John D'Emilio, *Lost Prophet: The Life and Times of Bayard Rustin* (Simon & Schuster, 2003, 420.

3. Ian F. Haney-López, "Protest, repression, and race: Legal violence and the Chicano movement," *University of Pennsylvania Law Review* 150 (2001): 205–244, at 214.

4. On Hispanic political participation, see Ricardo Ramírez, *Mobilizing Opportunities: The Evolving Latino Electorate and the Future of American Politics* (University of Virginia Press, 2013); S. K. Ramakrishnan, *Democracy in Immigrant America: Changing Demographics and Political Participation* (Stanford University Press, 2005); Sharon Ann Navarro and Armando Xavier Mejia, eds., *Latino Americans and Political Participation: A Reference Handbook* (ABC-CLIO, 2004); Marcelo M. Suárez-Orozco and Mariela Páez, eds., *Latinos: Remaking America* (University of California Press, 2009); Havidan Rodriguez, Clara E. Rodríguez, Rogelio Saenz, Douglas S. Massey, and Cecilia Menjivar, eds., *Latinas/os in the United States: Changing the Face of América* (Springer, 2007); Jan E. Leighley and Arnold Vedlitz, "Race, ethnicity, and political participation: Competing models and contrasting explanations," *Journal of Politics* 61, no. 4 (1999): 1092–1114; Atiya Kai Stokes, "Latino group consciousness and political participation," *American Politics Research* 31, no. 4 (2003): 361–378; Matt A. Barreto, "*ISí Se Puede*! Latino candidates and the mobilization of Latino voters," *American Political Science Review* 101, no. 3 (2007): 425–441. For a somewhat dated bibliography, see "Latino participation in United States politics," compiled by Danelle Crowley, revised by Margo Gutiérrez, BiblioNoticias no. 65, revised (October 1996) (http://www.lib.utexas.edu/benson/bibnot/bn-65.html).

5. Lisa M. Martinez, "Yes we can: Latino participation in unconventional politics," *Social Forces* 84, no. 1 (2005–06): 135–155, at 146. On political participation, education, and poverty, see Kevin Milligan, Enrico Moretti, and Philip Oreopoulos, "Does education improve citizenship? Evidence from the United States and the United Kingdom," *Journal of Public Economics* 88, no. 9–10 (2004): 1667–1695; Cliff Zukin, Scott Keeter, Molly Andolina, Krista Jenkins, and Michael X. Delli Carpini, *A New Engagement? Political Participation, Civil Life, and the Changing American Citizen* (Oxford University Press, 2006).

6. See David L. Leal, "Political Participation by Latino Non-Citizens in the United States," *British Journal of Political Science* 32, no. 2 (2002): 353–370.

7. On the literature of displacement, see John Tirman, "Nationalism in exile," *Boston Review* 26 (summer 2001): 21–23.

8. Quoted in Janell Ross, "Dream Act activists push into mainstream with American protest movement tactics," Huffington Post (http://www.huffingtonpost.com), August 21, 2012; reproduced verbatim from posting.

9. Roberto Gonzales, "Moving beyond the Single Story: Engaging a Comprehensive Strategy in Our Work with Undocumented Immigrant Youth," Lecture, "Children of Immigrants" conference, Harvard Radcliffe Institute (May 23, 2013); https://www.youtube.com/watch?v=8WWrdpJNldk.

10. Walter Nicholls, *The DREAMers: How the Undocumented Youth Movement Transformed the Immigrant Rights Debate* (Stanford University Press, 2013), 52.

11. Neidi Dominguez Zamorano, Jonathan Perez, Nancy Meza, and Jorge Guitierrez, "DREAM activists: Rejecting the passivity of the nonprofit, industrial complex," Truthout (http://www.truth-out.org), September 21, 2010.

12. Tom Hayden, "What's next for the Dreamers?" *The Nation*, February 11, 2013.

13. Juan Santiago, "Young illegal immigrants discuss future," Associated Press, August 16, 2012.

14. Daniel Gonzales, "A year later, immigrants face DREAM Act's limits," *USA Today*, August 13, 2013.

15. Elizabeth Llorente, "Judge dismisses ICE agents' lawsuit challenging Obama's deferred action," Fox News Latino (http://latino.foxnews.com), August 1, 2013.

16. On public support for Dreamers, see William T. Brown, "Border security, citizenship for military, DREAMers favored in poll," *Houston Chronicle*, February 7, 2014.

17. For statistics and analysis on immigrants and crime, see M. Kathleen Dingeman and Rubén G. Rumbaut, "The immigration-crime nexus and post-deportation experiences: En/countering stereotypes in Southern California and El Salvador," *University of La Verne Law Review* 31, no. 2 (2010): 363–402.

18. Sheryl Kornman, "Cops: City has 5,000 gang members; violence could be 'much worse,'" *Tucson Citizen*, February 24, 2009.

19. Federal Bureau of Investigation, Gangs (n.d.) (http://www.fbi.gov/about-us/investigate/vc_majorthefts/gangs).

20. Federal Bureau of Investigation, Reports and Publications: 2011 National Gang Threat Assessment—Emerging Trends (n.d.) (http://www.fbi.gov/stats-services/publications/2011-national-gang-threat-assessment).

21. Thomas W. Ward, *Gangsters without Borders: An Ethnography of a Salvadoran Street Gang* (Oxford University Press, 2013), 18.

22. Tani Marilena Adams, "Chronic violence and its reproduction: Perverse trends in social relations, citizenship, and democracy in Latin America," Woodrow Wilson International Center for Scholars, 2012.

CHAPTER 5

1. On the history of Guatemala, see Greg Grandin, *The Blood of Guatemala: A History of Race and Nation* (Duke University Press, 1982); William George Lovell, *Conquest and Survival in Colonial Guatemala: Historical Geography of the Cuchumatán Highlands, 1500–1821* (McGill–Queen's University Press, 2005); Greg Grandin, Deborah T. Levenson, and Elizabeth Oglesby, *A Guatemala Reader: History, Culture, Politics* (Duke University Press, 2011); Richard H. Immerman, *The CIA in Guatemala: The Foreign Policy of Intervention* (University of Texas Press, 1982); Stephen Schlesinger and Stephen Kinzer, *Bitter Fruit: The Story of the American Coup in Guatemala* (Doubleday, 1982).

2. Quoted by David M. Barrett, "Congress, the CIA, and Guatemala: Sterilizing a 'Red Infection,'" CIA Studies Archive Indexes (https://www.cia.gov/library/center-for-the-study-of-intelligence), volume 44, no. 5 (2007).

3. Nick Cullather, *Secret History: The CIA's Classified Account of Its Operations in Guatemala, 1952–1954*, second edition (Stanford University Press, 2006), 38, 39.

4. Zachary Karabell, *Architects of Intervention: The United States, the Third World, and the Cold War, 1946–1962* (LSU Press, 1999, 134.

5. Arbenz's resignation speech can be found at http://www.umbc.edu/che/tahlessons/pdf/historylabs/Guatemalan_Coup_student:RS06.pdf.

6. Patrick Ball, Paul Kobrak, and Herbert F. Spirer, *State Violence in Guatemala, 1960–1996: A Quantitative Reflection* (American Association for the Advancement of Science, 1999), 11.

7. Amnesty International report, 1982, quoted on p. 117 of Chris E. Stout, *The Psychology of Terrorism: Clinical Aspects and Responses*, volume 2 (Greenwood, 2002).

8. Felicity Lawrence, "Guatemala pays high price for global food system failings," *The Guardian*, May 31, 2011.

9. USAID, "Guatemala" (http://www.usaid.gov/guatemala/education).

10. Adrian Ventura's story is mainly quoted from the December 2009 issue of *El Quetzal* (a publication of the Guatemalan Human Rights Commission/USA) and from an interview conducted by John Tirman in April 2012.

11. LIO Campesino is an organization of indigenous farmers.

12. *Guatemala: Never Again!* Recovery of Historical Memory Project, Report of the Human Rights Office, Archdiocese of Guatemala (Orbis Books, 1999), chapter 2, passim.

13. Interview with Dianna Ortiz, Robert F. Kennedy Center for Justice & Human Rights (n.d.) (http://rfkcenter.org/dianna-ortiz-7).

14. Becky W. Evans, "In a remote Guatemalan village, links to New Bedford abound," New Bedford *Standard-Times*, March 6, 2008.

15. For general histories of Mexico, see William Beezley and Michael Meyer, eds., *The Oxford History of Mexico* (Oxford University Press, 2010); Gilbert M. Joseph and Timothy J. Henderson, eds., *The Mexico Reader: History, Culture, Politics* (Duke University Press, 2002); T. R. Fehrenbach, *Fire and Blood: A History of Mexico* (Basic Books, 1995).

16. Wendy Koch, "U.S. urged to apologize for 1930s deportations," *USA Today*, April 5, 2006. For scholarly accounts of "repatriation," see Francisco E. Balderrama and Raymond Rodriguez. *Decade of Betrayal: Mexican Repatriation in the 1930s* (University of New Mexico Press, 1995); George J. Sanchez, *Becoming Mexican American: Ethnicity, Culture and Identity in Chicano Los Angeles, 1900–1945* (Oxford University Press, 1993).

17. On the Bracero program, see Jorge Durand, "The Bracero Program (1942–1964): A critical appraisal" (2007) (http://meme.phpwebhosting.com/~migracion/rimd/revistas/rev9/e2.pdf); Kitty Calavita, *Inside the State: The Bracero Program, Immigration, and the I.N.S.* (Routledge, 1992); Marjorie S. Zatz, "Using and abusing Mexican farmworkers: The Bracero Program and the INS," *Law & Society Review* 27, no. 4 (1993): 851–864.

18. On neoliberalism, see Peter Kingstone, *The Political Economy of Latin America: Reflections on Neoliberalism and Development* (Routledge, 2011); Joseph E. Stiglitz, *Globalization and Its Discontents* (Norton, 2003); Saskia Sassen, *Globalization and Its Discontents: Essays on the New Mobility of People and Money* (New Press, 1999).

19. Mark Weisbrot, "NAFTA: 20 years of regret for Mexico," *The Guardian*, January 4, 2014.

20. Stiglitz, *Globalization and Its Discontents*, 8.

21. David Bacon, *The Right to Stay Home: How US Policy Drives Mexican Migration* (Beacon, 2013, Kindle Edition), Narrative One.

22. Tom Philpott, "Swine-flu outbreak could be linked to Smithfield factory farms," Grist (http://grist.org), April 26, 2009.

23. Douglas S. Massey and Magaly Sánchez, *Brokered Boundaries: Immigrant Identity in Anti-Immigrant Times* (Russell Sage Foundation, 2010, 39ff.; Pew Research Center Hispanic Trends Project, Survey of Mexican Migrants, Part One, 2005 (http://www.pewhispanic.org/2005/03/02/survey-of-mexican-migrants-part-one).

24. Source of visa statistics: US Department of State (http://travel.state.gov).

25. On Mexican drug cartels, see Evelyn Krache Morris, "Think again: Mexican drug cartels," *Foreign Policy*, December 3, 2013; Deborah Hastings, "Fleeing wrath of vicious cartels, record-breaking numbers of Mexicans seek political asylum in the US," *New York Daily News*, October 23, 2013; Larry Greenemeier, "As drug war rages, tweets reveal Mexicans' emotional numbness" (http://www.scientificamerican.com/article/as-drug-war-rages-tweets-reveal-mexicanse28099-emotional-numbness).

26. Leon Litwak, *Trouble In Mind: Black Southerners in the Age of Jim Crow* (Knopf, 1998); Litwak, *Been in the Storm So Long: The Aftermath of Slavery* (Knopf, 1979).

27. Douglas S. Massey, "Why Does Immigration Occur? A Theoretical Synthesis," in Charles Hirschman, Philip Kasinitz, and Josh DeWind, eds., *The Handbook of International Migration: The American Experience* (Russell Sage Foundation, 1999).

CHAPTER 6

1. David Nather, "Heritage Foundation: Immigration reform will cost $6.3 trillion," Politico (http://www.politico.com), May 6, 2013.

2. Elise Foley, "Chuck Schumer: Immigration reform would have passed 'in a pre-Tea Party world,'" Huffington Post (http://www.huffingtonpost.com), January 23, 2014.

3. Hana E. Brown, "Race, legality, and the social policy consequences of anti-immigration mobilization," *American Sociological Review* 78, no. 2 (2013): 290–314, at 303.

4. "Intolerance is alive and well," *Arizona Republic*, May 24, 1992 (quoted in Brown, "Race, legality, and the social policy consequences").

5. Ryan Kierman, "Conservatives frame immigration overhaul as next ObamaCare, as bill moves to full Senate," cnsnews.com, May 22, 2013.

6. National Immigration Law Center, "Access to Health Care and Benefits," July 8, 2013 (http://www.nilc.org/hlthcarebensS744.html).

7. Michelle Malkin, "While GOP leaders push amnesty, Dems rope more immigrants into welfare state," michellemalkin.com, January 28, 2013.

8. Michael Snyder, "Illegal immigration = More identity theft, more murder, more rape and more drug dealing," The American Dream (http://endoftheamericandream.com), June 24, 2013.

9. Tom Blumer, "Mind-boggling stats on illegal immigrants with criminal records the press rarely if ever publishes," NewsBusters (http://newsbusters.org), February 4, 2014.

10. "Text of Republicans' principles on immigration," *New York Times*, January 30, 2014.

11. Ulysses Arn, "Illegal immigrants don't deserve a pathway to citizenship they deserve #boots2asses," Red State (http://www.redstate.com), June 13, 2013.

12. Molly K. Hooper and Alex Lazar, "Immigration-reform critics fear citizenship pathway will spark rush to cross border," The Hill (http://thehill.com), February 13, 2013.

13. Joshua Linder, "The amnesty effect: Evidence from the 1986 IRCA," *The Public Purpose*, spring 2011: 13–31.

14. Raul Hinojosa Ojeda and Sherman Robinson, "Adding it Up: Accurately Gauging the Economic Impact of Immigration Reform," Immigration Policy Center, 2013 (http://www.immigrationpolicy.org/just-facts/adding-it-accurately-gauging-economic-impact-immigration-reform); Betsy Cooper and Kevin O'Neil, "Lessons from the Immigration Reform and Control Act of 1986," Policy Brief no. 3, Immigration Policy Center, August 2005.

15. Erin Siegel, "Immigration reform: What the last 'path to citizenship' did for immigrants," *Christian Science Monitor*, April 7, 2013.

16. Immigration Policy Center, "A Guide to S.744: Understanding the 2013 Senate Immigration Bill" (http://www.immigrationpolicy.org/special-reports/guide-s744 -understanding-2013-senate-immigration-bill).

17. Source of data on border apprehensions: US Customs and Border Protection, "US Border Patrol fiscal year apprehension statistics" (http://www.cbp.gov/sites/ default/files/documents/U.S.%20Border%20Patrol%20Fiscal%20Year %20Apprehension%20Statistics%201960-2013_0.pdf).

18. On cross-border shootings, see John Carlos Frey, "Over the line: Why are U.S. Border Patrol agents shooting into Mexico and killing innocent civilians?" *Washington Monthly*, May/June 2013. On investigation of deadly force and new guidelines, see Brian Bennett, "Border Patrol's use of deadly force criticized in report," *Los Angeles Times*, February 27, 2014[REMOVED HYPERLINK FIELD].

19. In the magazine *Mother Jones*, Ian Gordon traced the surge of unaccompanied minors to 2011.

CHAPTER 7

1. On polls in Everett and Somerville, see Daniel J. Hopkins, Van C. Tran, and Abigail Fisher Williamson, "See no Spanish: language, local context, and attitudes toward immigration," *Politics, Groups, and Identities* 2, no. 1 (2014): 35–51.

2. Source of data on visas for Mexicans: Douglas Massey, "Only by addressing the realities of North American economic integration can we solve the problem," *Boston Review*, May/June 2009.

3. Sources of Reagan quotations: "A Reagan legacy: Amnesty for illegal aliens," NPR, June 4, 2010 (http://www.npr.org/templates/story/story.php?storyId=128303672); Ryan Teague Beckwith, "What Reagan said about undocumented immigrants," mercurynews.com, January 28, 2013 (http://www.mercurynews.com/digital-first-media-td/ci_22467657/what-reagan-said-about-undocumented-immigrants).

4. Nicholas de Genova, "The legal production of Mexican/migrant 'illegality,'" *Latino Studies* 2 (2004): 160–185.

5. Cristina Rodriguez, "Immigration, civil rights, and the formation of the people," *Daedalus* 142, no. 3 (2013): 228–241, at 229.

6. Ibid., at 233.

7. Nicholas G. De Genova, "The Legal Production of Mexican/Migrant 'Illegality,'" *Latino Studies* 2 (2004); 161.

8. Cecilia Menjívar, "Liminal legality: Salvadoran and Guatemalan immigrants' lives in the United States," *American Journal of Sociology* 111, no. 4 (2006): 999–1037, at 1007–1008.

9. Hiroshi Motomura, "The rights of others: Legal claims and immigration outside the law," *Duke Law Journal* 59 (2010): 1723–1786, at 1731.

10. US Supreme Court, *Graham v. Richardson* (1971), quoted in Motomura, "The rights of others."

11. David Bacon, *Illegal People: How Globalization Creates Migration and Criminalizes Immigrants* (Beacon, 2008): 5.

12. Douglas S. Massey, "Why does immigration occur? A theoretical synthesis," in Charles Hirschman, Philip Kasinitz, and Josh Dewind, eds., *The Handbook of International Migration: The American Experience* (Russell Sage Foundation, 2008), 47.

13. On race and sentencing, see Patricia Warren, Ted Chiricos, and William Bales, "The imprisonment penalty for young black and Hispanic males: A crime-specific analysis," *Journal of Research on Crime and Delinquency* 49, no. 1 (2012): 56–80. Source of data on black-white wage differentials: Department of Labor, "The African-Ameri-

can labor force in the recovery," February 29, 2012 (http://www.dol.gov/_sec/media/reports/blacklaborforce).

14. Nick Bromell, *The Time Is Always Now: Black Thought and the Transformation of US Democracy* (Oxford University Press, 2013), 43.

15. Samuel P. Huntington, "The Hispanic challenge," *Foreign Policy*, March 1, 2004.

16. Ibid.

17. Samuel P. Huntington, *Who Are We? The Challenges to America's National Identity* (Simon & Schuster, 2004), 254.

18. Ibid., 142.

19. Jack Citrin, Amy Lerman, Michael Murakami, and Kathryn Pearson, "Testing Huntington: Is Hispanic immigration a threat to American identity?" *Perspectives on Politics*, March 2007: 31–48.

20. "Second-generation Americans" (http://www.pewsocialtrends.org/2013/02/07/second-generation-americans).

21. Bernie Reeve, "Why English Is Not the 'Official Language' of the United States," American Thinker (http://www.americanthinker.com), November 1, 2009.

22. Jack Citrin, Beth Reingold, Evelyn Walters, and Donald P. Green, "The 'official English' movement and the symbolic politics of language in the United States," *Western Political Quarterly* 43, no. 3 (1990): 535–559, at 557.

23. Jorge J. E. Gracia, *Latinos in America: Philosophy and Social Identity* (Blackwell, 2008), 124.

24. Signithia Fordham, "Dissin' 'the standard': Ebonics as guerrilla warfare at Capital High," *Anthropology and Education Quarterly* 30, no. 3 (2008): 272–293, at 275.

25. Ibid., 276.

CHAPTER 8

1. Anthony Bourdain, "Under the volcano," May 3, 2014 (http://anthonybourdain.tumblr.com/post/84641290831/under-the-volcano).

2. Martha Finnemore and Kathryn Sikkink, "International norm dynamics and political change," *International Organization* 52, no. 4 (1998): 887–917.

3. David Bornstein, "Immigrants welcome here," *New York Times*, February 19, 2014.

4. Kate E. Murray and David M. Marx, "Attitudes toward unauthorized immigrants, authorized immigrants, and refugees," *Cultural Diversity and Ethnic Minority Psychology* 19, no. 3 (2013): 332–341, at 340.

5. First poll, Public Religion Research Institute, July 23-27, 2014, http://publicreligion.org/site/wp-content/uploads/2014/07/PRRI-Religion-Politics-Tracking-Survey-July-2014-Topline.pdf; second poll, Pew Research Center. Aug. 20-24, 2014, http://www.pollingreport.com/immigration.htm.

INDEX